DECODING GENDER IN SCIENCE FICTION

DECODING GENDER IN SCIENCE FICTION

BRIAN ATTEBERY

Routledge
Taylor & Francis Group

NEW YORK AND LONDON

Published in 2002 by
Routledge
29 West 35th Street
New York, NY 10001
www.routledge-ny.com

Published in Great Britain by
Routledge
11 New Fetter Lane
London EC4P 4EE
www.routledge-co.uk

Copyright © 2002 by Brian Attebery
Routledge is an imprint of the Taylor & Francis Group.

Printed in the United States of America on acid-free paper.

Library of Congress Cataloging-in-Publication Data

Attebery, Brian, 1951–
    Decoding gender in science fiction / Brian Attebery.
        p. cm.
    ISBN 0-415-93949-6—ISBN 0-415-93950-X (pbk.)
        1. Science fiction, American—History and criticism. 2. Science fiction, English—History and criticism.
3. Sex differences (Psychology) in literature. 4. Androgyny (Psychology) in literature. 5. Gender identity
in literature. 6. Sex role in literature. 7. Women in literature. 8. Men in literature. I. Title.

PS374.S35 A84 2002
813'.0876609353—dc21

                                                                                                    2002024914

For Jennifer

CONTENTS

ILLUSTRATIONS

ACKNOWLEDGMENTS

Many people have read and commented on portions of this book; still more have helped me work out ideas in conversations, correspondence, and discussions at conferences. My thanks to all of these collaborators, and especially to Ursula K. Le Guin, Veronica Hollinger, Joan Gordon, Joe Sutliffe Sanders, Jennifer Eastman Attebery, Tamise Van Pelt, Karen Joy Fowler, John Kijinski, Susanna Sturgis, Justine Larbalestier, Dee Michel, Gwyneth Jones, James Morrow, and the late R. D. Mullen. Every member of the feminist-SF discussion group deserves acknowledgment, but there are too many to list here. I am indebted to scholars in the fields of SF and gender studies, and to writers of rich and challenging science fiction to an extent that is hardly covered by my bibliography.

As a complete novice in the field of illustrations, I relied on the good will and expertise of many people, including Vincent Di Fate, Jean Scrocco, Simon Ng, Justine Larbalestier, Forrest Ackerman, Ronda Mahl, and special collection librarians at the Harold B. Lee Library at Brigham Young University. Thanks to all.

Parts of some chapters have appeared in other publications: chapter 4 in *Science-Fiction Studies;* chapter 6 in *Femspec;* chapter 9 in a joint issue of *Journal of the Fantastic in the Arts* and *The Hungarian Journal of English and American Studies;* chapter 3 in *Speaking Science Fiction,* edited by Andy Sawyer and David Seed (Liverpool University Press, 2000), and chapter 8 in *Edging into the Future,* edited by Veronica Hollinger and Joan Gordon (University of Pennsylvania Press, 2001). Thanks to those publications for permission to reprint.

CHAPTER

SECRET DECODER RING

When this project began to take shape, I was surprised to find myself writing a book about gender and science fiction. There were already so many good studies out there, I thought. All the material has been covered. I'm not the person to do it. But every time I started researching a particular theme or period of science fiction, gender issues were shaping the fiction in weird, powerful ways that no one seemed to have mentioned. In the end, I gave up and decided to write about that interplay.

Science fiction is a useful tool for investigating habits of thought, including conceptions of gender. Gender, in turn, offers an interesting glimpse into some of the unacknowledged messages that permeate science fiction. Each reads the other in very interesting ways. Examining stories with a view to both their science-fictional qualities and their uses of gender generates new questions about both gender and genre. Then those questions can be addressed to those and other stories to yield further insights. The process is a particularly rewarding version of the hermeneutic circle—a decoding ring.

Both gender and science fiction are rather vexed terms: each is marked by rancorous debate over what it means, how it came to mean what it seems to mean today, what is allowed to count as part of it, how it ought to be studied—and who gets to speak to these issues. In his study of *Critical Terms for Science Fiction and Fantasy,* Gary K. Wolfe lists thirty-three definitions for science fiction, many of them directly contradictory. Some, for instance, consider it a subset of fantasy, while others see fantasy as a branch of science fiction. Definitions of gender are equally controversial. Is it a grammatical term, a synonym for sexual differentiation, a class system, or, as Kate Bornstein has suggested only half facetiously, a cult (Bornstein 103)?

Donna Haraway points out that even the distinction between social *gender* and biological *sex,* central to many discussions of the topic, is meaningless in languages such as German, in which a single term indicates both (128). In French, to complicate matters further, one can distinguish gender from sex but not from literary form. What is your *genre:* masculine, feminine, or science fiction?

Among multiple definitions, I have chosen ones that treat both gender and science fiction as sign systems. Gender is a way of assigning social and psychological meaning to sexual difference, insofar as that difference is perceived in form, appearance, sexual function, and expressive behavior. Science fiction is a system for generating and interpreting narratives that reflect insights derived from, technological offshoots of, and attitudes toward science. These rather stiff and wordy descriptions are not the only legitimate definitions for either term. They are not even necessarily the ways I find myself using the words in conversation. I offer them as clarification of my method, as a way of saying "if we define gender this way and science fiction thus, we can make these discoveries."

My choice is partly determined by the double subject matter: these are definitions that highlight the relationships between science fiction and gender and place the two categories on comparable footings. In addition, I like to think in terms of signs because decades of reading SF have given me the habit of looking at my fellow humans as interestingly weird creatures, alien beings. The first thing to do in confronting a dangerous alien is to figure out what it means by beeping or waggling its antennae. Before we can program the universal translator, we have to learn the code.

Both gender and science fiction, then, can be seen as codes: cultural systems that allow us to generate forms of expression and assign meanings to them. Both codes overlap with and depend on language itself, the master code through which all other cultural systems are transmitted, verified, and (as I am doing here) analyzed. Whenever we call something a code, we are implicitly making a comparison between it and language. We begin to look for individual "words" or signs; we expect to find a "grammar" for organizing those signs; we identify social and linguistic contexts within which those signs have meaning, and we interpret or "translate" individual "messages."

Codes have another interesting property. They can be used to send a message and at the same time to conceal it from those who are not conversant with the code. The Navajo code talkers of World War II are a famous example of the way a linguistic code can become a secret code when a group of insiders makes use of it in front of outsiders. Both gender codes and the specialized vocabulary and narrative techniques of science fiction frequently fulfill the social function of marking boundaries between those who know the code and those who don't. One can easily label oneself an outsider by misusing a key element—by, for instance, wearing an earring in the wrong place or abbreviating science fiction as sci-fi rather than SF.

The gender code is vastly more pervasive than that of SF. Like language, it is something we start learning the day we are born. Its rules and processes become part of the structure of consciousness, so that we find it difficult to think consciously about it. It is rooted in biology but shaped by culture to such a degree that it is impossible to untwist the thread and say which strands are inborn—and which are acquired and arbitrary. There is no "natural gender" any more than there is a natural language.

Like individual speech sounds, one gender is meaningful only to the degree that it differs (or is treated as if it differs) from another. Speech features are conveniently sorted into binary oppositions: voiced and voiceless consonants, active and passive verbs. Likewise, gender is usually conceived as a pair of mutually exclusive "opposites": masculine and feminine. Such a schematic diagram is just about as true to the range of individual expressions of gender as a structural diagram of phonemes is to the full range of sounds people actually produce. If you are from rural Georgia and I from Northern Ireland, our versions of the word "bird" will hardly resemble one another, even though most speakers of English will understand them as variations on the "same" sound. Just so, my way of expressing masculine gender barely overlaps with those of a Masai warrior or a Mormon patriarch. We all act out the signifiers "man," "husband," "father," and "son," according to our own regional and personal dialects. Most of what we have in common is the degree to which we differ from our various cultures' definitions of the feminine. Legal systems and other institutions typically respond to simplified "phonemic" expression of gender while disregarding "phonetic" differences in expressing it.

The gender code permeates the linguistic one: masculine, feminine, and neuter are, after all, grammatical terms. Within most cultures, when women and men speak, they make slightly different stylistic choices among linguistic possibilities, and even when a man and a woman utter the same sequence of words, listeners are likely to interpret their meanings differently. The differences are rarely to the woman's advantage: he is being forceful, we say, but she is shrill; he is asking for directions, she is issuing a sexual invitation.

Nonverbal signs in the gender code can include clothing, hairstyles, cosmetics, posture, gesture, vocal pitch and inflection, use of chemicals to mask or enhance body odors, and patterns of eye contact. Within this code, the body itself becomes a sign. Its meaning shifts according to presentation and context.

Signs within the gender code are fairly easy to pinpoint, but it is another matter to decide what is being signalled. Take something like a shaved head.

Depending on whose head it is and what other signs are present, it may denote aggression (for instance in skinheads), helplessness (in concentration camps), conformity (in military contexts), nonconformity, sexual availability, lesbian separatism, hypermasculinity, a medical condition, youth, age, or effacement of gender. The sign may even indicate more than one meaning at a time. The meanings it points to may themselves be signs representing some further meaning: for instance, the bald head may be a sign of androgyny, but androgyny itself (as I will discuss later) is nothing but a sign and a particularly slippery one at that.

Hollywood has offered us quite an array of bald heads, each signifying something different. In *Star Trek: The Motion Picture,* actress Persis Khambatta's shiny scalp was a sign of sexual availability, whereas Mira Furlan's Delenn, in the series *Babylon V,* became sexually desirable only after a metamorphosis that replaced her alien baldness with human locks. Sigourney Weaver's shaved skull in *Alien³* was part of her distancing from ordinary humans, while the baldness of Captain Jean-Luc Picard, played by Patrick Stewart on *Star Trek: The Next Generation,* contributed to the character's grave and vulnerable humanity, especially in contrast with the various ridges and ruffles that indicate alien races in the *Star Trek* universe.

In printed science fiction, even more than in the movies, the generic code proves to be apt at revealing aspects of the gender code that are usually exhibited, shall we say, less baldly. The genre's storytelling conventions encourage writers to ask questions about the biological basis of sexual division and allow them to explore alternative formulations of society and the individual psyche. The code, in other words, generates utterances along the lines of "What if X were the case instead of Y?" or "What happens if we follow X to its logical conclusion?" The Y's and X's that are being explored may be laws of physics and new inventions, or they may well be chromosomes and marriage customs.

Furthermore, these explorations take place within another code, that of narrative. The nature of storytelling demands that ideas be embodied in characters within social contexts, undergo alteration over time, be aligned in patterns of conflict, and achieve some sort of resolution. This is a powerful set of operations. Societies use mythic stories to express their relationship to the world. Historians have begun to notice that narrative is an essential part of the cognitive equipment of their discipline no less than it is of literary art. Psychologists since Freud have observed that selfhood is a matter of telling one's own story. Even the natural sciences rely on narrative models to make sense of such phenomena as evolution, reproduction, and the origin of the universe.

So storytelling is a way of thinking about things, and science fiction is a form of storytelling that invites us to challenge standard notions of nature and culture. SF's unique innovation within the code of narrative is to incorporate signs derived from science and technology in such a way as to evoke a sensation of strangeness—not mere novelty but a reordering of categories. Ideally, this reordering carries over from the fiction to the reader's own experience and thus become the "sense of wonder" invoked in fan discussions of the best SF stories. The pull toward strangeness invites the SF writer to investigate aspects of society, self, perception, and the physical universe that are difficult or impossible to represent through conventional realism.

This invitation does not mean that all SF exploits the form's potential. Even though nothing has to be assumed in a science fictional world, in practice, contemporary cultural habits and attitudes usually get taken for granted. No writer can concentrate on every aspect of the imagined world at once, and the weirder one particular element is, the more likely other elements will be allowed to fall into familiar patterns. A 1950s story about methane-breathing aliens is all too likely to show them talking like 1950s engineers. As Joanna Russ has pointed out, visions of future society well into the 1960s have space-suited men coming home to the wife and kids in an orbiting suburbia (81).

Until the 1960s, gender was one of the elements most often transcribed unthinkingly into SF's hypothetical worlds. Even if an author was interested in revising the gender code, the conservatism of a primarily male audience—and the editors, publishers, and distributors who were trying to outguess that audience—kept gender exploration to a minimum. SF, especially in the United States, has been in the peculiar position of being both a popular entertainment and an arena for testing ideas. Its writers are expected to provide both escapist adventure and challenging thought experiments. For this reason, SF has never been easy to class either as literary art or as a popular genre along the lines of the women's romance novel or the Western. No single formula defines SF, although as Frank Cioffi has observed, many of its stories rely on formulaic plots (40–41).

SF's role as a commercial product has always tended to push it toward safe predictability and a reinforcement of existing social roles, but its own internal dynamics invite more daring variations in story, characters, setting, and social implications. Among writers who focus on technology and the physical sciences—writers of so-called "hard SF," the conservative side of the equation usually dominates. Moreover, SF texts aimed at the broadest possible audience—novels that break out of category to become best sellers, for instance, or nearly all SF movies—tend to reinforce the sexual status quo. However, when the intended audience consists of a smaller population of experienced and venturesome SF readers and the format is "soft SF," emphasizing human biology, sociology, or unusual forms of perception, then SF is more likely to challenge than to uphold gender norms. That is when the field begins to generate the "dangerous visions" celebrated in the title of Harlan Ellison's influential 1967 anthology.

Back in the 1930s and '40s, when the pulp magazine market severely restricted SF's ability even to imply sex, let alone offer subversive visions of male and female identities, a few writers found ways to investigate gender issues. Catherine L. Moore and Theodore Sturgeon, in particular, made use of the SF code to send deeply encrypted messages about sexual identity and desire. Their work alerts us to the fact that most signs in the SF code—robots, aliens, psychic powers, death rays, and so on—can also function as gender markers. A story like Moore's "No Woman Born" (1944) is unusual for its era in that the signs of gender are reallocated. Its heroine, transferred into a mechanical body, unites three characteristics rarely seen in combination: femininity, power, and artifice. Those same attributes might have remained transparent if they had been distributed more conventionally. If, that is, the powerful mechanical body had been marked as masculine rather than feminine, it would have seemed to most readers to have no gender at all. Only Moore's reassignment of the categories makes them noticeable.

It is no longer so easy for gender markings to be invisible. Beginning in the 1950s, several factors, including a shift in market dominance from magazines to paperback books and the formation of a separate market for juvenile SF, led to a partial breakdown of sexual taboos. At the same time, the number of women writers (and probably readers, though this is harder to verify) began to increase. Like C. L. Moore before them, these writers, including Judith Merril, Katherine MacLean, Andre Norton, Margaret St. Clair, Miriam Allen de Ford, and Zenna Henderson, quietly challenged assumptions about which sex is rational, which aligned with nature, which capable of empathy, and which prepared for violence. Their stories, without necessarily being feminist or even including female characters, still tended to force awareness of gender roles and to foreground habits of projecting sexuality onto the nonhuman universe. They helped pave the way for a wave of powerfully feminist SF in the late 1960s and 1970s: Sonya Dorman's "When I Was Miss Dow" (1966), Ursula K. Le Guin's *The Left Hand of Darkness* (1969), Suzette Haden Elgin's "For the Sake of Grace" (1969), Suzy McKee Charnas's *Walk to the End of the World* (1974), Carol Emshwiller's "Abominable" (1980), Joanna Russ's *The Female Man* (1975), Marge Piercy's *Woman on the Edge of Time* (1976), and James Tiptree, Jr.'s "The Women Men Don't See" (1973).

In the wake of these stories, it is virtually impossible for an SF writer to take gender for granted any more. If a writer wishes to portray unchanged sex roles in the future or in an alien society, that fact has to be explained somehow. It's the result of biological imperatives, for instance, or reactionary social pressures. The more conservative examples of hard SF in the 1990s are likely to offer such explanations while paradoxically depicting women as pilots, assassins, politicians, and so on. Evidently a single tough woman (shown in leather on the cover illustration) can be accommodated without threatening existing sexual arrangements.

At the other end of the spectrum, there is now a significant body of SF that makes the redefinition of gender a primary concern. An award for SF that explores and expands gender roles was instituted in 1991 and named for James Tiptree, Jr. The name is an appropriate sign for defiance of gender stereotyping, for James Tiptree, Jr., designates the authorial persona adopted by Alice Hastings Sheldon. Sheldon became Tiptree so convincingly that despite the feminist implications of many Tiptree stories, a number of critics were convinced that no woman could write in such an obviously "masculine" style.

The founders of the Tiptree Award and most of the winners to date have been women, although the official description by award founders Pat Murphy and Karen Joy Fowler does not specify the winner's sex. Not all fiction by women challenges gender assumptions, nor is all gender-bending necessarily feminist in its implications. However, those who are denied power or autonomy within a social system are more likely to be aware of its workings than are those who benefit from them. Hence, women have made up a majority of the pioneers in feminist and gender-investigating SF, from C. L. Moore and Katherine Burdekin in the 1930s to Tiptree winners Gwyneth Jones and Nicola Griffith and a host of others in the 1990s.

Indeed, women writers and their ways of representing female roles within SF constitute a whole field of study in themselves. This book is indebted throughout to the work of feminist critics such as Joanna Russ, Beverly Friend, Marleen Barr, Robin Roberts, Sarah Lefanu, Elizabeth Cummins, and Jenny Wolmark. The field of gender studies grows out of the feminist insight that women and men play roles that are not inborn but culturally determined. Those roles are skewed so as to place authority in the hands of men, often by defining such powerful concepts as law, reason, tradition, creativity, and divinity as inherently masculine. The task of feminist women writers and critics has been to force these assumptions out of concealment, to show where they lurk in custom and language, and thereby to carve out a space for women to talk together, explore their experiences, and use those experiences to create new identities and patterns for social interaction.

Although gender criticism as a field grows out of feminist reading, and although the need for a more equitable treatment of women is always a part of the gender picture, the study of gender in literature is not restricted to the examination of women writers and the representation of women characters. Once women begin to demonstrate their independent existence, males too become gendered. Men are forced to reexamine themselves, and the comforting image of a stronger, more creative, more rational sex breaks down. What is left in its place is a record of some (mostly) masculine triumphs—the Sistine Chapel, American democracy, space flight, Magic Johnson on the basketball court—and also some really shameful behavior. Men, it turns out, belong to the sex that rapes and abuses, that rationalizes its own tendency to violence, that cannot clean up after itself, that whines about any loss of prerogatives, and that consistently disparages women and any of its own members that are perceived to be womanish.

This last trait may the most difficult to eradicate, for as ethnologists and psychologists have pointed out, the transition to manhood in most cultures has required a violent separation from a matrix (literally a womb) of femaleness. The pubescent boy becomes a man by rejecting the world of the mothers and embarking on a journey to find his name and learn the secrets of the male warriors, a pattern that emerges everywhere from tribal rituals to classic American novels. But when women, too, can be adventurous, autonomous, and audacious, then the carefully constructed masculine self loses its foundation. Being a man becomes more complicated when it isn't enough not to be womanish.

The redefinition of masculinity has taken many forms, from imitations of women's consciousness raising to mock tribal gatherings. A considerable body of recent scholarship testifies to the need for new ways of thinking about maleness, now that it can no longer be mistaken for the universal condition of "mankind." In SF by men, one recent trend has been the dismantling of traditional father figures and their replacement by various groupings of mentors who may be male, female, or other.

Other? The traditional formulation of gender allows for male and female—or, more precisely, male and not-male—with no room for anything beyond this contrasting pair. Yet within the gender code, certain ways of expressing maleness or femaleness can serve to destabilize the binary pair. Such disrupters include cross-dressing, homosexuality, and surgical alteration of the body. Any of these variations can serve as a third gender option, thereby changing the positions of the other two. When there is a triangular relationship, it is more difficult to define one sex as the Self and the other as the Other, or one as complete and the other as lacking. Depending on one's commitment to the existing gender code, such third terms may be seen as dangerous deviance or overdue liberation. Marjorie Garber points out that the third term is not actually a *term* at all, in the sense that the binary pair is made up of opposing terms. Instead, it is "that which questions binary thinking and introduces crisis" (11) by challenging the very structures of thought. Much as the third actor on a stage, added by Sophocles to classical tragedy, the third functions as the emissary of disorder, the messenger who brings the news that nothing is as it seems (Garber 12).

It is not only defenders of male authority who are made uncomfortable by the destabilizing implications of a "third sex." There are varieties of feminism founded on the idea of an uncrossable boundary between the sexes, and some of those who believe in an essential (and superior) womanhood, notes Bornstein, condemn androgyny and transsexualism with a positively Puritan rigor (75). Likewise, gay and lesbian activists who assert that one's sexuality is inescapably fixed upon one's own or the opposite sex may be uncomfortable with fictions about a sex that is neither opposite nor the same.

In fiction that purports to represent the real world, there are few ways to represent the category—or anti-category—of "thirdness." As mentioned above, the role of disruptive third can be taken by characters who possess epicene features; or who cross-dress; or who are, as in Balzac's frequently analyzed story of sexual misinterpretation, "Sarrasine," actually castrated males.

*We can suspend our proclivities toward order and dualism

In each of these cases, however, it is possible to force the ambiguous character into a more conventional category; by the story's end, the author or reader (or both in collusion) discovers the "real" gender of the character and reinterprets events accordingly. Genuine hermaphroditism, as in the famous nineteenth century case of Herculine Barbin, does not seem to translate readily into realistic fiction. Perhaps this is because such cases come to us encrusted with medical/scientific language—chromosomes, genitalia, physical anomalies, in-utero influences, etc.—and are so firmly defined as rare exceptions that they naturally gravitate toward the form of literature devoted to science and the exceptional: science fiction.

For in SF, androgyny and other sexual alternatives need not be illusions to be dispelled or exceptions to be avoided but can instead represent plausible features of an extrapolated future or an alien world. SF writers are more than willing to disrupt the binary gender code with such concepts as a literal third sex, a society without sexual division, gender as a matter of individual choice, involuntary metamorphosis from one sex to another, gender as prosthesis, and all manner of unorthodox manifestations of sexual desire. Readers are asked to accept these features as literal truths about the imaginary universe of the fiction, but at the same time they are invited to map the new fictional (dis)order onto the world of experience.

In such deliberately disorienting stories as Le Guin's *The Left Hand of Darkness* (1969), about a world of androgynes; Tiptree's "And I Awoke and Found Me Here on the Cold Hill's Side" (1972), in which aliens of uncertain gender send out such powerful sexual signals that they coopt desire between humans; or Samuel R. Delany's *Stars in My Pocket Like Grains of Sand* (1984), in which the pronouns "he" and "she" are assigned according to whether one desires or is desired, one is reminded that gender is both capricious and ubiquitous. It colors every perception, governs every exchange. The gender code is not something we apply to the world; it is part of our way of knowing the world. Historians and philosophers of science such as Sandra Harding, Donna Haraway, and Evelyn Fox Keller have pointed out that science itself, despite its pose of impersonality, incorporates gender distinctions in its language, its social structure, and even its epistemology.

As an outgrowth of science, SF is well positioned to function as meta-science, examining different ways of knowing. As an essentially realist mode—that is, one which constructs convincingly faked histories—it is capable of investigating history's shifting alignments of power. As a form of popular romance, it exploits, channels, and stimulates desires. Desire, power, and knowledge are thus not only expressions of gender, but also fundamental operations of the SF code. In order to explore the full range of interactions between the two codes, we need to look at recent feminist and gender-bending SF in the broader context of the genre's history, to see how concepts of the masculine, the feminine, and none-of-the-above have shaped the fiction of discovery, power, desire, selfhood, and alienness.

Gender is not merely a theme in SF; I hope to show that it is an integral part of the genre's intellectual and aesthetic structure. A focus on gender brings out certain transitional moments and counter-movements that have not figured prominently in most histories of the genre. What I originally imagined as a structural study of selected works has become, in effect, an alternative history of SF. Alternative histories have always been a popular subgenre within SF. It is fun to imagine what the world would be like if the Vikings had set up permanent settlements in North America or if Anne Boleyn had produced a male heir for Henry VIII. Besides being entertaining, such histories can open up new viewpoints on actual events: standard history may be written by the winners, but alternative history can be written by forgotten allies or losers or innocent bystanders.

Although I have kept my alternative history of the genre consistent with documentary evidence, I find myself contradicting widely accepted "facts" about its origins and development, particularly those that concern the centrality of certain writers and stories. A story may be a touchstone to some readers, reading with their particular interests, and largely irrelevant to others. Setting aside differences of taste, historical judgments still inevitably reflect the historian's perspective. Even in a scientific experiment, after all, what the observer sees is affected by where he, she, or it stands.

Literary criticism, like science, is performed by male or female individuals using gender-biased tools. I am not an indeterminately-sexed alien looking indifferently at these quaint efforts to come to terms with the gendered human condition. My reading of SF is grounded in my experience in a male body and a masculine social role. I respond powerfully and involuntarily to images and scenarios that address those experiences. I have only second-hand knowledge of what it is like to be a daughter, a mother, a woman in the workplace, or a woman in love, and in reading about such experiences I have to perform a complicated set of imaginative translations. In sum, the readings I offer in this book are neither objective nor universal.

Yet I read fiction not only as my individual situation determines, but also as I have been taught. From the very beginning of my formal training as a student of literature, the language I was taught to use and the perspectives embedded in that language, were masculine through and through. Outside of class, however, I was given another kind of education within stories by writers like Andre Norton, Madeleine L'Engle, and Eleanor Cameron. Later the tastes formed by reading their work led me to Patricia McKillip, Suzette Haden Elgin, Kate Wilhelm, Joan Vinge, Joanna Russ, and Ursula K. Le Guin. Eventually I discovered that some of these fiction writers—notably Cameron, Russ, and Le Guin—were also able critics working toward a feminist reading of fantasy and science fiction. From both the fiction and the criticism, I learned something of reading with an eye to gender assumptions, inequalities of power, and differences in metaphoric structures.

So I, as a reader, am a chimera, a science-fictional construct incorporating many identities and many voices. When I read and write about my reading, I catch myself echoing something of Russ's sardonic wit or Le Guin's inclusive humaneness. Their voices have become part of my reading self to such a degree that it is difficult to sort out and acknowledge the borrowings. Bakhtin's insight about the dialogic nature of fictional discourse also fits my experience of academic discourse. An essay such as this is a many-voiced dialogue in which direct quotation and scholarly documentation represent only the most obvious forms of indebtedness.

In writing about gender, I have attempted to let some of those other voices come through, especially those that speak from experiences and identities other than my own. This has meant not only reading women writers and critics but also discussing ideas with friends and trying out drafts of chapters on willing commentators. I got used to this way of operating when I took part in two projects, both of which involved working through issues of gender and SF. The first was the editing of an anthology, *The Norton Book of Science Fiction,* along with Ursula K. Le Guin and Karen Joy Fowler. The second was serving as a judge for the 1994 Tiptree Award, along with Pat Murphy, Susanna Sturgis, Lucy Sussex, and Ellen Kushner. In both cases, I had the privilege and pleasure of learning from my collaborators new ways of reading SF and new reasons to value particular kinds of fiction.

These experiences thus offer an answer to an accusation still occasionally leveled (by my students, for instance) against feminist criticism: that all it amounts to is condemning older literary works for not sharing the critic's views. It is, of course, true that the critic must read in historical context. One cannot expect most SF of the 1930s to do a very good job of representing women, let alone to give them the variety of roles they play in more recent stories. However, one can read 1930s fiction with an awareness of the mostly concealed interactions of gender and with, therefore, an even greater appreciation for the occasional stories that make artful use of those interactions.

I have tried, in my analysis, to incorporate something of the sense of discovery and pleasure arising from discussions with my fellow editors and judges. Decoding gender can be fun, whether one is tracing the hidden assumptions in a straightforward adventure story or sorting out the perspectives in a complex novel of cultural conflict. In the discussions that follow, I aim at finding ways to enjoy a wide variety of texts: short and long, new and old, covertly sexist and overtly feminist.

I sometimes treat whole groups of stories as if they constituted a single statement about gender, for in SF the individual story often serves primarily as a response to or an embellishment of an earlier idea. Indeed, in some ways all of SF constitutes a single encyclopedic repository of images, tropes, character types, and narrative moves. Damien Broderick and other critics have borrowed Philippe Hamon's term *mega-text* to describe the collective quality of the SF universe (Broderick 57). Some stories are more or less disposable in themselves but significant in their contribution to the SF code. Others, while no less dependent on the megatext, assert themselves more firmly as expressions of a single artist's vision. With the latter sort, I look for the ways the writer has woven familiar tropes into rich and original designs, some of them so compelling that they change the way we see the world outside the text.

For I would like to see SF's changes in the gender code emerge from fiction into the world of perception and action. By transforming existing sexual practices and power structures, SF lets us see that there might be other, more humane, ways of arranging matters. My motive in writing this study is not merely to introduce readers to a number of curious and pleasing narratives but also to encourage them to look through these fictional lenses and see which offer visions of a future worth steering toward.

In framing the individual essays that make up this book, I have looked for approaches to the subject of gender that have not already been thoroughly mapped out by critics. I have also sought out cases in which the codes of gender and SF most powerfully transform one another, changing the meaning of the most fundamental signs in both. If I am writing history, it is not the smooth evolutionary narrative that sometimes presents itself as the true course of the genre. I see history generally in terms of lurches, bumps, divided tracks, and half-camouflaged gaps. To represent these I have framed the genre's story as a set of defining moments, some of which may seem to reverse directions taken in the others.

I begin with the emergence of SF as an offshoot from a related genre, Gothic fiction. Many historians of SF, especially Brian Aldiss, have identified Mary Shelley's *Frankenstein* as a particularly influential text: a story in which Gothic storytelling formulas are linked with scientific issues to create a new kind of fiction. Shelley's sex is noted as an odd aberration in the history of an essentially masculine pursuit. However, in the history of the Gothic, women writers are not exceptional. From Ann Radcliffe to the Brontës, women made key contributions to the genre. Anne Williams identifies a feminine Gothic tradition that differs structurally and thematically from the masculine Gothic of Matthew Lewis or Edgar Allan Poe. In chapter 2, I trace this difference into the newer genre of SF. The masculine tradition of Poe and Hawthorne posits one sort of science and one sort of narrative fulfillment; another is hinted at in Shelley and in the forgotten work of her contemporary Jane Webb Loudon.

The basic storytelling tropes pioneered at the beginning of the nineteenth century continued to proliferate throughout that century and up into the 1920s and '30s, when specialty magazines gave the genre a locus and a name. Chapter 3 examines stories published in and out of the SF magazines at the beginning of what is often called the Golden Age of science fiction. By the year 1937, SF had accumulated an extensive vocabulary of meaningful images, such as the robot, the alien, and the spaceship, and had developed a grammar for organizing those iconic images into emotionally rewarding narratives. After 1937, under the leadership of editor John W. Campbell, SF writers began to approach SF's tropes with more literary sophistication. The stories of that year, then, represent a maturing but not yet self-conscious genre. In them, the engines of desire and fear and curiosity are running full throttle, unmuffled by self-censorship. Individual plot devices and scientific props were carefully vetted by fans in the letter columns of the magazines, and yet the overall story structures and their gender implications were almost completely ignored. Simply by reversing those emphases, by paying most attention where the story invites us to pay least, one can trace patterns of masculine frustration and fulfillment that still underlie SF's masterplots, though today they may be better disguised or employed ironically.

Chapter 4 takes up one of the most powerful of those masterplots, the story of the emerging superman. Favored by John W. Campbell and popular with fans, this scenario posits a Darwinian competition between ordinary human beings and a superior mutated race (who just happen to share a number of features with SF fans). Most superman stories of the 1940s and '50s rely on a sexual dynamic derived from Darwin's popularizers, in which evolutionary developments are demonstrated in males, whose sexual competition is thus also a struggle for racial advancement. By the mid-1950s, however, some writers had begun to question both the evolutionary model and the narrative formula. One story by Philip K. Dick, for instance, "The Golden Man," transforms the superman story into a vehicle for questioning the definitions of both masculinity and superiority. His darkly humorous tale points the way toward new levels of potential meaning within existing tropes.

Chapter 5 is about an absence that becomes a dazzling presence within SF: the feminine counterpart of the superman. Early male writers rarely imagined women in the role of *Homo superior*. If they did so, it was usually in terms of a slippery, indefinable threat. When women writers like C. L. Moore began to toy with the idea, they kept the indeterminacy but rewrote it as possibility or multiplicity. I call this trope, not the superwoman, but the wonder woman, because it reflects a whole gamut of wonderment, beginning with Freudian bafflement over just what it is that women want and ending in feminist speculation about what they might become.

In chapter 6, the focus is on imagined societies dominated by or entirely composed of a single sex. Male or female, utopian or dystopian, the single-sexed society has long been one of the primary ways to perform thought experiments on gender. The best known of these *Gedankenexperiments* are the feminist utopias of the 1960s and '70s. Their relationship to the matriarchal dystopias of pulp SF has occasionally been noted; I suggest that there is also a close link to male-bonding stories from the 1950s such as Robert A. Heinlein's *Space Cadet*. In the logic of utopian writing, each formulation opens up contrary possibilities, one generation's ideal becoming the next generation's nightmare, and vice versa. Some of SF's most misogynistic concepts may have opened the way for some its most influential feminist texts.

Many readers became aware of the power of SF to question gender after the publication of Ursula K. Le Guin's *The Left Hand of Darkness.* That book offered a vision of an androgynous society that continues to be debated today. Is it restrictive or liberating; is its depiction of androgyny psychologically realistic or illusory? Chapter 7 looks at the way the debate has been conducted in subsequent fictional texts, and at the shifting nature of androgyny itself. Looking at androgyny as a sign, rather than as a real or imaginary phenomenon, we can see how the meaning of the sign can alter depending on both the fictional context and the narrator and author's own gender. Women and men have different views of the no-man's-land between them, and a writer like Raphael Carter, who claims neither gender, offers yet a different formulation.

Chapter 8 focuses on SF in the postmodern era. Most versions of postmodern epistemology ask us to pay attention to what Hayden White has called the "content of the form." Rather than seeing figures of speech and narrative forms as neutral carriers of meaning, postmodernist critics like Jean Baudrillard and Donna Haraway call our attention to the power of tropes to shape reality, or at least our conceptions of it. Two recent sequences of novels, by James Morrow and Gwyneth Jones, can be read as thought-experiments conducted on metaphor itself. Using an analytical model derived from the work of George Lakoff and Mark Johnson, I examine the way both writers call attention to the metaphoric basis of scientific thought and social organization. Lakoff and Johnson call this "the body in the mind," because the most fundamental metaphoric systems are informed by images of the human body. In the work of Jones and Morrow, the gender of that metaphorized body becomes evident. At the same time, these writers posit alternative figures of speech: other ways of thinking about the body and other kinds of bodies to think with.

If chapter 8 takes us up to the postmodernist present, chapter 9 concerns SF's future, which is already being negotiated in various venues, including the publishing industry, movies and television, the college classroom, and the Internet. As the future itself becomes both a dominant cultural metaphor and a valuable commodity, it becomes imperative for every subset of society to stake a claim within that future. Who's going to be in charge? ask women and Asians and Latinos. Will we be there at all? ask lesbians and gay men. Will our stories continue to matter? ask members of the white, male technological elite who have traditionally formed SF's primary audience. Borrowing the notion of cultural negotiation from Stephen Greenblatt's analyses of Elizabethan theater, this final chapter looks at what happens when symbols move from one cultural arena to another. Some ideas cross cultural barriers freely and some get left behind. Sometimes the payments offered in return—money or prestige or a different set of cultural icons—become the force directing the future of the genre.

Each of these chapters is one more variation on my theme: that signs such as the images and storytelling tropes of SF enable us to sort out the world and help us make sense of experience. The history of the genre, at least in my alternative version, reflects the ongoing hope that if we change the signs, the world might follow. SF is not usually very successful when it tries to predict solutions to particular problems, but it is very good at playing insightfully with social issues.

A popular mode of storytelling hardly constitutes a reliable source of hard facts about the origins and nature of sexual differentiation—but then, there is no such source. Ethnological observations about gender roles are contradictory and hopelessly tangled up in observers' expectations. The same is true about animal behavior studies, with the added complication that there is no agreement about which animal species we are supposed to resemble: violent baboons, gentle bonobos, chimps, gorillas, lions, gazelles, or Surinam toads. Biochemistry and genetics give us a lot of information about the mechanisms that underlie sexual behavior but not much about the ways those mechanisms translate into individual sexual identities or social systems, and observations in these fields, too, are tainted by the tendency to impose current social norms on the data. What are often called "biological imperatives" turn out, on closer inspection, to be something more like "biological interrogatives." Our genes offer many possible ways of expressing them, rather than insisting on a single pattern of development.

History likewise provides us with plenty of examples of gender arrangements, but no explanation as to why these arrangements have come about except as a result of tradition—in other words, of earlier history. What history teaches, as Gertrude Stein pointed out, is simply that history teaches. Any number of different lessons about gender roles can be drawn from looking at, say, twelfth-century Iceland or nineteenth-century Pueblo society. The eternal verities, like the snows of Dylan Thomas's Welsh Christmas, turn out to be "eternal since Wednesday."

Any discipline that claims to explain the origins of gender coding should be looked on with a mixture of interest and suspicion, with the suspicion increasing in proportion to the strength of the claims. Such accounts are essentially what Thomas Laqueur has termed "just-so stories": fables in which an imagined distant past serves as both a metaphor and a rationale for present customs (226). Similar stories have been offered to explain the origins of other codes, like language, which has been explained as evolving from expressive "bow wows," imitative "ding dongs," and other sorts of protolinguistic utterances. Where there is no evidence, storytelling at least helps organize our imaginings.

SF is not so different from the storytelling engaged in by sociobiologists and anthropologists, save for the fact that it tends to focus not on origins but on ends, not on where we came from but on where we are going. And because where we are going depends partly on where we are willing and able to imagine ourselves going, SF can offer important insights into the limits of the imaginable and the ways those limits are changing, from housewives in space to gender-free utopias, and beyond.

Furthermore, the conventions of SF allow it to represent gender as what I claimed it to be at the beginning of this chapter, a code. In other areas of literature and life, gender rarely operates as an independent sign system. It is constrained by habits of thought and speech, economics, power, desire, and the stubborn physicality of bodies. But there are no bodies in fiction, only words that call bodies to mind. SF encourages us to play with those words, changing their forms and applications, literalizing old metaphors and generating new ones, and generally treating gender as if it were simply and completely a code. By doing so, it opens up new ways of talking gender: new things to say and new ways to say them.

CHAPTER

FROM NEAT IDEA TO TROPE

hat does it mean to define science fiction as a code, as I have done here, and what does such a perspective allow us to discover about SF and especially about its relationship to gender? To answer those questions, I am going to venture back into the genre's early history, to the time when a number of writers were more or less independently—and accidentally—inventing the form.

Some of these writers, such as Mary Shelley and Edgar Allan Poe, are recognized as major precursors of modern SF, while others, like Jane Webb Loudon, have had little direct influence on later developments. The difference lies primarily in whether or not they were able to match up fictional elements with images and ideas from science in such a way that each component, the fiction and the science, represents and illuminates the other. That is to say, in addition to the many decisions any writer of narrative must make—about language, focus, incident, and character—writers of SF take on the additional challenge of using those same decisions to contribute to an ongoing conversation on scientific issues. When Victor Frankenstein takes one look at his monstrous creation and hightails it out of the lab, his actions reveal his character and advance the plot, but they also invite the reader to think about the borderline between death and life and about the implications of using science and technology to blur the boundary. Victor (or the mad scientist), the Creature (or monster, or superman), even the appraising look that passes between them—all of these elements, by helping to develop the plot, also become enrolled in the science fictional code. And, once having entered the code, the same signs become available to later writers, who have been giving them a good workout from Mary Shelley's time to this.

Several elements are required to make up any code. First, there have to be recognizable signifiers: sounds, gestures, visual images, or any other supply of things that can be distinguished from one another and reproduced freely. Next, there must be a systematic set of rules for combining the signs into messages—a grammar. Additionally, there must be rules for interpreting the messages; that is, for translating them into other codes and for applying them to experienced situations. "That is a cow," can be translated into "Den där är en ku"; it can also be uttered in appropriate circumstances, as when somebody is trying to put a saddle on the wrong animal in the pasture. Finally, at least two people must understand the rules, so that one can send and the other receive a message.

So in order for science fiction to become a code in the first place, it had to accumulate a set of signs, develop an orderly way of combining those signs, establish relationships with other sign systems and with categories of experience, and create a community of writers and readers who understood the code in the same way. Furthermore, these things all had to take place pretty much simultaneously. If the signs exist but no one knows the rules, nothing happens; it's like trying to start a fire with fuel and heat but no oxygen. Fortunately, new literary genres, like new languages, can reuse parts of existing ones. In fact, one code can form and develop within another without anyone noticing, until at some point people suddenly realize that they have not been speaking Latin for some time, but something that will eventually be renamed French or Spanish. The new code isn't likely to be noticed until someone comes along attempting to make sense of it by the old rules and failing.

Imagine, for example, trying to read a science fiction story using the interpretive strategies that work for something like detective fiction. SF and Detective are both what can be called secondary codes: they exist as elaborations of the more fundamental and more extensive codes of narrative and of language. A set of words (part of the language code) is combined in such a way as to send a message about a character (part of the narrative code) performing an action (another narrative sign). If one is reading in the Detective code, that character might be interpreted variously as Victim, Suspect, Detective, Criminal, or Red Herring. If she is the Detective, her action might be an act of Interrogating the Witnesses, Locating a Clue, or Reenacting the Crime. If she is performing one of the other roles, she might be Revisiting the Crime Scene or merely Innocently Bystanding. Experienced readers of detective stories are so proficient at assigning these meanings that writers can play with them the way poets play with conventional usage, creating figures of story rather than mere figures of speech. Characters can shift or combine roles, so that the detective may also serve as a suspect or even a victim. A single action might function "literally" as the planting of a false clue and "figuratively" as the legitimate revelation of a deeper level of the mystery.

But this neat and coherent system breaks down when applied to the wrong sort of story. Take, for instance, a story frequently listed as one of the early works of SF, Nathaniel Hawthorne's "Rappaccini's Daughter" (1844). In this story we find a young protagonist, Giovanni Guasconti, who is trying to figure out what is going on in the garden outside his window. He might do for a detective. Then we have a scientist, Rappaccini, who has something to hide: could he be the murderer? The young woman in the garden: victim? But these characters fail to perform actions appropriate to character-signs within the Detective code. No bodies are found, no wills concealed, no secret love affairs brought to light. There is a death, perhaps even a murder, but it is by no means clear who has committed it. In terms of that particular code, the story almost, but doesn't quite, make sense.

There is a reason that the reading almost works. Detective fiction and SF spring from the same parent genre, the Gothic romance, and family resemblances among the three are strong. One can imagine the situation in "Rappaccini's Daughter" being handled by Poe as either an exercise in ratiocination or a descent into horror: imagine Beatrice Rappaccini dissolving into a pool of poison, leaving only her rich clothing and two rows of phosphorescent teeth. In many of Poe's stories, in fact, Gothic, science fictional, and detective codes alternate or coincide: "The Murders in the Rue Morgue" works simultaneously as SF, Gothic, and mystery, and no single reading strategy can quite make sense of *The Narrative of Arthur Gordon Pym*.

Brian Aldiss emphasizes the Gothic heritage in his pioneering history of science fiction, *Billion Year Spree* (upgraded in its revised edition to a *Trillion Year Spree*). Aldiss's definition of the genre even includes the controversial proviso that SF "is characteristically cast in the Gothic or post-Gothic mode" (25). Aldiss specifically mentions the Gothic propensity for exotic scenes and shocking revelations as useful models for SF (35), but other features may have been equally significant in the development of the younger genre.

Hawthorne's works, like Poe's, certainly support Aldiss's claim of close kinship between the SF and the Gothic. Although "Rappaccini's Daughter" is not quite readable as a detective story, there is virtually nothing in it that cannot be interpreted in terms of older Gothic conventions. The setting is exotic Italy at the beginning of the Renaissance, Beatrice Rappaccini makes an effective imperiled heroine, her father resembles the many ambiguous mages and alchemists who call down devastation on their descendents, and Giovanni is the naive protagonist who stumbles upon the mystery (for it is indeed a mystery, though not one soluble by any act of sleuthing).

Some of the signs distinctive to the Gothic code are described by one of its more alert readers: the fictional Henry Tilney, in Jane Austen's Gothic parody *Northanger Abbey:*

> you must be aware that when a young lady is (by whatever means) introduced into a dwelling of this kind, she is always lodged apart from the rest of the family. While they snugly repair to their own end of the house, she is formally conducted by Dorothy, the ancient housekeeper, up a different staircase, and along many gloomy passages, into an apartment never used since some cousin or kin died in it about twenty years before. (Chap. XX, 209–10)

The Gothic writer's repertoire thus includes, as Henry points out, such elements as the endangered young lady, the ancient and gloomy mansion, and the enigmatic servant—all present in "Rappacini's Daughter." Henry goes on to list other features for his eager listener, Catherine Morland, who fancies herself a Gothic heroine. She can expect to find "a ponderous chest which no efforts can open," "the portrait of some handsome warrior, whose features will so incomprehensibly strike you, that you will not be able to withdraw your eyes from it," "a violent storm," "a secret subterranean communication between your chamber and the chapel of St. Anthony, scarcely two miles off," "the remains of some instrument of torture," and a manuscript containing the "memoirs of the wretched Matilda," the source of whose wretchedness will remain forever a mystery, since Henry breaks off laughing (XX, 210–13).

These elements are often referred to as "Gothic machinery," implying that their only function is to manufacture, like some sort of push-button gadget, the shivers and goosebumps that Catherine and the rest of the audience were seeking. In his travesty of the form, "How to Write a Blackwood Article" (1838), Edgar Allan Poe emphasizes both the conventionality of the Gothic code and the automatic way it generates the intense sensations for which it is known. For Poe, or rather for his stand-in, Miss Psyche Zenobia, writing an effective Gothic piece simply requires assembling a bizarre and threatening situation, such as that of "a young person who goes to sleep under the clapper of a church bell, and is awakened by its tolling for a funeral" (197); an appropriate tone, such as "the tone elevated, diffusive, and interjectional" (199); and, to fill up space, a generous supply of, "first, *Piquant Facts for the Manufacture of Similes;* and, second, *Piquant Expressions to be introduced as occasion may require*" (200).

This is all close enough to Poe's actual practice to cast some doubt on his good faith as an artist: is he no more than a master of what he calls, in another sketch, the exact science of diddling? Does he consider his chosen form to be a sort of verbal card trick? But Poe is never a reliable guide to his own intentions: if we take him at his word in "The Philosophy of Composition," the haunting incremental repetitions of "The Raven" result from a computer program for generating evocative sound patterns—no meaning intended here, folks.

Nonetheless, readers of Poe's Gothic verse and fiction have persisted in finding something significant in their many mouldering towers and hollow-eyed heroes. His limited repertory company is capable of expressing acute insights into psychological responses, especially those called up by desperate situations. And that is where the Gothic mode or code excels: in its ability to convey human experience not at its most typical but at its most extraordinary. In capable hands like those of Poe, Hawthorne, E. T. A. Hoffmann, or Mary Shelley, such Gothic elements as madmen, mirrors, lovers in disguise, and incestuous desires are not merely tokens in a game of Goosebumps. Rather they serve to frame questions about aspects of human behavior and psychology buried under layers of Enlightenment reason and nineteenth-century respectability. Again and again in Gothic tales one finds repressed images and emotions erupting into the streets and parlors of middle-class reality. The Gothic code provides ways of talking about the unmentionable or inconceivable by locating it in the past, in the haunts of aristocrats, under monks' robes and nuns' habits, or in the eyes of ancestral portraits. Religious ecstasy, sexual obsession, violence, ancient superstitions: all that offends against the middle class faith in family, progress, and enlightened self-interest can be invoked, flirted with, and (temporarily) exorcized within Gothic narratives.

Reading Hawthorne's tale in these terms, one finds the shadowy past figured forth in Giovanni's gloomy chambers, in the shattered fountain he sees below his window, and in the elderly and secretive housekeeper or landlady (Henry Tilney's old Dorothy, renamed Lisabetta). Archaic beliefs are represented by the house's association with one of Dante's damned souls and by the legend recounted to Giovanni by Rappacini's chief rival, Professor Pietro Baglioni, of a beautiful woman imbued with poisons and sent as a deadly gift to Alexander the Great. Both Beatrice and the garden she tends represent unbounded and therefore threatening sexuality—or perhaps the threat is merely Giovanni's obsession projected onto her vivid beauty. Violence is hinted at throughout, but in small, subtle ways: the death of an insect exposed to Beatrice's toxic breath; the fearful movement of Rappacini through the deadly garden he has created, as "of one walking among malignant influences, such as savage beasts or deadly snakes, or evil spirits, which, should he allow them one moment of license, would wreak upon him some terrible fatality" (166); and Beatrice's gentle touch on Giovanni's wrist, that nonetheless leaves a bruise, "a purple print, like that of four small fingers, and the likeness of a slender thumb upon his wrist" (181).

The reading is coherent and reasonably satisfying. As a message in the Gothic code, "Rappacini's Daughter" says something about the lure of the morally ambiguous, as when Giovanni, musing on what he takes to be Beatrice's wickedness, is overwhelmed by "a wild offspring of both love and horror that had each parent in it, and burned like one and shivered like the other" (174). There are also messages about hypocrisy (Giovanni's), jealousy (Baglioni's), and purification by self-sacrifice (Beatrice's). Even the symmetry of the story's structure and the vividness of its images can be read as messages in the Gothic code, for an important part of meaning is aesthetic. But after everything in the story that can possibly be read as part of the code is noted and translated, there is still a little residue, a detail here and there that seems to say nothing of significance.

The fluent reader of Gothic knows what to make of Rappacini's intense gaze into the poisonous flowers, "as if he was looking into their inmost nature," but might be less certain why he should be interested in "discovering why one leaf grew in this shape, and another in that, and wherefore such and such flowers differed among themselves in hue and perfume" (166). Inmost natures are familiar signifiers, but leaf shapes, unless they are clearly assigned some symbolic meaning—if they are shaped like a baby's hand, say, or a blade pointed at someone's heart—don't register in the code. The poisonous garden, with its ironic echoes of Eden, functions well within the Gothic code, but what need is there to explain that certain of the plants "were probably the result of an experiment, which, in one or two cases, had succeeded in mingling plants individually lovely into a compound possessing the questionable and ominous character that distinguished the whole growth of the garden" (178)? Rappacini's studies, insofar as they resemble alchemical meddling, fit into the Gothic mode, but his idea "that all medicinal virtues are comprised within those substances which we term vegetable poisons" (170), a theory that he seeks to validate not by reference to ancient philosophers or theories of correspondences but through observation and experiment—such a theory is likely to send the contemporary reader's thoughts on a detour into the pharmaceutical potential of rain forest flora.

These leftovers could, perhaps, be explained as part of the atmosphere Hawthorne is trying to create: having chosen to set his Gothic tale in a medieval university, he can add verisimilitude by letting his characters actually engage in some serious study (and some serious academic rivalry). If his protagonist had been a student of painting, rather than natural philosophy, Hawthorne could similarly have incorporated bits of information about brushwork and glazes—not too much, just enough to make us believe in the setting.

The science of Rappacini, however, is not entirely reducible to corroborative detail. It is too consistent, too interesting, and too necessary to the plot. The poisonous garden, with its single human blossom, is not just a Gothic device. It is what science fiction readers are wont to call a Neat Idea: that is, a scientific datum or hypothesis that calls up, in the right sort of imagination, a host of fascinating "what-ifs."

Hawthorne's notebooks show that his was the right sort of imagination. H. Bruce Franklin cites a number of entries in which Hawthorne can be seen turning over various scientific Neat Ideas to see which might be transformed into fictional What-Ifs. Here, for instance, is one of the notebook entries that show "Rappacini's Daughter" beginning to take shape:

> Madame Calderon de la B (in Life in Mexico) speaks of persons who have been inoculated with the venom of rattlesnakes, by pricking them in various places with the tooth. These persons are thus secured forever against the bite of any venomous reptile. They have the power of calling snakes, and feel great pleasure in playing with and handling them. Their own bite becomes poisonous to people not inoculated in the same manner. (Hawthorne, *The American Notebooks,* ed. Randall Stewart, cited in Franklin 9)

Franklin points out that Hawthorne, despite his habit of imposing symbolic value on every plot twist, was usually careful to ground those plots in the science of his day: "The long line of doctors, chemists, botanists, mesmerists, physicists, and inventors who parade the wonders of their skills throughout Hawthorne's fiction rarely strays far from historically accepted achievements or theories" (10). Even such a tale as "The Man of Adamant," about a heart that miraculously turns to mineral, can be traced to a scientific report, written by Hawthorne himself, about a new method for "converting animal substances into stone" (*The American Magazine of Useful and Entertaining Knowledge,* 1836; cited in Franklin 10).

We may be justified, then, in seeing yet another code at work in "Rappacini's Daughter," a code made up not just of the leftover bits of scientific information but of all of the other narrative elements as well, reinterpreted in light of that information. Calling the tale a work of science fiction is a little anachronistic in that neither the SF readership nor its specialized reading habits existed in Hawthorne's day. It is, however, an anachronism justified not only by the insights it can offer into the story but also by the role that Hawthorne and his contemporaries played in bringing the SF code into existence.

As SF, "Rappacini's Daughter" is not so much about Giovanni's obsessions and moral dilemmas as it is about Rappacini and his achievements. Unlike his rival Baglioni, Rappacini is willing to "sacrifice human life, his own among the rest, or whatever else was dearest to him, for the sake of adding so much as a grain of mustard-seed to the great heap of accumulated knowledge" (169). A mysterious figure who is discussed by other characters but hardly speaks himself until the end of the story, Rappacini turns out to be the only character who sees the world in material and pragmatic, rather than mythical and moral, terms. He is able to manipulate the natural world because he ignores inherited categories such as "poisonous" and "harmless" and because he is willing to violate the integrity of species to produce new combinations of traits. His practical goal is to give his daughter power, to make her "able to quell the mightiest with a breath" (192). The idea of taint or sin, which dominates the thinking of the others, seems not even to have occurred to him.

And thus Rappacini can stand for modern science, while the others stand, depending on the reader's viewpoint, either for superstitious obstruction or for wise restraint. One can extrapolate from Rappacini's science to inoculations and antibiotics, in which case the opponents seem ignorant and shortsighted. Alternatively, one can see Rappacini pointing the way toward biological warfare and eugenics, in which case their intervention seems providential. Beatrice is either saved by the efforts of her lover and his mentor or needlessly sacrificed to their masculine pride.

And it *is* a specifically masculine pride, for all the signs that Hawthorne has found to embody his Neat Idea are deeply divided along lines of gender. The two scientists and the acolyte for whom they are competing are all masculine. Even the potion Giovanni administers to Beatrice has male sexual associations: it is, after all, a fluid transmitted from a man to a woman in order to consummate their relationship and to transform her body.

An opposing femininity is represented minimally in Lisabetta, whose sexuality is attenuated by age and subordinated to her masters' commands; somewhat more strongly in the garden, where Rappacini has been working to impose his will, overturning natural order; and most assertively in Beatrice, whose desirable body becomes the battleground not so much between father and suitor as between rival scientific factions.

Such gender coding is not unique to "Rappacini's Daughter." Another story of Hawthorne's that responds well to a science fictional reading is "The Birth-Mark" (1843). In this story, also, the scientist aspires to create a superior human being. This tale, as well, designates a female character as the object of the scientist's manipulations, and she too dies at the end, the victim not only of her husband's ambitions but also of her own acquiescence. Readings of "The Birth-Mark" ignored this aspect of the story for many years, until Judith Fetterly pointed out in *The Resisting Reader* that it isn't just "a story of misguided idealism, a tale of the unhappy consequences of man's nevertheless worthy passion for perfecting and transcending nature" (Fetterly 22). It is also "the story of how to murder your wife and get away with it" (35), brilliantly interwoven with themes of men's reduction of women to physical appearance (24), their denial of their own bodily existence and projection onto women of the body's imperfections (28–29), and the male scientist's resentment of and subversion of a nature perceived as powerfully female (27).

Fetterly's reading is so coherent and so well able to account for the many clues planted within the story that I have never been able to (or wanted to) go back to the way I was taught to read "The Birth-Mark." Rather than subverting the author's intention, this "resisting" technique arguably brings it to fruition. A gendered reading enriches the themes by locating them within a social and cultural matrix. What must be resisted is not the story itself but a way of interpreting it sanctioned by generations of critics, including Cleanth Brooks and Robert Penn Warren, Richard Harter Fogle, Robert Heilman, F. O. Matthiessen, Arlin Turner, Millicent Bell, William Bysshe Stein, and Simon Lesser (Fetterly 191–92). For these critics, it was clear how "we" were supposed to interpret Aylmer and his quest: "We are not, of course, to conceive of Aylmer as a monster, a man who would experiment on his own wife for his own greater glory," say Brooks and Warren in *Understanding Fiction* (1943, cited in Fetterly 191). In order for Judith Fetterly to be able to stand back and say, yes, he is too a monster, she had to un-include herself in that "we," which is a masculine collectivity even though one of the critics she cites is female.

Fetterly's rereading is part of an ambitious undertaking by critics in the 1970s and '80s to learn to read as women rather than as honorary men. A large part of this project was learning not to ignore certain signs in narrative and other codes. Feminist readers had to learn to say what went without saying, to point out what was too obvious to be seen. One such invisible sign was the fact that Hawthorne's scientists were men, and their experimental subjects women. Of course, one wants to say. Scientists *were* men in Hawthorne's day (well, mostly). But Hawthorne does not let us off so easily. Beatrice Rappacini has been taught by her father, is perhaps even "already qualified to fill a professor's chair" (171). Why shouldn't she do so, especially at a time when the profession of science is just beginning to be established? Yet Hawthorne has her deny any such knowledge or ambition: "I know no more of them than their hues and perfume . . . do not believe these stories about my science" (179).

Is Beatrice telling the whole truth here? (If so, she is unique among the actors in the story.) Or does she have reasons to deny what the story itself suggests: that she knows the garden and its contents as well as or better than her father. (This reading also accords with Hawthorne's other dark and "gorgeous" women, like *The Blithedale Romance*'s Zenobia, who reflects his uneasy admiration for the formidably intellectual Margaret Fuller.)

Too much knowledge would damn Beatrice in Giovanni's eyes just as certainly as her poisonous perfume and too opulent beauty. To assume the identity of a scientist might also require that she adopt her father's chilly materialism rather than finding in the flowering shrub a fellow being, a sister, or even a lover: "Approaching the shrub, she threw open her arms, as with a passionate ardor, and drew its branches into an intimate embrace; so intimate, that her features were hidden in its leafy bosom, and her glistening ringlets all intermingled with the flowers" (171).

Judith Fetterly's example invites a similar resisting reading of "Rappacini's Daughter," in which the central action is a conspiracy to divert Beatrice Rappacini from becoming what she has the potential to become: a scholarly new Eve, unfallen and armed with the serpent's knowledge as well as its poison. She could be the founder of a new science, one based in kinship and sympathy rather than objectification and use-value. Such an outcome is a threat to Giovanni, her father, and the embryonic scientific culture in which they take part. No wonder Rappacini seeks out an unwitting ally, a handsome young man who will keep her safely within the embrace of paternal power. Hawthorne uses the language of gesture to express Rappacini's controlling intent: "He paused—his bent form grew erect with conscious power, he spread out his hand over them, in the attitude of a father imploring a blessing upon his children" (191). But Beatrice being what she is, such a blessing can come only in the form of death. No other application of masculine force can contain her.

Reading "Rappacini's Daughter" in this way requires taking into account not only the operations of the science fictional code, but also the code of gender. What I have tried to do in reinterpreting the story is what Fetterly does so well with "The Birth-Mark": namely, invoke one code to amend the perspective imposed by another. Read simply as parables of science, both Hawthorne stories align themselves with the aspirations (if not the methods) of their protagonists, but read as examinations of the relation of gender and science, they offer a more complex and ironic perspective on the characters and their ideals.

Having now summarized the same story four times, with four radically different results, I can only conclude that there is no such thing as a simple plot summary. The very thing literature teachers tell students to avoid, as distraction from real critical work and a waste of the reader's time, may actually be the heart of critical interpretation. Every act of retelling is also a translation that reveals which codes the story invites or allows us to apply in order to generate meanings. The more codes at work, the more possible translations.

By framing his Neat Ideas not just in story form, but specifically in the form of Gothic tales, Hawthorne can take advantage of the way the Gothic code wraps human disguises around abstractions like knowledge, power, and desire, not only attaching such principles to characters but also making them interact in dramatic and suspenseful ways. A large part of the drama comes from the unequal apportionment of these qualities by gender. Female characters in Gothic fiction are typically naive, curious, beautiful, and powerless, while males are experienced, desirous, dangerous, and propertied, the ancestral mansion being essentially an extension of the man who owns it. These are quite conservative groupings of features, but the Gothic mode does not leave them untouched. The dynamics of the Gothic plot require that whatever order is apparent at the beginning of the story be subjected to various transgressions, unmaskings, and wild transformations before a new stability can be achieved at the end.

An emphasis on shifts and shocks means that the Gothic code can be used to make many different, even contradictory statements about gender. If it sometimes reinforces the heroine's submission to patriarchal demands, it can just as easily validate her rebellion against them. It can assert the unbridgeable gap between women and men or reveal gender differences to be mere illusion.

Anne Williams, in her study of the poetics of the Gothic tale, concludes that the conventions constituting the form can be arranged to form two quite different patterns of plot and meaning. Whereas Ellen Moers had earlier identified a "female Gothic" that differed from the presumably genderless norm in its emphasis on childbearing and family relationships (96, 105), Williams describes two Gothic traditions, one feminine and one masculine, in terms of their resemblance to two traditional tales. The masculine version is structured like Perrault's "Bluebeard," which was revived as a Gothic-style stage production in 1798, during the heyday of the Gothic novel (Williams 38). Male writers typically use the Gothic to tell a story of female curiosity punished, of male rebellion taken beyond all limits, and of a final descent into bodily horror: blood, gore, and dissolution. Female writers, on the other hand, generally tell of female curiosity leading through a period of terror to redemption of the male and a marriage that means spiritual rebirth for both partners (103–105). Thus, the paradigm for the feminine Gothic is the story of "Cupid and Psyche" or "Beauty and the Beast" (146). As Williams uses them, the names "feminine" and "masculine" correspond only approximately with the sex of the writer. The feminine Gothic carries on in mass-market romance fiction, written by writers of both sexes, though always published under feminine pen names (270 n. 4). Contemporary versions of the masculine Gothic include the works of Stephen King and Clive Barker—but also stories by Anne Rice, Kathe Koja, and Poppy Z. Brite.

Particular Gothic motifs may be incorporated into either story pattern, but with different meanings. In a number of Gothic tales, for instance, male characters are paired with female doubles, with whom they end up trading traits or even merging. Poe's Roderick Usher and his twin Madeline, representing the masculine pattern, collapse into a dark singularity. In the feminine version, Emily Brontë's Heathcliff and Catherine share one passionate soul between them and are united in a ghostly marriage. Fitting even more neatly into the feminine paradigm is Charlotte Brontë's *Jane Eyre,* in which Jane and Rochester find happiness only after exchanging roles as provider and dependent, pursuer and pursued.

"Rappacini's Daughter" flirts with the idea of a marriage based on a similar exchange of qualities, but ultimately opts for the masculine Gothic ending of death and despair. What Giovanni cannot face, finally, is becoming another Beatrice. "Thou has done it!" he accuses her. "Thou has made me as hateful, as ugly, as loathsome and deadly a creature as thyself,—a world's wonder of hideous monstrosity!" (189). Does the virulence of his response reflect his distaste for her poisonous nature—or his disgust at her femaleness and at finding himself apparently infected by it? The two reactions are inseparable. The gender coding within the story makes them one and the same.

But neither the story's gender-coding nor its resultant emotional charge were anywhere to be seen in the original Neat Idea. Hawthorne's journal entry talks only about "persons . . . inoculated with the venom of rattlesnakes" and "people not inoculated in the same manner." If there is any gender difference between the venomous "persons" and the defenseless "people," the former would seem to be more likely to be men and the latter women, on the grounds that snakes and power have conventionally masculine associations. Not until the bit of weird natural history has been run through the (masculine) Gothic machinery does it begin to function as a compelling study in female power, male paranoia, and the relation of both to scientific exploration.

What about other Neat Ideas drawn from early nineteenth-century science? Does the Gothic and its treatment of gender similarly shape their embodiment in fictional form? Here are some of the What-Ifs that have made it into SF's retrospective canon: What if someone made an artificial being so lifelike it could fool people into thinking it was real? What if dead bodies could be given back their vital spark? What if an apparently empty drop of water were revealed to be an entire world with living human beings in it? What if one were to hypnotize a person right at the point of death and if the mesmeric trance carried over into the next state?

Each of these Neat Ideas actually shows up in more than one narrative written during SF's first half-century. Hawthorne wrote about an artificial butterfly in "The Artist of the Beautiful" (1844); Melville invented a bell-ringing automaton in "The Bell-Tower" (1855); and E. T. A. Hoffmann introduced to the world the beautiful clockwork Olimpia in "The Sand-Man" (1816). Fitz James O'Brien's "The Diamond Lens" (1858) looks in on the residents of a microscopic world, as did an earlier story, now lost, by a writer named William North (Franklin 322). Hawthorne wrote a journal entry about "questions as to unsettled points of History, and Mysteries of Nature, to be asked of a mesmerized person" (Franklin 9), which became the science-fictional premise of *The Blithedale Romance.* Poe added the notion of making the hypnotic subject a dead or dying man in "Mesmeric Revelation" (1844), and then again in "The Facts in the Case of M. Valdemar" (1845). He also wrote a joking version of the revived corpse story in "Some Words with a Mummy" (1845). More serious treatments of the latter Neat Idea show up in Jane Webb Loudon's *The Mummy!* (1827) and, most famously, in Mary Shelley's *Frankenstein* (1818).

Interestingly enough, all of these Ideas concern the same transgressing of the boundary between inert matter and living beings that is central to Shelley's novel. This concern was a good excuse to bring in recent experimentation with mesmerism and electricity (with accompanying occult gestures, leaping sparks, and galvanic twitches) as possible clues to the true nature of the Ghost in the Machine. The scientific questions also lent themselves to dramatization along Gothic lines, not least because of the host of gender-coded images and actions authorized by close attention to issues of reproduction, creativity, and the body itself.

Take, for instance, the notion of the artificial or mechanical being. An assemblage of cogs, springs, and flywheels would seem to be pretty irrelevant to questions of gender. In Hawthorne's hands, though, the artisan who has fabricated a mechanical facsimile of a butterfly is attempting to win the love of a young woman and the respect of her father, his mentor. The butterfly's glittering wings are for Owen Warland, as they are for the living insect, a form of sexual display. However, the butterfly's beauty is no match for the masculine qualities displayed by his rival, the brawny blacksmith Robert Danforth.

Danforth gets the girl and thereby succeeds in reproducing himself: it is his equally macho little son who delivers the final blow to Owen's creation.

Hawthorne identifies the artificial being as at least nominally masculine, through its role as Owen's love offering. Yet by conventional definitions of gender, he continually undercuts both the machine's and its maker's claims to masculinity with such terms as "delicate" (41), "etherealized" (50) and "exquisite susceptibility" (58). The result is that he effectively marks off a different sort of gender distinction, in which Owen and the butterfly represent one pole, the blacksmith and his son the other. Annie Hovenden, who admires Owen's work but opts for more substantial pleasures, is the intermediary between these opposing "genders." Ultimately, Owen both fails and succeeds in his reproductive quest. Even though he ends up alone and his miraculous mechanical offspring is crushed by Danforth Junior, he has reached his goal. Choosing to compete on the ideal rather than the physical plane, he has, unaided by nature or by female counterpart, given birth to an idea.

Melville's version of the automaton story also begins with sexual competition between males and ends by revising conventional gender distinctions. In "The Bell-Tower," the protagonist, Bannadonna, attempts to create the ultimate masculine display in the form of an enormous clocktower. As Bruce Franklin points out, Melville, always cheeky in his use of sexual imagery (as in "The Paradise of Bachelors and the Tartarus of Maids," "I and My Chimney," and, of course, *Moby-Dick*), leaves little doubt as to the phallic implications of Bannadonna's "erection" (146–47). Bannadonna has invested in the tower not only his sexual energy but also his self-image, which is then validated by the admiring watchers below: "their homage not the less inspired him to self-esteem" (152). The final stage of his project, the casting of an enormous bell, requires the death of another man, a recalcitrant workman, whom Bannadonna smites with his "ponderous ladle" (153) and adds to the molten metal in the bell mold.

But from the moment of this murder, the story's gender symbolism grows steadily murkier. Although Bannadonna's ambition is couched in specifically masculine terms, he is competing for no particular woman. The only female figures in the story are the representations of the hours cast in relief on the bell: "twelve figures of gay girls, garlanded, hand-in-hand" (155). One of these is slightly flawed, reflecting the presence of the murdered workman's body in the bell's alloy. The flaw gives the girl's face a somber look, leading an observer to compare her to Deborah, the Biblical judge. If she is Deborah, asks another, "Where's Jael, pray?" (158). Who is to drive the spike through the offending man's head? The answer is the automaton, the clockwork slave that Bannadonna has designed to journey around the bell twice a day, striking each hour at a different place. As Bannadonna pauses to alter the offending face of Una, the one-o'clock girl, the mechanical figure performs its assigned function, accidentally killing its designer.

But what gender is actually represented in each of these metal beings: Bannadonna's judge and his executioner? Una's form is female, but her flaw marks the presence of a male body. Jael was a woman, but the bell-ringing automaton, once freed from its disguising shroud, appears more insect-like than either masculine or feminine: "It had limbs, and seemed clad in a scaly mail, lustrous as a dragon-beetle's" (160), and if it is motivated by any human spirit, it would be the ghost of the workman.

Or is the workman really a workwoman? One of the underlying themes in the story is slavery. From the epigraph, which states that, "Like negroes, these powers own man sullenly; mindful of their higher master; while serving, plot revenge" (151) to the explanation that Bannadonna intends on "stocking the earth with a new serf" (162), the sexually tinged relationship between Bannadonna and his creature is analogous to that of the American master and his slave. The image of the androgynous figure finally rising up to strike its master dead may be an echo of one of the climactic scenes in Harriet Beecher Stowe's recently published *Uncle Tom's Cabin,* in which the slave owner Simon Legree, having struck down the innocent Tom, is finally brought to justice by his slave mistress Cassy, who appears, like Melville's bell-ringer, genderless, shrouded in a sheet, and weirdly "gliding" (367). One might say that both Cassy and the automaton acquire power by cross-dressing, not between the sexes but across the boundary between human and non-human.

The nineteenth-century American experience shows that the enslavement of one human being by another affects the gender code in many ways: because female slaves are expected to work like men they do not fit the feminine gender role (hence Sojourner Truth's query, "Ain't I a woman?"); even middle-class wives are considered the property of their husbands and thus, like slaves, are something less than fully human; male slaves must behave with feminine acquiescence, leaving them permanently in the category of "boys," rather than men; and the repressed knowledge that slaves are sexually available to their white masters shadows every interaction between the races.

Because of this tangle of gendered identities, the ambiguous sexuality that marks much of Melville's fiction (and is a frequent Gothic device as well) lends itself here to an appropriately unsettling examination of the idea of mastery. The resulting indictment also takes in the male scientist's domination of feminine nature, which is described as both ravishment and usurpation: "In short, to solve nature, to steal into her, to intrigue beyond her, to procure some one else to bind her to his hand;—these, one and all, had not been his object; but, asking no favors from any element or any being, of himself, to rival her, outstrip her, and rule her" (162–63). Bannadonna, like Frankenstein, has tried to "rival" and "outstrip" female creativity and has given birth instead to an avenging monster.

In each of these examples from the emerging genre of SF, scientific ideas acquire immediacy and urgency by being translated, after the manner of the Gothic, into stories of vexed gender identities and ambiguous sexual relationships. The same is true of all the other stories listed above. E. T. A. Hoffmann builds into his tale of the automaton Olimpia so many threads of sexual anxiety and gender miscoding that Freud made "The Sand-Man" the basis of his theory of the Uncanny, the sudden vision of something familiar rendered strange and unsettling. Hoffmann's story also introduces into SF the idea that the perfect woman might have to be manufactured by men, so that she would be all glittering surface and no troubling inner life. Olimpia is the ideal mirror for flattering male vanity:

> She neither embroidered, nor knitted; she did not look out of the window, or feed a bird, or play with a little pet dog or a favourite cat, neither did she twist a piece of paper or anything of that kind around her finger; she did not forcibly convert a yawn into a low affected cough—in short, she sat hour after hour with her eyes bent unchangeably upon her lover's face, without moving or altering her position, and his gaze grew more ardent and more ardent still. (105)

Freud could just as easily have used O'Brien's "The Diamond Lens" to illustrate his theory of the sexual fetish. The protagonist of that story kills a neighbor to acquire the diamond that will allow him to spy on nature's smallest mysteries; viewing a drop of water through the lens he becomes a voyeur, the unseen admirer of microscopic Animula, a beauty "beyond the loveliest daughter of Adam" (301). Though the scientist claims to wish that he and the unknowing object of his desire could meet, the pleasure he describes in watching her seems to be primarily invested in the (phallic) instrument which keeps her imprisoned and under his control. He is in love with "the marvellous power of my microscope" (303), for which he has committed murder, and at the making of which "I stood trembling on the threshold of new worlds" (300). This masturbatory reverie ends only when he allows his animalcule's liquid universe to evaporate, in a chapter provocatively titled "The Spilling of the Cup" (303).

Poe's stories of mesmerism are not without their sexual symbolism, but it is a little more difficult to name the syndrome. The hypnotizing of M. Valdemar by the narrator is described as a grotesque sort of seduction, commencing with a "lateral stroke" of his forehead that has little effect until he "exchang[es] the lateral passes for downward ones" (109). This phase continues with no more effect than a sigh until his "continu[ing] the manipulations vigorously" results in "stiffened" limbs (109). The moment of Valdemar's death is marked by a horrific parody of arousal: "The upper lip, at the same time, writhed itself away from the teeth, which it had previously covered completely; while the lower jaw fell with an audible jerk, leaving the mouth widely extended, and disclosing in full view the swollen and blackened tongue" (111). Finally, "amid ejaculations of 'dead! dead!' absolutely bursting from the tongue," M. Valdemar's body undergoes its final dissolution into "a nearly liquid mass of loathsome—of detestable putridity" (114).

Putting this scene together with Poe's other "Mesmeric Revelation," though, in which a deathlike trance is revealed to compensate its subject with "keenly refined perception" and "wonderfully exalted and invigorated" faculties (1030), we can interpret M. Valdemar's orgasmic death as a blissful farewell to the burden of the body. The circle of men who view the transformations in both stories, and especially the masterful hypnotist who performs it, are the midwives assisting in the birth of a purified spirit. In the latter tale, the mesmerized subject reveals that there are two sorts of bodies, "the rudimental and the complete, corresponding with the two conditions of the worm and the butterfly" (1037). Lurking behind this dichotomy is the polarity of gender, with the gross material body coded, as it is in many traditions, as feminine, and the spirit, freed by the actions of both death and science, as masculine. Because the condition of release can also be described in terms of movement from place to place, some of Poe's stories about journeys into more rarefied realms, such as Hans's balloon voyage to the moon in "Hans Pfaal" (1835) and the narrator's pilgrimage to the artificial paradise of "The Domain of Arnheim" (1842) may represent another way of sending the same message, with gender embodied in landscape rather than character. This spatial version of masculine transcendence would be replayed time and again by later SF writers starting with Jules Verne.

When the Gothic version of gender-coding interacts with a scientific Neat Idea in each of these stories, the result is a richly layered and compelling narrative. By contrast, other attempts from the same era to build scientific thinking into literary forms are strained and tedious. There were many such experiments, including Erasmus Darwin's epic poem about plant reproduction, tracts describing future utopias, satires on new geological theories, imaginary travelogues depicting other planets, and Poe's meandering dialogues on space and time ("The Conversation of Eiros and Charmion," 1839; "The Colloquy of Monos and Una," 1841; and *Eureka,* 1848). None of these has much more than curiosity value today, regardless of the writers' inventiveness and concern for fact.

The stories that continue to reward a reading within the SF code are the ones in which the Neat Idea has become something else. Once the scientific concept has put on human garb, once it is worked into a sequence of events invoking not only scientific curiosity but also desire, sexual anxiety, and gender, it has been transformed into a narrative figure, a trope. Tropes are higher-order signs, signs that conduct meaning from one level of reference to another within a given message. Like the clue in a detective story that functions as both a piece of the intellectual puzzle and a pointer toward some psychological or social insight, the science fictional trope carries its scientific freight while doing—*by* doing—something else.

The term *trope* disturbs many SF writers and fans. It seems to deny the genre's ability to refer literally to scientific exploration and technological breakthroughs. It flattens out the distinction between seriously considered extrapolation and the shoddiest space opera. It shifts attention away from the ideas themselves and directs it toward literary niceties, manner at the expense of matter.

SF's tropes, however, are neither mere ornaments nor a transparent medium through which the real ideas can be communicated. The narrative tropes I have been identifying in early nineteenth-century fiction are not some accidental and unfortunate holdover from the gaudy Gothic past. By fusing concept and character, putting idea into action, the trope makes possible a new kind of meaning. This new kind of meaning is close to what Darko Suvin talks about as the SF *novum*, which he defines as a novelty or innovation within the text that dominates the entire fiction and thereby constructs "an imaginative framework alternative to the author's empirical environment" (Suvin 66). It sounds almost as if Suvin is talking merely about scientific content, as if the novum were equivalent to what I have been calling a Neat Idea, but Suvin further qualifies his definition. The coherence of such a novum—and hence its ability to mean anything at all—is dependent on a whole set of presuppositions that are "not external to the statement, but necessarily implied in and by it" (63). These presuppositions, shared by writer and reader, include ideas about the physical world, social realities, and the organization of lived experiences (64).

It is the narrative trope that, by forming links between ideological presuppositions and various images and ideas borrowed from science, allows those ideas to function as novums. To reshape the world one must first invoke the world. The world invoked by early SF stories is organized primarily by being divided up among contrasting social classes, races (such as Melville's symbolically represented masters and slaves), occupations (such as Hawthorne's diametrically opposed artists and blacksmiths), and genders. Any idea that the writer wants to examine will necessarily be located in terms of its impact on class, race, occupation, and gender. What we find in Hoffmann, Hawthorne, Melville, O'Brien, and Poe is a set of tropes that not only anchored their particular novums for an audience who shared their reality but continued to energize writers throughout their century and well into this one.

Hawthorne's image of the alluring, threatening Beatrice Rappacini—of woman-as-alien standing within a landscape that is her other self—reappears in stories by countless later SF writers, from Edgar Rice Burroughs to Ray Bradbury. The sexual competition between a scientist and his unimaginative but powerful rival is a staple of magazine fiction of the 1930s. Likewise, the image of the scientist as male mother, defying Mother Nature to give birth to a new form of humanity, passes on from Hawthorne, Melville, and Shelley to a host of writers in the pulp magazine era and after.

At least two elements in Hoffmann's "The Sand-man" were to reappear in later SF. The perfectly pleasing artificial woman is a central trope in stories like Lester del Rey's "Helen O'Loy" and, with an ironic spin, Ira Levin's *The Stepford Wives.* Dr. Coppelius, Hoffmann's tormenting father-figure, is echoed in nearly every SF movie villain from *Flash Gordon*'s Emperor Ming to Dr. Strangelove. The robot or android's powerful androgyny, which is only hinted at in Hoffman37

n's tale, becomes in Melville's version a fully developed part of the trope, available to writers such as C. L. Moore, Isaac Asimov, and Philip K. Dick.

Hawthorne, Melville, and O'Brien all helped to develop the recurring image of the machine as an extension of male sexuality, although not every later writer invested the trope with as much ambiguity. Melville's bell-tower needs only a rocket engine underneath it to become the sort of sexual challenge issued by space opera heroes like "Doc" Smith's Lensmen. The effortless way those space opera heroes zip around the farthest reaches of space—"Doc" Smith calls it the inertia-free drive—is a variant of the bodiless state achieved by Poe's mesmerized heroes. A more recent variation on the same theme is the escape from the body into cyberspace.

So long as those tropes are allowed to remain invisible, their function is necessarily normative. Working as unchallenged assumptions, they reinforce existing patterns of associations and social arrangements, such as the identification of masculinity with the perceiving self. Yet as tropes, as working parts of a code, they may also be used to call presuppositions into question. The unconsidered trope is rather like a dead metaphor or a conventional simile: the "head of the company" is "busy as a beaver" increasing profits. Yet even these figures can be brought back to life through such techniques as paradox and irony, if that head is described as sitting backwards on the company shoulders (or in another part of the anatomy entirely) or if the busy beaver is engaged in clear-cutting stands of old-growth pine. Dead tropes can be revived and redirected deliberately by someone who is aware of both their conventionality and their ideological implications. They can also be redirected by being uttered in unexpected contexts: when, for instance, the expression, "That took a lot of balls," is applied by a woman speaker to a woman subject.

The dismay felt by many longtime readers of SF at hearing their favorite form described as a set of tropes may indicate discomfort with having those tropes opened up for examination or subjected to irony. And the way they have been deployed in recent years by women writers like Joanna Russ, Carol Emshwiller, and Alice Sheldon leaves little doubt as to ironic intent, especially in the last case, after Sheldon's successful decade-long masquerade as the male writer James Tiptree, Jr. The revelation of her sex not only forced a reinterpretation of all the Tiptree stories, but also of the conventions that he/she was employing. The case is a perfect illustration of the way the meaning of an utterance is affected by the identity of speaker and listener and the circumstances in which it is uttered. As sociolinguists like Mikhail Bakhtin have pointed out, those circumstances are not incidental to the code, but fundamentally part of its operation.

The Tiptree case may also explain why another woman writer, Mary Shelley, was able to play such an important part in transforming the Gothic code into SF, while her contemporary Jane Webb Loudon vanished from sight for a century and a half. In Shelley's case, we have a female writer using tropes in a way that could be taken for masculine. Not only are the primary narrators and viewpoint characters of *Frankenstein* all men, but the story's tropes are all at least apparently drawn from masculine experience.

Shelley presents her Neat Idea in terms of the same sort of conflicts and identities we have seen in Hoffmann, Hawthorne, Melville, and Poe. Like those writers, Shelley portrays her male scientist, Victor Frankenstein, seeking self-definition through attachment to a male mentor. Like Hawthorne's protagonists, Dr. Frankenstein is forced to choose between his scientific interests and his ability to play prospective husband and father. Like Melville's Bannadonna, he attempts to take over the prerogatives of both the human female and feminine nature: to use technology to become a solitary male mother. As in "The Sand-man," the created being returns in a guise both fearsome and desirable. Finally, Shelley's story ends in a Poe-like escape from the organic realm into a more ethereal existence—in the novel represented by the vast reaches of the Arctic—coupled with the violence and abjection that pervades the male Gothic formula.

Loudon's *The Mummy!*, by contrast, alternates between masculine and feminine viewpoints. No male character steps forward to act as narrator, leaving the reader to guess at the speaker's gender (the first edition was published anonymously), or, once the author's name became known, to confront a feminine authorial persona with no intervening masculine sensibility. The central issue in the plot is which of the female heirs to the throne of a future England will become its queen. Indeed, the first sentence of the novel states, "In the year 2126, England enjoyed peace and tranquillity under the absolute dominion of a female sovereign" (Loudon 3). Although this female rule is altered by the end of the story to a joint rule by the rightful heir and her chosen consort, the emphasis on choosing the right mate and the happy outcome of the choice put the story in the category of female, rather than male, Gothic.

Even the mysterious title character, the resuscitated pharaoh Cheops, fails to act up to the horrific standard set by Frankenstein's Creature, on whom he is obviously modeled. His appearance is properly sepulchral—"his ghastly eyes glaring with unnatural lustre upon the terrified courtiers, who ran screaming with agony in all directions, forgetting every thing but the horrid vision before them" (87)—and he does spook around in the background of every scene, periodically emitting "demon-like laughs" (108). Yet the Mummy, unlike his predecessor, murders no one, but works instead to bring the rightful heir to the throne and to get her married to the right man. Whereas Frankenstein's Creature is a dark double of his creator, parodying his desires and mocking his ambitions, Cheops is relatively indifferent to the bumbling scientist who administers the shock that brings him back to life. If he is a double of anyone in the story, it is the missing mother of Elvira, the heroine. As Alan Rauch points out in his introduction to the recent reissue of the novel,

Thus, in spite of his gender, the Mummy acts as a kind of mother figure throughout the novel. Though he hardly suggests the figure of mothers described in conduct books and didactic works for children, the Mummy's purpose is to instill the kind of values and to exercise the kind of discipline that would make those mothers proud. Unlikely 'mommy' though he may be, the Mummy's moral stance, 'to assist the good and punish the malevolent,' has everything to do with nineteenth-century conceptions of parental responsibility. (xxv)

There is no way to read this figure, a sort of (possibly unconscious) narrative pun, as an embodiment of masculine desire. Yet the gender arrangements of the time would have prevented readers from seeing a mother figure as emblematic of the workings or ambitions of science. Loudon herself finally draws back from explaining the reanimation in secular, scientific terms; instead, Cheops explains at the novel's end that "The power that gave me life could alone restore it" (299). As Paul Alkon points out, this recantation leaves the novel's status as a work of SF in question: "Thus what seems like a scientific achievement turns out to have been a genuine miracle whose moral is clear: do not attempt to meddle with nature" (39).

Despite its innovative use of futuristic inventions and a number of strikingly visualized scenes, then, *The Mummy!* did not generate tropes that other writers could build on, the way they were able to build on Hawthorne, Shelley, or Poe. Loudon's novel shows that even a writer working within the Gothic tradition could fail to invest scientific ideas with the kind of narrative urgency that helped create and expand the SF code—if the expressions of gender were not of a sort that readers were ready to recognize and respond to.

From a reader's perspective, narrative codes operate not as a set of conventions to choose among, but as sets of questions to be used in making sense of the text. As a genre emerges, readers are taught further questions by each new work. These questions, in turn, can generate new meanings even in earlier examples of the form. The questions SF readers are accustomed to asking as they read include not only the fiction reader's usual "Who are they?" and "What are they doing?" but also "What world is this?" and "What ideas about the universe underlie these characters and their actions?" Once the SF code was available, Mary Shelley's novel, which earlier readers viewed as run-of-the-mill (though more than usually sensational) Gothic fiction, became not only a pioneering work in the new genre but also one of its most rewarding examples. Loudon's novel, which is considerably less successful in making its characters and situations carry scientific significance, fails to respond to the same sorts of the questions and remains merely a curious display in the museum of SF history.

However, SF readers like Brian Aldiss were not the only ones to take new interest in Shelley and her work. Feminist critics, bringing a different set of questions, found *Frankenstein* to be an important statement of ideas about gender. Many of these questions concern the apparent absence of a feminine perspective in the novel: by asking, basically, "Where is she," Ellen Moers, Sandra Gilbert, Susan Gubar, Elaine Showalter, and others have identified themes and techniques that link the novel to Mary Shelley's experiences and to her culture's treatment and perception of women. "She"—that is, not only Shelley's female voice but a whole range of meanings grouped under the sign of "woman"—is there throughout the novel. She is the silenced or murdered female characters Justine, and Safie, and Elizabeth. She is the barren landscape of Alp and Arctic—Mother Nature withholding her blessing from men and their depredations. She is the monstrous Other, the Creature whose fate is predetermined by bodily form. And she is the rebellious scientist himself, defying nature and tradition to bring to birth a new life. These readings have established the novel as a significant feminist myth.

Some of the same sorts of questions, especially when combined with those that drive SF readings, make a more interesting text out of *The Mummy!*. Even the novel's weaknesses, such as the way its main plotlines fail to come together (the reader is wrenched from scenes of atmospheric horror to episodes of domestic comedy and jolted between futuristic travelogue and battles out of Tudor history)—even these failings become interesting as indicators not only of Loudon's inexperience but of her vexed relationship to her material.

Loudon says in her introduction that her ambition is twofold: "I have long wished to write a novel, but I could not determine what it was to be about. I could not bear any thing common-place, and I did not know what to do for a hero" (xxxvii). The male muse who appears to her offers a solution to the first problem: she may avoid the commonplace by imagining her way into the future, where "the scenes will indeed be different from those you now behold; the whole face of society will be changed; new governments will have arisen; strange discoveries will be made, and stranger modes of life adopted" (xxxviii–xxxix). In that future, he says, she will also find her new kind of hero—but neither Loudon nor her muse tells us who that hero might be. She leaves it to the reader to decide whether Roderick, the dashing king of Ireland, best fills the bill, or maybe the sardonic Mummy himself, or perhaps neither of these but one of the women: ambitious Rosabella or tenderhearted but increasingly independent Elvira, both of whom take turns as England's queen. However, the very novelties that form the story's backdrop, from overeducated servants to high-speed balloons, work to shift our choice away from the more traditional sort of hero represented by Roderick. The Mummy, for his part, relinquishes his powers and his centrality to the plot by the novel's end. The new kind of hero, which Loudon can almost, but not quite imagine, may well be the female hero who is to emerge a century later in the works of C. L. Moore, Leigh Brackett, and their successors.

It turns out that raising questions of gender brings *The Mummy!* closer to *Frankenstein* than it would first appear. Both employ the image of the monster to investigate issues of power, perception, and gender. Both connect scientific arrogance with the absence of the maternal in nature and society. Both use the strangeness of their settings and incidents as a way of disconnecting gender signs from their conventional meanings. Do Shelley and Loudon, then, represent, as with the Gothic, a female SF distinct from the male tradition of Hoffmann, Hawthorne, and Poe? Not really, or, at any rate, not at that time.

Frankenstein succeeded in establishing the new SF code to the extent that it is male science fiction. That is, the tropes set up within the novel allow themselves to be read, first and foremost, in terms of male bodies and a masculine scientific enterprise, indistinguishable in this respect from Poe's or Hawthorne's. The feminist reading of the novel is as much a resisting reading as Fetterly's reinterpretation of "The Birth-Mark." Loudon's work falls down as SF precisely with respect to the features that most mark it as an exemplar of nineteenth-century femininity: its emphasis on courtship and marriage, its validation of traditional mores, and its reinscription in terms of the supernatural. *The Mummy!* points the way toward a more genuine fusion of SF with women's points of view, but such a fusion had to wait more than a century and eventually involved redirecting masculine tropes more than rediscovering early feminine perspectives like Loudon's.

What we find in the first SF is not two separate codes, but rather a single language structured along gender lines. From their Gothic precursors, the women and men who invented SF learned how to pose philosophical questions and to express psychological insights by putting male and female characters through the emotional wringer. The characters, along with their various disguises, terrors, transformations, obsessions, and guilty secrets, derive their impact from being grounded in social realities. The social pressures felt most intensely concern sexual arrangements (standard and forbidden) and gender roles (ordinary and transgressive). The Neat Idea was eventually to shed some of its Gothic garishness but not its sexual subtext.

Even after SF separated itself from the Gothic, writers necessarily kept on imagining the future, the alien, the machine, and the superhuman in gendered ways. They do so still, only now the attention of many SF writers has turned to those very gender-laden tropes and their implications. Part of what they are investigating is the code itself. And that, as Robert Frost might say about the code not taken, has made all the difference.

ANIMATING THE INERT: GENDER AND SCIENCE IN THE PULPS

Many of SF's essential tropes—from robots to time travel—were dreamed up by nineteenth-century writers such as Mary Shelley, Nathaniel Hawthorne, Edgar Allen Poe, Jules Verne, Jack London, and H. G. Wells. Yet not until Hugo Gernsback named and tamed it in the 1920s did SF consolidate into a popular genre commanding a loyal and insatiable audience. Gernsback started the first English-language all-SF magazine, *Amazing Stories,* in 1926 and coined the term *science fiction* three years later.

The taming of the mode was a result of the popular marketplace converging with Gernsback's enthusiasms. Nineteenth-century SF was a set of wild mutations from such stock as the gothic novel, the utopian tract, the travel story, and the newspaper hoax. Gernsback, in turn, was the Luther Burbank who selected and stabilized a commercially viable variety. The SF he published was more coherent and consistent than much of what had gone before, but at the expense of some distinction in style and content.

Amazing Stories and the publications that soon joined it on drugstore shelves resembled a number of other genre magazines, collectively known as pulps for the low-grade paper they were printed on. Pulp magazines of all sorts offered competent storytelling and a measure of novelty within a predictable structure of plot, setting, and character. Writing for one pulp category was much like writing for another. Indeed, many of Gernsback's early contributors also sold to Western or detective magazines.

Unlike other popular formulas, though, pulp magazine SF began almost immediately to develop mechanisms through which the readership could exert a direct influence on authors and editors. These mechanisms included letter columns, fan organizations, conventions to which author guests were invited, and homemade critical publications called fanzines. Fans did not object to the formularization of SF, but they did, in collusion with sympathetic editors like Gernsback, make the formula less interchangeable with other forms of adventure fiction by demanding that the scientific content be both valid and essential to the plot.

Within a decade of Gernsback's first issue, editors, fans, and writers had reached consensus as to what type of story reflected the role science was to play in framing the future and dramatized the role of the scientifically-minded individual in bringing about social progress. The evolving formula had to meet a number of criteria. To provide the vicarious enjoyment demanded of all modes of popular romance, it had to generate heroes who were more attractive, more capable versions of the average reader and to give those heroes adventures in exotic settings. It had to compensate for readers' insecurities by demonstrating that their technical know-how could, under the right circumstances, bring them riches, respect, and sexual gratification. At the same time, it had to suggest that these rewards were the natural result of scientific principles and that by attaining the necessary knowledge the hero was benefitting not only himself but also humanity. And, finally, the fictional formula was expected to invoke the same kind of awe that accompanies genuine discovery: the sense of strange new worlds opening outward before one's gaze.

To satisfy this last criterion, which became known among fans as the Sense of Wonder, the other elements had to be essentially invisible, or so the letters columns of the SF magazines would indicate. A story of interplanetary exploration was typically met with questions about the accuracy of information about orbits and gravitational fields and with praise for the author's ability to translate scientific theory into vivid description. Plot, characterization, and style went without comment, except when the plot led into dangerous territory such as too close attention to the hero's love life. Then the letters reprimanded the author for diverting attention from more important issues.

Yet the stories that best satisfied fans were more than scientific travelogues: in their action and characters they embodied a cluster of beliefs and desires regarding the natural world and men's place in it. Similar desires and beliefs are expressed in such venues as popular science magazines, biographies of scientific saints like Edison or Einstein, newspaper features on technological breakthroughs, and occasional realist fiction such as Sinclair Lewis's *Arrowsmith*. All of these contribute to a shared understanding of science's procedures, social contexts, and discoveries. Like science fiction, considered as a collective body, science itself constitutes a megatext within which individual utterances function. The scientific megatext is a sort of unbound encyclopedia of scientific facts together with interpretations of their human implications. SF depends on its readers' knowledge of the scientific megatext just as Christian devotional poetry depends on knowledge of the Bible. A reader who doesn't supply the larger connections will miss most of the significance, making the narrative appear thin and unconvincing. Such a reader will also be unable to tell good examples from bad.

Like the Bible, however, the scientific megatext is not merely a compendium of knowledge; it is also a master narrative that invites believers to recast their own lives along the lines of the stories of saints and true believers. Even in raw form, in laboratory reports and field notes, scientific information has frequently been accompanied by narrative kernels such as the story of the experiment gone wrong or the miraculous solution offered to the researcher in a dream. But only with the rise of modern SF were these scattered story fragments bound together into an overarching master narrative.

A story requires characters, setting, point of view, and theme. Narrative form, as Hayden White has pointed out in regard to the writing of history, has a content of its own. It turns places into settings; people into characters. What SF has done by embedding scientific understanding in a masterplot is to propose a meaning for it, a meaning coded in terms of heroes and villains, conflict and resolution, frustration and fulfillment. Indeed, it was SF writers, especially those working in the 1920s and '30s, who largely set the pattern for the scientific hero and his quest. Plotlines from the pulp magazine era still dominate popular thinking about science, from political debates about Star Wars to soft drink ads depicting the triumphs of lonely lab workers.

It is difficult to get a sense of how SF looked during those formative years. Autobiographical writings by people like Damon Knight, Jack Williamson, and Frederik Pohl convey something of the excitement of early fandom and the adventure of writing one's way into the unknown, but their memories reflect personal and political biases, and their reminiscences are smoothed by hindsight. Historical anthologies distort the past by improving it, offering only those stories that continue to function (and not necessarily on their original terms) years after their first publication.

To try to get a closer glimpse of SF's Wonder years, I attempted a thought experiment in time travel. My destination was 1937, which seems to represent both the culmination and the end of the pulp era. My method: to read all the SF published over the course of that year, in something like its original context.

As of 1937, Gernsback's pioneering effort had grown into an industry. His *Amazing Stories* had been joined by *Thrilling Wonder Stories, Astounding Stories,* and, at the end of the year, the adult British *Tales of Wonder.* Having launched and lost control of both *Amazing* and *Thrilling Wonder Stories,* Gernsback himself was out of the picture as an editor by the late '30s, but his successors at those two magazines, T. O'Conor Sloane at *Amazing* and Mort

Weisinger at *TWS,* followed his lead in choosing stories and developing writers long on adolescent adventure, exotic scenery, and scientific hardware but short on character development and style. By 1937, *Astounding,* under the guidance of F. Orlin Tremaine, had begun to cast off its early garishness and was known for a more thoughtful brand of scientific extrapolation, paving the way for a revolution in the field. That revolution really began when John W. Campbell, Jr., took over as editor at the end of the year.

After 1937, Campbell fostered a new generation of writers, including A. E. Van Vogt, Robert E. Heinlein, Theodore Sturgeon, and Isaac Asimov, who created a new style of SF. Some of these writers fostered themselves, as well, by joining together in mutually supportive, mutually critical fan organizations such as the Futurians, a club organized, interestingly enough, in 1937. The work of these so-called Golden Age writers is subtler than that of their predecessors: more polished stylistically, more character-driven, tighter in construction, more self-aware: indeed, more like the fiction published in the *Saturday Evening Post* and other non-pulp publications. Golden Age SF did not abandon the scientific megatext, but it presented it less transparently than did SF of the pulp era.

One of the challenges, then, of reading one's way back into the 1930s is to unlearn the lessons taught by Campbell and his writers: to forget that scientific information could be sneaked into the narrative or simply assumed, to get back to a state of eager anticipation for the next ingenious gadget or strange new world. Even reading the old magazines from cover to cover cannot quite reproduce the experience, for they are now *old* magazines. Carefully turning crumbling yellow pages in the hushed reading room of a special collections library is not the same as thumbing through a crisp new copy of *Amazing Stories* on a news rack. Nor is it easy to reproduce the cultural context of 1937. Hitler isn't around, nor his American counterpart Father Coughlin; the Depression can be glimpsed vaguely through a curtain of Hollywood musicals and old newsreels; science has gone on to give us antibiotics and a trip to the moon with one hand and nuclear bombs and biological weapons with the other. All the signs that make up the science-fictional code have shifted their meaning, especially the markers of gender. Hence, the old magazines, also inevitably, provide a fragmentary and distorted view of a vanished time, but it is at least a different view that may compensate for some of the biases of the memoirs and anthologies.

For instance, reading stories in their original magazine context changes one's sense of what a "story" is and how it functions. In anthologies, where they have been selected for variety of content and style and framed by biographical anecdotes or critical comments, individual stories look like self-contained aesthetic objects. In their original habitat, however, boundaries seem much thinner. An idea proposed in story A gets further development in story B. Characters reappear, sometimes with the same name (for a popular character would often star in a whole series of adventures) and sometimes altered from Professor Stone to Professor Brown. Scenery is particularly transferrable from story to story, as if a dozen movie crews were filming on the same lot. All laboratories are one laboratory; all spaceships variations on a theme.

Indeed, when one reads an issue of *Amazing Stories* or *Thrilling Wonder Tales* cover to cover, complete with ads, editorials, and letters from readers, reading the hacks along with the more ambitious writers, one gets the sense that it is all one thing. Rather than self-sufficient objects of art, the individual stories are part of a continuous stream of discourse, like the "flow" that television programmers aim for. Individual TV series exist only as part of a continuity of sound and picture designed to keep the set turned on and tuned to a single channel all day long. A show that stands out too much or fails to merge with its commercials betrays its primary function. A properly integrated show inhabits the same world as its advertising and welcomes guest actors from neighboring dramas.

The reappearance of characters, images, and plot devices in SF story after story likewise helps to maintain a flow. The story of Professor Jones's time machine is part of the same whole as the letter from a reader who wants to know whether electricity might be broadcast without wires. The story has its meaning within the same discourse about the ways we come to know the natural world and the place of the scientifically-minded individual within society. Furthermore, this conversation about science also incorporates the scantily clad maiden in the cover illustration and the ads for razor blades or a body-building course—"No skinny man has an ounce of SEX APPEAL, but science has proved that thousands *don't have to be SKINNY!*" (*Astounding Stories,* April 1937, inside front cover) These elements suggest that the message is about gender as well as science, or rather that any statement about science also entails a message about gender.

One way to assemble the message emerging from the juxtaposition of ads, illustrations, editorials, and adventure stories is to retell the stories as if they were one story, ignoring just those differentiating elements that drew readers' conscious attention and provided material for endless arguments about why the latest Stanton A. Coblenz story is or is not as good as the previous one. Take away such features as planetary climate and spaceship propulsion systems and what is left is the recurring story of a young man and his initiation into the masculine mysteries of science.

The hero of this story is sometimes a student, sometimes an experienced adventurer with a checkered past. To create a scientific hero, SF writers had to write both within and against popular tradition, calling on popular images of the romantic lead while denying popular associations between intellectual activity and age and impotence. "He was not aged and bearded, nor spectacled," begins Joseph Wm. Skidmore in describing the hero of "Murder by Atom,"

Figure 1. Science Proves. Advertising in *Astounding Science Fiction* contributes to the magazine's flow of information about gender by first raising anxiety about masculine identity and then promising a scientific solution.

> On the contrary, he was young, virile and athletic. His fine figure and handsome face had tugged the heartstrings of many a fair maid. Not to record that Millstein was a Don Juan; his heart was entirely wedded to his scientific research and the undoing of dangerous criminals. (13)

The negative phrasing of these assertions indicates some unease. The hero may be virile and athletic, but he is also branded by his intellectual superiority. In one story, his difference from other young men is expressed in terms of unusual perceptions: he can see into the ultraviolet portion of the spectrum. For this reason, even though "I was normal in my desires, wanting to play and laugh as all children do . . . [i]ntimate friendships were denied me, for casual friends soon came to notice my—queerness!" (Eando Binder, "Strange Vision," 46).

The scientific elite to which this hero aspires is represented by a second recurring character: the Professor. Unlike the hero, the Professor *is* "aged and bearded [and] spectacled," but he makes up for his lack of sex appeal by being wealthy, famous, and in possession of some powerful technological secret. The relationship between the hero and his mentor is generally the most powerful emotional tie in the story, and is explicitly acknowledged as such: "I loved Professor Brett Kramer at sight. He was an odd man—and I like the odd," says the hero of K. Raymond's "The Comet" (99).

Unlike other emotional attachments, this tie between younger and older males does not distract readers from the Sense of Wonder, for it is equated within the story with the love of knowledge: "However, if my story proves the greatness of him I loved, Professor Brett Kramer, and further advances his own beloved astronomical science, I shall die content." (Raymond 105).

The love between assistant and mentor is not always untroubled. The younger man can be rival as well as protégé, and the Professor sometimes responds by making the hero the subject of his experimentation. The scientist in A. R. Long's "The Mind Master," for instance, attempts to displace the mind of his young assistant and take over his body. The Professor's research generally involves one of three related goals: personal immortality, freedom from physical limitations, and the creation of life. When he pursues his quest selfishly, using the hero as a tool, the story ends in combat between the two, but when he designates the hero as the one to fulfill his dream, the story results in the peaceful passing of the scientific torch. The hero becomes a surrogate son, and the pact is sealed by marrying him to the Professor's daughter, the third recurring character.

Just how the Professor managed to acquire a daughter is a mystery, since there is rarely any evidence of his ever having had a wife. Sometimes, indeed, she is merely a surrogate daughter, an assistant or secretary. The important thing is that she take on the chief Daughterly functions:

(1) being explained to:

"Seed spores? Mars?" Lucy was clearly baffled.
"Let me explain." (Fearn, "Seeds" 18)

(2) making coffee:

The girl busied herself at the [spaceship's] electric stove and soon they sat down to a steaming meal of scrambled eggs and coffee. (Farley 22)

(3) getting rescued:

"Ray!" she shouted hoarsely, striving vainly to tear free from the merciless grip on her arms. "Ray! Save me! They're taking me away—to Meropolis!" (Fearn, "Menace" 22) and

(4) marrying the hero.

At other times, the Daughter is herself a product of the Professor's science. The Professor tends to be scornful of ordinary reproductive methods:

"Do you mean that you can create living creatures?"

"Pooh! Anybody can do that with the help of a female of the species. What I mean is that I have found the life force. I can animate the inert." (Beynon 122)

Hence, he frequently seeks, Frankenstein-like, to bypass sexual reproduction, or at least woman's part in the process. "He could produce the spermatozoön from his own body. If he could create the egg, with all its incalculable, character-determining genes, from inert matter . . ." (Macfaydon 67). The resulting offspring is sometimes merely a figurative daughter—a newly created world, for instance—but other times a literal woman, fully human even if, as in one case, she was formed by stimulating the glands of a marmoset (Winterbotham 31–36). Even worse, the Daughter in Festus Pragnell's "Man of the Future" has been artificially evolved from a cobra. Whether adopted or immaculately conceived, though, the Daughter brings as dowry her father's secret knowledge and his blessing on the young aspirant.

The marriage and final clinch of hero and heroine is, of course, a staple of most popular genres, but it is evident in most of these stories that the bond between the hero and the Professor's Daughter is secondary to attachment between the men. "The friendship of man for man," states one hero sternly, "is more enduring than love for a woman" (Schachner 134). The Daughter represents a safe form of sexuality. She helps keep the love between the men from being interpreted sexually, and, by being marked as the eventual but always unconsummated object of desire, she distracts us from any other sexual implications in the action of the story.

For sex is nowhere and everywhere in pulp SF, even, as the title of one story intimates, in the lab. There is a "Cupid of the Laboratory" even though

the reference to 'Cupid' might give rise to unfortunate misconceptions, which are hereby promptly dispelled. No—this account has nothing whatever to do with love or love-making. In fact, there is not one female in the entire story. It treats exclusively of two altogether staid and serious-minded chemists whose thoughts and efforts were as far removed from women and the unclothed little rascal with the bow and arrow as anything could possibly be. (Lemkin 79)

In this case, the Professor and the hero are working together to produce an artificial life form—a budding mass of copper-based "oozy matter." The relevant deity here is probably Venus rather than her son Cupid. Copper is the metal associated with Venus, and its female qualities were contrasted by alchemists with the male metal iron In the story, masculine iron penetrates and destroys the formless, fecund creature of copper. Nonetheless, there are, as the narrator says, no women here; sex is rigidly excluded—and therefore omnipresent. When women are excluded from the laboratory, everything the scientist studies threatens to become a substitute woman.

The scientist whose sexuality is manifest only in his work, who is "married to his experimenting" in "virgin fields of research" (Binder, "Chemical" 91) had been a central character in the scientific megatext long before the advent of magazine SF. Evelyn Fox Keller points out that the master narrative of science has always been told in sexual terms. It represents knowledge, innovation—and even perception as masculine; while nature, the passive object of exploration, is coded feminine. Since the time of Francis Bacon, scientists have seen themselves as seducing or ravishing Nature of her secrets (Keller 34). Bacon, speaking in the voice of the older scientist, promises the younger acolyte that he can become both Nature's husband— "My dear, dear boy, what I plan for you is to unite you with things themselves in a chaste, holy and legal wedlock" (Keller 36)—and her master—"I am come in very truth leading to you Nature with all her children to bind her to your service and make her your slave" (Keller 39). This equation of love with mastery, knowledge with domination, remains embedded in the scientific master narrative, affecting not merely the occupation of science, but also the knowledge produced thereby.

Yet Keller's analysis, which is seconded by Sandra Harding, Margaret Wertheim, Londa Shiebinger, and other historians and critics of science, has been challenged on the grounds that the scientific method incorporates mechanisms to compensate for observers' limitations and preconceptions. Scientific observations are, in theory, repeatable by anyone, male or female; scientific explanations must meet the demands of logical analysis. Where is the gender bias in Newton's laws of motion, or Planck's constant?

According to Harding, such examples themselves illustrate the way science depends on a gendered model but finds it necessary to deny its own social contexts. For one thing, the examples are skewed. The subject/object split that characterizes physics (at least before Heisenberg) hardly pertains to fields like psychology or primate behavior studies, in which the object of study clearly resembles the observer. However, even those endeavors, though clearly dependent on interpretation and therefore apt to project the scientists' own cultural conditioning on the object of study, claim to base their findings on purely neutral observation, just like those of their colleagues in the physical sciences.

"If they are not careful to establish their conformity to the standards of positivistic science," says Susan J. Hekman, the social and behavioral sciences are in danger of being "relegated to the sphere of 'feminine' enterprises" (96). They are already feminized by being classed as soft sciences, as opposed to the more predictive and experimental hard sciences. Scientific ideas may be gender neutral, but they can only be framed and communicated in terms of the speaker's physical being and social experience, as indicated by the terms *hard* and *soft*. The hardness of hard science is that of the male body—or rather that body socially constructed as the opposite of female pliancy and permeability.

Underlying all empirical knowledge are sense impressions conveyed through organs of the body, and those organs—eyes, ears, tongue, lips, fingertips—are implicated in the knower's social and sexual identity. Looking through a microscope at the inner structure of a cell is an act that carries with it associations with other sorts of looking, including the voyeur's gaze. To send out sensors to probe other worlds is to extend the sense of touch beyond the limits of the body. There is no way to imagine or to talk about such investigations without calling on the experience of the body—and the body upon which scientific knowledge is grounded in our culture is male. Indeed, it is only because science is so firmly anchored in the male experience that it can deny the traces of that body and claim to be the product of pure consciousness. In a sense, only the female body is perceived *as* a body. The male body usually lies hidden in the concept of pure mind, as in Emerson's image of the transparent eyeball.

The SF community borrowed the language of *hard* and *soft* from science at least as early as 1957, when P. Schuyler Miller used the term *hard science fiction* in a review column in *Astounding* (Stableford, "Last" 1). But long before that time, fans expressed their preference for fiction that foregrounded the discourse of physics and related fields. A story called "Hoffman's Widow" was criticized by some readers of *Amazing Stories* for basing its plot on anthropological rather than astronomical speculation (June 1937, 144). Yet the same fans who objected to this story were willing to accept fiction with dubious scientific content or none at all. What they seem to have objected to is being forced to pay attention to the social structures within which science and its creations must operate. Better to let those structures be taken for granted, so that the story could get along with the business of sweeping the reader from adventure to adventure.

Critics have pointed out that what makes a story feel like hard SF often has less to do with its scientific content than with a particular stance that Kathryn Cramer calls "technophilic" (24). This stance involves much more than a mere fondness for gadgets. If a story makes the reader feel that he (using the gendered pronoun advisedly) is part of a technologically-minded elite, someone who can contemplate the real workings of the universe without fuzzy thinking or sentiment, then it is hard SF regardless of its scientific accuracy. It is no accident that one of the touchstone stories for hard SF is Tom Godwin's "The Cold Equations" (1954), for in that story the lines are drawn with absolute clarity. Either one is in tune with the "cold equations" that govern the physical universe, and is willing to let those equations guide human action as well, or one is a naive victim, like the "girl" stowaway of the story, who is ultimately jettisoned from the spaceship to allow it to complete its mission.

Not all hard SF is so grim. The grand space sagas of E. E. "Doc" Smith take their heroes from triumph to triumph as they invent ever more powerful instruments for perceiving and manipulating the universe, and writers are still mining the lode Smith opened in the 1930s. Eleanor Arnason's witty term for this tradition is "Very Large Hard Equipment sf" (22).

At this point it is very difficult not to invoke Freud and begin making comments about the shape of guns and spaceships. I would rather not do so, if only because Freudian readings always seem to end up, regardless of point of origin, at the same primal scene. Nevertheless, both the feminist readings of science and the SF stories I have been talking about force me to talk about symbolic as well as literal gender, about ways of invoking femininity and masculinity other than the direct representation of male and female characters.

So I will try to edge my way around the issue by focussing on a less obviously male anatomical feature. The most pervasive masculine symbol in 1930s SF is not the cigar-shaped space cruiser, but rather, as the neo-Freudian Jacques Lacan might have predicted, the eye. The eye is the scientist's most important piece of equipment, without which it would be difficult or impossible to interface with telescopes, microscopes, graphs, computer monitors, and other perceptual aids. Unlike, say, voices or genitalia, male and female eyes differ hardly at all, and yet when eyes get adopted into symbol systems like language, the meaning of the female gaze differs dramatically from that of the male. More precisely, women are rarely represented as looking or seeing.

This difference is particularly obvious in the movies. Laura Mulvey, in an essay on "Visual Pleasure and Narrative Cinema," drew on Freud and Lacan to point out how deeply embedded in Hollywood tradition is the gendered distinction between the one who sees and the one who is seen. Camera angles and editing turn the lens into a symbol of masculine desire and control. An actor looks at an actress, and the camera colludes, letting the audience share his point of view but rarely hers. The woman becomes a spectacle to be consumed by the triple gaze of actor, camera, and audience (595).

In pulp SF, women's eyes, like their bodies, are defined as something to be looked at, by men. They are typically described in terms of coyly dropped eyelids, sweeping lashes, luster, and soulfulness rather than acuity, focus, or force. Men's eyes, by contrast, seize upon objects and control them. As in the movies, too, the male gaze is strongly associated with technology. The eyes of male characters in SF are given extended range and enhanced power by various mechanisms: microscopes, telescopes, spy rays, view screens. These in turn are sources of greater knowledge. Thus, the eye—or rather the symbolic representation of the eye—is both a marker of sexual difference and a sign of scientific prowess. It is not surprising, then, that SF is full of eyes and eyelike imagery.

The eyes of the scientist hero reveal his unusual powers of observation and deduction. The hero of Eando Binder's "Strange Vision," mentioned above, can see parts of the spectrum that are invisible to ordinary humans. This ability sets him apart from his peers but also gives him access to secrets of nature. In Edmond Hamilton's "A Million Years Ahead," the hero and his rival are transformed into men of the future, and the alteration is signaled primarily through their eyes: "But the face! It was godlike in terrible beauty, the features perfectly regular, the mouth a straight, merciless line, the eyes enormous glowing ones through which looked a cold, vast mind whose shock was felt tangibly" (94). When the two supermen fight, the weapon of choice is the eye:

> As he understood the meaning of that command, Fraham's eyes became terrible. Hellfires of furious revolt flamed in them, a surge of terrific mental resistance.
>
> But Sherill's commanding eye held steady, beating the other down again with hypnotic command. (96–97)

These eyes are not just passive receivers of light. They grow larger, they shine with an inner light, and they can be used to control others through sheer force of will. There is a strong suggestion that, as in folk belief, the eye makes its own light, sending out beams or rays that bathe the object and make it visible.

If the naked eye is not powerful enough to defeat an opponent, its power can be augmented through technology. When the hero of John Russell Fearn's "Menace from the Microcosm" is cornered and looking desperately for a weapon, "immediately the scientist in him came uppermost. He jumped across to a case of instruments and brought out a microscope" (23). Later in the story he switches to a gun, but still seems to operate it by ocular power: "His eyes narrowed as he clutched the molecular gun, most deadly weapon in Earthly science . . ." and later, "Price, eyes shining like steel across the sights, pressed the firing button" (26–27).

The molecular gun itself is a more powerful eye, sending out a destructive ray, and its target is the weaker eye of its opponent: "The beam, no thicker than a lead pencil, stabbed into the enormous face of the ruler of Uk, drove clean into his single eye and through it into the depths of his fiendish brain" (28).

Sometimes the eye is detachable. In Arthur K. Barnes's "Green Hell," the hero's lost rank is represented by a token of "metal, cut in the form of an all-seeing eye, mirroring the sun and its planets. . . . Ellerbee clutched it tightly and thrust his shoulders back. It was plain what that token meant to him—respect, honor, manhood, all those things that had been stripped from him years before" (100).

A similar token of manhood is the Lens, "a lenticular polychrome of writhing, almost fluid radiance" (12), awarded to Kimball Kinnison, hero of E. E. "Doc" Smith's *Galactic Patrol*, serialized in *Astounding Stories* beginning in October of 1937. The third of Smith's popular Lensman series, *Galactic Patrol* is the installment in which the Lens is revealed to be more than merely the token of membership in the Patrol and a superior communications device, but rather a quasi-living symbiote that confers superhuman powers on selected Lensmen.

The power of the hero's lens, like that of his eye, is indicated by its size and brightness. The more mental power he brings to it, the "tighter" and "higher" the beam he can project. (It's hard to believe the phallic imagery was completely unnoticed by early readers). In the previous installment, *First Lensman,* Smith had made an explicit connection between the Lens and gender:

> Women's minds and Lenses don't fit. There's a sex-based incompatibility. Lenses are as masculine as whiskers—and at that, only a very few men can ever wear them, either. Very special men, like you three and Dad and Pops Kinnison. Men with tremendous force, drive, and scope. Pure killers, all of you; each in his own way, of course. No more to be stopped than a glacier, and twice as hard and ten times as cold. A woman simply can't have that kind of mind! (38)

Wearing the Lens, Kinnison can penetrate thoughtscreens; enter another's mind to control his actions; perceive any object directly, "as a whole, inside and out," without light or instruments (103); and eventually use his mind as a weapon to "hurl no feeble bolts" at an enemy (182). The power of the Lens is only limited by the capacity of the user's mind: one must "have enough jets to swing it" (*Galactic Patrol* 141). Its ultimate power is the ability to start from "one fact or artifact belonging to any given universe" and "construct or visualize that universe, from the instant of its creation to its ultimate end" (*First Lensman,* 30). The ambiguity of the phrase "construct or visualize" suggests that visualization *is* construction, that the act of seeing, developed to the ultimate degree, is also an act of bringing into being. Thus, the eye, or its more powerful analog the Lens, is an organ of generation as well as perception and destruction.

In the discourse of pulp SF, then, eyes (and the rays they project) stand for a complex cluster of ideas: identity, status, intellectual prowess, force of personality, destructiveness, and creativity, all conceived of in gendered or even sexual terms. Accordingly, the masculine act of seeing bestows on its object the complementary gender. As in Bacon's metaphor, the male scientist looks at a feminine universe, which thereby becomes both his mate and his property.

In George H. Scheer's "The Crystalline Salvation," the space that the scientist's gaze penetrates is a very feminine one indeed. It is a hollow crystalline planetoid into which the heroes' ship floats "at very low velocity, into a rosy-hued cavern of enormous proportions" (113). Once inside this womb, "Our minds were soothed, and we could think of nothing else save the quieting influence which had come upon us like a healing salve. We did little talking, for it seemed that talking broke an almost holy stillness. Here was rest and peace and quiet, such as we had never dreamed of before" (113).

But feminine space is not always so compliant. John Edwards' "The Planet of Perpetual Night" takes place on a world that cannot be seen, at least at first. Not even that eye in the sky, the sun, can shine through its veils: "The sun—his rays do not pierce that at all; nor do the beams of your fog-piercing headlights. It is one great mass—yet your instrument says practically no great mass near? Then what is it? What is this that gives no light, which no light can penetrate—which reflects nothing?" (24) Since the penetrating sun is given masculine gender here by the Germanic scientist (although *sun* is actually a feminine noun in German), the resisting, invisible, massive body must be feminine. And sure enough, when the ship lands, it finds "something soft" in which it "skidded and wallowed to a standstill" (25). This world is not only soft and dark but "as warm as tea" (38).

The men contrive a ray that they hope will break through the gloom of this "Etherless Zone" (45). The operation of this ray can only be described as the climax of the story: "Watching closely the blue beam, Dr. Davidson noted that it was slowly but surely pushing its sputtering way down to the surface below, moving and thrusting like a shaft of solid fire through the strange black shroud which obstructed its progress like a solid thing" (52).

When the gaze of the scientist penetrates female space, the result can be erotic or cataclysmic or both at once. Dr. Davidson's blue beam has the unfortunate effect of destroying the earth. In contrast, the hero of Fearn's "Metamorphosis" uses technology to achieve a permanent and ecstatic union with the feminine universe:

> As he arose out of this gulf he became aware of two things: one, that his body was a form of glowing, bluish energy; and, secondly, that he existed in an apparent endless sea of misty light, incredibly beautiful light possessing the misty translucence of a pearl. It came to him as a momentary shock when he realized that everything he saw was not accomplished by eyes, but by the pulsing of electric radiation. He had no nerves, no sexual power, no emotions, was nothing but a somewhat heavier form of the endless sea of pearly light surrounding him. (110)

The act of seeing can lead not only to (symbolic) sexual release but still further, to impregnating the universe. "Let us suppose," suggests Henry Kuttner in "When the Earth Lived," "that a scientist has discovered a ray which creates life. He is experimenting with the atom. He turns this ray upon an atom—an extremely complex one—under his microscope. He creates life" (94).

Because the scientific gaze is so insistently masculine, whatever it touches upon is feminized. Not only alien spaces, but aliens themselves must play the role of female Other to the male observer. The dark, female world of "The Planet of Perpetual Night" is inhabited, and the narrator takes great care to mark its people as feminine. Their voices are "treble-piping"; altogether they make "a confused medley of thin, high-pitched notes" (28). They are small: "about as high as his shoulder" with "short plump bodies" (29). Their touch, like that of the planet itself, is soft, unnervingly so: "Then the two waiting men felt soft hands—or feelers, they could not tell which—running over their leather uniforms" (28) and later "The invisible orator spoke at length to his two puzzled listeners, and finished the address by running his light hands down their arms to the finger-tips—a proceeding which made them feel creepy in the blackness" (30). Blind, because their world is lightless, the aliens are not rival possessors of the masculine gaze. They acquire knowledge by direct bodily contact, an act that has sexual connotations, especially when the men are obliged to reciprocate: "The patting and stroking continued for a time to the accompaniment of soothing voices, and the two relieved men joined in by returning the implied compliments—but they were thankful for the blackness which hid their acute embarrassment!" (29).

Part of the unease here is that these beings are not explicitly female, and the unmarked gender is, by convention, masculine. For instance, despite the analogy with worker bees and ants, the insect-like aliens of Walter Rose's "By Jove" are all assigned masculine pronouns. The only exception is the queen, who is "no revered 'She-who-must be obeyed' of an adoring community, but is instead that absolute nadir of the feminist ideal, a specialized breeding machine . . ." (95). In other words, anyone or anything *not* explicitly portrayed as performing a female sexual function is a "he."

The same pattern governs the ambiguously sexed alien orator of "The Planet of Perpetual Night." In the darkness, it is impossible to determine whether "his" quasi-sexual touch is heterosexual or homosexual. No wonder one of the men exclaims that "This is a queer gang, Gene" (29)! Nonetheless, at the end of the story, the all-male crew rescues the aliens and carries them off to Venus, perhaps with the hope that they will be the right gender for hybridizing:

> "We'll be a very mixed lot—the Venerians, ourselves, and about a hundred-and-fifty of these poor little devils who have lost their planet as well! I doubt whether they will survive there, unless we can manage to keep them in total darkness. . . . It is a big job before us, and God knows how it will turn out! But we must face up to it . . . no women, except the Venerians . . . I wonder. . . ." and his voice trailed away as he gazed abstractedly at the gleaming crescent of the new world swinging majestically in Space before their speeding craft. (57; ellipses in text)

The feminization of aliens can be represented even more explicitly (and not merely by keeping them in total darkness). The scientist of "The Endless Chain" has used his ray machine to destroy most of humanity during a war. All that are left are himself and Soan, not a "man of Avalon," but "a stranger from the plateau, in the form of a true man" (MacFaydon 66). Soan asks Lomas, the scientist, "How can a scientist and a madman start a new race? Eh?" (63), but that is not Lomas's greatest concern:

> Lomas stared at the lunatic; he could change the sex of Soan without much difficulty. Although his own field was inorganic chemistry, he knew a little biology, and the changing of sex was a very elementary technique; he was familiar with it. But the prospect of fair Avalon overrun by a mad

race who muttered incomprehensibilities and could not feed themselves revolted him. (64)

In other words, he is willing to overlook Soan's sex. (As Joe E. Brown, in *Some Like it Hot,* says to a cross-dressed Jack Lemmon, "Nobody's perfect.") The problem is Soan's inferior race.

If I were trying to demonstrate that science fiction is nothing more than a set of male sexual fantasies decked out in exotic decor, I would stop here. But that is not the case, even in the pulp magazines of 1937. Despite its masculine bias and lack of sophistication, the fiction of this era already possessed the potential to develop into a powerful tool for questioning assumptions about gender.

The picture I have drawn needs correction on four main points. First, there were always stories that did not fit the model: SF generates formulas but has never been confined within them in the way that other popular genres tend to be. Second, the audience and authorship of SF, even in 1937, was not exclusively male. Third, a more self-consciously literary tradition of SF, heir to the nineteenth-century scientific romance, existed outside the SF magazines but attracted many of the same readers, who were thereby alerted to new possibilities in the form. Fourth, the very narrative structures I have been outlining can lend themselves to subversive uses, and in the hands of the more astute writers prove to be the foundation for a very different sort of SF about gender.

Even among the stories in the four magazines publishing in 1937, few fit every point of the description offered above, and a handful go off in different directions entirely. For instance, the "hero" of the story is, in a couple of instances, actually a couple, with the woman taking an active role in the adventures (Williamson, Willey). Other stories fail to follow the standard story line at all, particularly those set in the distant past or the far future. The more distant in time, the more variation in gender relationships, including visions of a fully androgynous humanity: "Little difference could be seen to distinguish them in sex, since they wore almost identical clothing, and it seemed both had an equal degree of femininity in their bearing and manners" (Scheer, "Last" 71).

A surprising number of women were included in the readership of the 1930s, at least among those whose comments were printed in letters columns. Mrs. Charles Bohant of Astoria, Oregon, for instance, mentions in June, 1937, that not only is she a subscriber to *Amazing* but that she has given a birthday subscription to her sister (136). Women readers, though never more than a small percentage of the correspondents, kept their male counterparts aware that there might be other points of view on gender issues, and indeed, engaged them in a debate over the appropriateness of women characters in SF. Justine Larbalestier, who has traced this debate from the 1920s to the 1950s, sees it as evidence that "social constructions of sex have always been under negotiation in science fiction" (xiii).

Starting in 1938, the redoubtable Mary Byers took on a number of male readers over the claim, issued by a very young Isaac Asimov, that "When we want science-fiction, we don't want swooning dames, and that goes double" (*Astounding Science Fiction,* September 1938, 161). Byers responded that she was all for getting rid of such "hooey," but that "less hooey does *not* mean less women; it means a difference in the way they are introduced into the story and the part they play" (*Astounding Science Fiction,* December 1938, 160).

The women readers' viewpoint was reinforced by the fact that at least three of the most popular writers of the late 1930s were women. Despite the unmarked gender of their bylines, Leslie F. Stone, A. R. Long, and C. L. Moore were known by at least some of the readership to be female: letters refer to "Miss Moore," "Miss Long," and "our distinguished authoress, Leslie F. Stone" (*Amazing Stories,* February 1937, 137).

Of the three, Amelia Reynolds Long did the least to challenge male-centered storytelling conventions; her humorous tales follow the convention of the all-male spaceship crew. Stone does challenge a few assumptions in a prehistoric story called "The Great Ones." None of the male writers of caveman stories seem as aware as she that tasks in a hunting-gathering society need not be divided by the gender conventions of contemporary American society:

> The women left the meager, rock-bound slope of the tor, their few rough tools left between the furrows. The fishermen at the water's edge swarmed up the beach, the day's catch left where it lay. The weavers and the skin-workers threw down their handiwork and grabbed at their sleeping babes; while the old men, who had been squatting around the community fire, caught up lighted brands before herding the young children that had been playing nearby into the caves. (75–76)

Stone also makes a subtle comment on the "ascent of man" motif that characterizes these prehistoric tales: "For it is by dreams such as these that *man, so to speak,* has pulled himself upward by his boot straps!" (89, emphasis mine). If we read carefully, we see that both the dreams and the boot straps (made by those female "skinworkers"?) might well have belonged to women.

But the woman writer most interested in reexamining ideas of the feminine, Catherine L. Moore, published no SF stories in 1937, though readers of *Astounding Stories* were still buzzing over her novelette, "Tryst in Time," in the last issue of 1936. I will be discussing Moore elsewhere, so I won't try to stretch my sample year to fit her in here. Nonetheless, her presence was part of the full picture in 1937, helping to keep the discourse of SF open to alternative ways of writing and reading gender.

The readership of the SF magazines was never exclusively male; nor was it entirely lowbrow or juvenile—indeed, a brief experiment in incorporating a juvenile adventure comic strip in *Thrilling Wonder Stories* early in 1937 met with howls of protest and was quickly dropped. One element of the magazines' "flow" that indicates the presence of a more sophisticated readership is the occasional announcement or brief review of a new book. While always associated with SF, these books represent a wider range of style and form than is present within the magazines themselves. Books reviewed in *Amazing Stories* during 1937 include a novel about ancient witchcraft called *The Undying Mother,* by Jessie Douglas Kerruish (February 1937, 133); *Noonmark,* by Julia Boynton Green, described as "poems by someone who has been published in this magazine" (August, 1937, 132); and Olaf Stapledon's 1935 novel *Odd John,* described as "a splendid fantasy" (April, 1937, 134). Only the last could be called strictly SF, and it is SF of a decidedly nonformulaic sort.

The time lag in reviewing means that none of the 1937 reviews refer to books published that year, and yet it was a banner year for SF novels. The scientific romances published in 1937 all focus on gender more explicitly than most of the magazine SF, and all offer perspectives different from that of the pulp formula. H. G. Wells issued an odd tale called *Star Begotten:* one of his last SF works and nowhere near as effective as his early novels, but still an interesting exercise in SF paranoia. Its premise, that selected humans are, in effect, alien changelings, their chromosomes reprogrammed by cosmic rays, is given a gender twist when the protagonist decides that his own wife is one of these aliens, primarily because of her "unfathomable" failure to fit his expectations of feminine behavior (524).

A similar paranoia fuels William Sloane's *To Walk the Night,* in which the beautiful, unreadable Selena really is an alien masquerading among humans in order to prevent discoveries that could threaten her people. What is most interesting about Selena is that her masquerade can be read as a metaphor for any woman's adoption of a feminine role. At the beginning she gives all the wrong signals: she is unconcerned about her clothing and hair, her walk is a "long, free stride" (101), her fingernails are "untinted, and short—not even polished" (95), and most damningly she is "too intelligent" (75). Later, she has learned to pass as an ordinary woman, although "there was something familiar about her new gestures, and in a moment it came to me that they were Grace's, flawlessly imitated and employed at just the same moments" (101). Sloane's narrator never trusts her, always views her as a threat to himself and his friend Jerry, who marries her. He seems to be vindicated when she causes Jerry's death. However, we cannot entirely trust a narrator who says, "A certain amount of ingenuous ignorance, I decided, was a great factor in feminine charm" (163). Selena comes across, despite the narrator's judgments, as a complex and sympathetic being, who must not only cope with being a stranger in a strange land but also deal with people like the narrator, who fears her simply "For what you are" (225).

A third novel from 1937 was Murray Constantine's *Swastika Night,* a dystopia set in a distant, Nazi-ruled future. One important feature of the book is its analysis of Nazi ideology in terms of its worship of an exaggerated and violent masculinity. It is, in essence, an all-male society, for women are reduced to the status of domestic animals, kept in compounds. Constantine's remarkable alertness to the role of gender in the Nazi mythos was highlighted when Murray Constantine was discovered, fifty years after the book's publication, to be a pseudonym for Katherine Burdekin.

Also published in 1937 was Olaf Stapledon's *Star Maker,* widely regarded as one of the major works in the genre. *Star Maker* is a strange, shapeless, visionary story in which the major relationship is the partnership between the universe and the various intelligences that inhabit, observe, and ultimately recreate it. Starting with one man who emerges from his house after a quarrel with his wife to gaze at the night sky, the novel sweeps outward into space, continually broadening its perspective until it embraces not one but a series of universes from beginning to end.

The recurring movement throughout the book is the confrontation with ever stranger forms of life and consciousness. The narrator greets each of these with bafflement or even disgust at first, but gradually learns to share each alien perspective, so that the book's central consciousness soon ceases to be merely that of the man on whose vision we are eavesdropping. He first links up with a being much like himself, a philosophical old man of a nearly human species, and the experience is both pleasurable and enlightening: "All the experiences of each took on a new significance in the light of the other; and our two minds together became a new, more penetrating, and more self-conscious mind" (70). As other, stranger entities are brought into the composite mind, it becomes able to travel further and further afield. They encounter "feathered, penguin-like men" (80), centaur-like creatures (81), and "Human echinoderms" (82), each with different customs, perceptions, and philosophies.

At this point, though, all are still described as "men." Not until the traveling intelligences leave the human form behind does the narrative describe merging with a clearly female being, and then it is a member of a symbiotic race in which one member of each symbiotic pair is female, one male (105). Incorporating this race proves to be a great advance in the narrator's development, for immediately afterward we are introduced to bird-like composite beings, hive minds, plant people, and even the vast consciousness of the stars themselves. Eventually, the group mind encompasses the entire universe, and its quest is for the principle of creation, the Star Maker, who seems sometimes to be a loving parent and sometimes the spirit of cool contemplation. Just as the scope becomes impossibly grand, the perspective unsustainably Olympian, the narrator returns to earth again to contemplate the workings of these cosmic forces in the lives of ordinary human beings.

Stapledon appropriately begins and ends his starry odyssey with a marriage, for it is, throughout, a story of unlike minds meeting and marrying to the benefit of both. In direct contrast to Bacon's idea of the scientific marriage with only one active partner, Stapledon's protagonist comes to see that "this our delicate balance of dependence and independence, this coolly critical, shrewdly ridiculing, but loving mutual contact, was surely a microcosm of true community" (12). Thus the marriage of complementary beings forms a metaphoric basis for understanding not only the universe but also the ones who are looking at the universe.

The existence of non-formulaic fiction outside of the SF magazines, the existence of individual magazine stories that stretch the boundaries, and the presence of women in the SF boy's club all remind us that no matter how strongly the conventional images and actions of pulp SF suggest existing patterns of male domination, they may be read otherwise. Narrative has the power to alter any such patterns: indeed, one of the most fundamental operations of narrative is to represent change. Once the male scientist, with his phallic, nature-skewering gaze, is placed in a narrative setting, he is subject to every sort of transformation. He can be doubled, split, mirrored, inverted. The hero's role can be divided between friends; the older scientist can be a machine or an alien. Most importantly, the universe can look back. This is just what happens in one of the best stories published in any SF magazine in 1937, Don A. Stuart's "Forgetfulness." Although Stuart's tale remains entirely within 1930s pulp conventions, it also anticipates the gender exploration of later generations of SF writers.

"Forgetfulness" contains the standard elements: a spaceship landing on an unknown planet; a heroic captain, "tall and powerful; his muscular figure in trim Interstellar Expedition uniform of utilitarian, silvery gray" (140); a young scientist whose masculinity is less obvious and must be asserted during the course of the story; an alien race coded as feminine; a breakthrough of understanding that also implies power over the thing understood. Yet all of these elements are reshuffled by the narrative so that the ultimate effect is to question rather than reinforce standard gender codings.

There is no question that the invading spaceship stands for conventional masculinity. It is a "mighty two-thousand-five-hundred-foot interstellar cruiser" (139) crewed by the "young, powerful men of Pareeth" (140) who are led by Shor Nun, "commander, executive, atomic engineer" (143). The only exception to this array of space brawn is the astronomer Ron Thule, who is set apart by being imaginative, empathetic, and self-doubting, seeing himself as a "strange little man from a strange little world circling a dim, forgotten star" (142). As the group's astronomer, he has no role in the landing force: "The men you mentioned are coming. Each head of department, save Ron Thule. There will be no work for the astronomer" (141).

The world that is being invaded is described in terms of conventional femininity: smooth, gentle, rounded, "a spot where space-wearied interstellar wanderers might rest in delight" (140). The residents of this world seem almost a part of the landscape, living in "a village of simple, rounded domes" that cluster "irregularly among the mighty, deep-green trees that shaded them from the morning sun" (139). The aliens themselves are of ambiguous gender: though all are "men," they are marked by colorful clothing and a gentle, almost passive demeanor. Their spokesman, Seun, is "an almost willowy figure" (140) with "a slim-fingered hand" and "glinting golden hair that curled in unruly locks above a broad, smooth brow" (141).

Seun's people live in the shadow of their ancestors' city, which seems to represent their lost glory: full of mysterious machines and "stupendous buildings of giants long dead" (142). Questioned by Commander Shor Nun about these monuments, Seun answers "Its operation—I know only vague principles. I—I have forgotten so much" (145). Watching Seun, the astronomer feels sympathetic "vague, inchoate stirrings of ideas that had no clarity; the thoughts were formless and indistinct, uncertain of themselves" (145). This vagueness suggest both feminine intuition and the softness ascribed to the soft sciences.

The turn in the story comes when Seun takes the visitors into the city and Shor Nun is overcome by the sight of machines that extend, apparently, into infinity: "Shor Nun . . . clawed at his eyes; he fell to his knees, groaning. "Don't look—by the gods, don't look—" he gasped" (149). In response, Seun demonstrates his ocular power:

> "Shor Nun, look at me, turn your eyes on me," said Seun. He stood half a head taller than the man of Pareeth, very slim and straight, and his eyes seemed to glow in the light that surrounded him.
>
> As though pulled by a greater force, Shor Nun's eyes turned slowly, and first their brown edges, then the pupils showed again. The frozen madness in his face relaxed; he slumped softly into a more natural position—and Seun looked away. (149)

This confrontation of gazes foreshadows the story's conclusion, in which it is revealed that Seun's race has forgotten only that which is no longer necessary. They now know so much that Seun can virtually hold the universe in his mind, shifting its contents around at will. With a glance, he creates a lens-like object that is both eye and weapon:

> His eyes grew bright, and the lines of his face deepened in concentration. . . . Quite suddenly, a dazzling light appeared over Seun's hand, sparkling, myriad colors—and died with a tiny, crystalline clatter. Something lay in his upturned palm: a round, small thing of aquamarine crystal, shot through with veins and arteries of softly pulsing, silver light. It moved and altered as they watched, fading in color, changing the form and outline of light.
>
> Again the tinkling, crystalline clatter came, and some rearrangement had taken place. There lay in his hand a tiny globe of ultimate night, an essence of darkness that no light could illumine, cased in a crystal surface. Stars shone in it, from the heart, from the borders, stars that moved and turned in majestic splendor in infinite smallness. (157)

Using this artificial eye, Seun "rearranges" the universe so that the men and ships of Pareeth are suddenly back home. They have been shifted not only through space but through time as well, to just after the expedition's departure, thereby stealing from them "eighteen years of our manhood" (163). Yet Seun leaves them with a compensating gift. In place of Ron Thule's telescope, he has placed a device (a little brother to his own lens) that enables Thule to see other star systems with miraculous resolution—but only vacant systems, so that they might not attempt another invasion.

Stuart's story gets much of its effect through its subversive use of the gender code of pulp SF. If the masculine self is defined in terms of looking at the universe, then what happens when the scientist sees himself held in the eyes of the alien? When the feminine, the indistinct, the Other turns out to be the controlling Self? When the male society that the young hero seeks to join is revealed to be a group of powerless outsiders? When passivity is strength and vagueness is deeper understanding?

This story illustrates that the sexual symbolism of pulp-era SF is a language—the code rather than the message. It isn't "about" male anxiety and genital competition. Seun's crystal isn't really a phallus or even an eye. What it represents is exactly what the story says it represents: knowledge of the universe. It resembles an eye because we conceive of knowledge primarily in terms of vision, imagined to be a male prerogative. The men in the story

Figure 2. Fun with Your New Head. Male anxiety cured by technical training in *Astounding Science Fiction*, March 1936.

respond to the crystal as if it indicated Seun's masculinity and signaled a challenge to their own, because the signs for knowledge, vision, and masculinity form a complex, interrelated system, in which each can stand for the others.

The scientific megatext incorporates those traditional sign systems, but the SF version of the master narrative does not merely incorporate the signs; it plays with them. In Stuart's hands, the gender coding of self, universe, knowledge, and power passes through a complex set of mirrorings and reversals, with the effect of bringing underlying assumptions to the surface where they may be challenged. Every time we think we know what is happening, the story undermines our knowledge. We are even invited to misread the identities of the worlds—the planet that the story places in the position of alien space is actually Rrth, or earth—and of the author himself. Don A. Stuart was a pen name of none other than John W. Campbell, Jr., whose stories under his own byline have little of the innovation or subversiveness of his Stuart stories. To further complicate the matter, the authorial mask that allowed Campbell to refuse "to take the standard axioms for granted" and to "give the feeling and humanity to his stories that had been lacking" (del Rey 3) was actually the name of his wife, Dona Stuart Campbell, which suggests some blurring of gender boundaries if not a conscious attempt to attain a feminine point of view.

Stuart's "Forgetfulness" was one of the first works to demonstrate SF's ability to investigate the key role of gender in constructing models of self, society, and universe. It helped point the way for later generations of SF writers, who have turned the form into a powerful tool for examining the effects of science on cultural patterns and vice versa. Looking at the story in their original context reveals that SF has this ability not in spite of its gender coding but because of it, and because of the way narrative tends both to coopt and to destabilize other systems of meaning.

"Forgetfulness" suggests that science is a lens that looks both outward and inward. All the while we are scoping out the universe, says Stuart, we are seeing our own reflections—and maybe being looked at as well. When other writers within the American magazine tradition began to exploit this double vision, the line between the literary scientific romance and pulp SF disappeared. As the genre moved into the Campbell era and beyond, it matured not by jettisoning early SF's characteristic plot devices but by complicating and examining them. And the same is true of the cultural freight carried by those devices, especially their troubling, hopeful messages about sexuality and gender.

CHAPTER

SUPER MEN

Looking for significant scientific hooks to hang their narratives on, SF writers often turn to Darwin. The story of evolution, itself a powerful narrative used to justify social as well as biological change, offers a framework within which a favored group can be made to represent the winning side in a contest for racial survival. Writers who incorporate this framework uncritically end up transcribing its biases directly into their fiction. However, the story of evolution may be also retold in such a way as to undercut its assumptions, especially those regarding sexual difference.

One form of evolutionary SF deals with prehistoric, rather than futuristic, settings. Caveman fiction typically depicts the rise of a younger, smarter (and, alas, often fairer-skinned) branch of humanity at the expense of poor stupid Neanderthals. Most caveman SF actually depicts the concept of evolutionary change in very un-Darwinian terms: not as a series of random mutations and environmental selections but as advancement toward a goal, variously postulated to be the human race, human intelligence, or, more sinisterly, one particular class of human beings.

This pattern comes as no surprise. Prehistory, like history, is written by the winners. Another branch of evolutionary SF, though, grows out of the observation that nothing in Darwin's theory guarantees us this privileged place on the pinnacle. Human beings may not be the supreme achievement of evolution after all. We may be more like the Neanderthals than we would like to think, destined to be supplanted in turn by insects, by machines, or by something like ourselves only more so. This last variation is the superman, arguably the preeminent story form for 1940s and '50s SF.

Superman stories began appearing almost with the first examples of the genre. Dr. Frankenstein's Creature is intended to be a superior being, and despite a botched execution is nevertheless a sort of superman: smarter, faster, stronger, and bigger than the humans who reject him. There is even the implication that the Creature could have been the progenitor of a new race, if only Victor Frankenstein had not destroyed the Creature's female counterpart. But the new Adam had no Eve, and so the race was aborted.

Other stories from the nineteenth and early twentieth centuries suggest variations on the superman theme, mostly focusing on physical superiority. Nathaniel Hawthorne's Frankenstein-like scientist Rappacini fed his own daughter on poisons that turned her into an invulnerable but poisonous beauty. H. G. Wells likewise hypothesized that supermen are what they eat: in his *Food of the Gods* (1904), children given a superior diet became a race of supersized superbeings.

Edgar Rice Burroughs created a number of supermen who attain physical prowess through historical accident, such as Tarzan's apprenticeship to the great apes or John Carter's translation to the lighter gravity of Barsoom in *A Princess of Mars* (1917). The best known bearer of the name, *the* Superman of comic-book, television, and movie fame, likewise benefits from circumstance, for Superman is technically an alien, rather than a superhuman. On his own world he has no extraordinary strength. An earlier story by Superman's creators is more typical in that its hero is not an immigrant but a native-born mutation (Andrae 92). Outside the comic books, Philip Wylie's *Gladiator* (1930) is one of the last stories to represent superhumanity solely in terms of superior physical development.

In *Back to Methuselah* (1921), George Bernard Shaw couched the superman theme in terms of immortality, implying that if one could only live long enough, one would learn enough to leave ordinary humanity behind. Robert A. Heinlein picked up the same theme in his stories about Lazarus Long, beginning with "Methuselah's Children" (1941). Heinlein also develops Friedrich Nietzsche's notion that the superior being would be marked as much by force of will as by any specific ability. Lazarus Long's superior genes do not make him particularly strong or allow him to read minds; his intelligence is high but not beyond the bell curve of normal human intelligence. He does, however, possess what many Heinlein heroes possess: absolute conviction that he knows better than anyone else, along with the author's collusion in making his ideas pay off.

A more ambiguous strain of twentieth-century superman begins with J. D. Beresford's *The Hampdenshire Wonder* (1911), which describes the somber fate of a solitary child of genius. Other superbeings marked primarily by increased intelligence appear in Olaf Stapledon's *Odd John* (1935), Heinlein's "Gulf" (1949), and Edmond Hamilton's "The Man Who Evolved" (1931). Hamilton's protagonist, who undergoes millions of years of evolutionary advancement in a few moments, pays a price for his intellectual advancement with a corresponding physical deterioration, growing

> thin and shriveled, the outlines of bones visible through its flesh. His body, indeed, seemed to have lost half its bulk and many inches of stature and breadth, but these were compensated for by the change in his head.
>
> For the head supported by this weak body was an immense, bulging balloon that measures fully eighteen inches from brow to back! It was almost entirely hairless, its great mass balanced precariously upon his slender shoulders and neck. (31)

Perhaps the unpleasantness of this image of the spindly, egg-headed genius led to the eventual absorption of the superintelligent superman into the category of psychic superman, a favored mode of Golden Age writers like A. E. Van Vogt and Henry Kuttner. Working around the time of the first atomic explosions and with a dawning awareness of the mutagenic properties of radioactive fallout, these writers equipped their supermen with a combination of advanced intelligence, extrasensory powers, and some form of physical oddity. The last serves to emphasize the strangeness of their supermen, explicitly labeled "mutants" in stories like Van Vogt's *Slan* (1940) and Kuttner's "The Piper's Son" (1945). In these texts, the Darwinian story of competition was made more urgent by fears of atomic war (Carter 160).

From the late 1930s through the mid-50s, a remarkable number of writers took up the notion that humans might well give birth to their own replacements. The results ranged widely, from paranoia to cautious optimism, and from devout belief to satire. Indeed, the superman theme is one of the best illustrations of the way SF writers trade ideas, as Philip Klass has observed, like jazz musicians borrowing and embroidering on one another's riffs (Letson, 61).

In this case, however, one reason so many artists ended up playing the same tune is that there was an especially persistent patron, like the fellow at the back of the bar shouting "Play 'Melancholy Baby' " at every break. This patron was John W. Campbell, Jr. He not only requested innumerable versions of "Homo Superior" but even asked for particular arrangements.

In letters to contributors, Campbell repeatedly suggested the theme of the mutated superman, often with psionic abilities (such as telepathy or clairvoyance). Writing to Poul Anderson in 1952, for instance, Campbell suggested a story about a superior race, *Homo inquisitivus,* whose activities in the distant past might have been the source for classical myths (Chapdelaine

83–87). To Henry Kuttner, he suggested a similar treatment of werewolf legend (Chapdelaine 121). It was under Campbell's influence that Isaac Asimov introduced a telepathic mutant into his Foundation series (Berger 93) and Jack Williamson incorporated telekinesis in his ". . . And Searching Mind" (Williamson 165). Campbell undoubtedly played a role in shifting E. E. "Doc" Smith's later Lensman books, especially *Children of the Lens* (serialized in *Astounding* in 1947), away from simple shoot-'em-ups in space and toward emphasis on the mental evolution of the Kinnison family. Smith later attempted, in *The Galaxy Primes,* to tailor a psi story specifically to suit Campbell's tastes, but Campbell rejected the novel and it was serialized in *Amazing Stories* (Moskowitz 24).

James Blish's story "Let the Finder Beware" (1949), expanded into the novel *Jack of Eagles* (1952), appeared in *Thrilling Wonder Stories* rather than in Campbell's *Astounding,* but Blish, like Smith, was certainly aware that the theme he was using was Campbell's favorite. In his critical disguise as William Atheling, Jr., Blish comments in 1957 that "from the professional writer's point of view, the primary interest in *Astounding Science Fiction* . . . continues to center on the editor's preoccupation with extra-sensory powers and perceptions ("psi") as a springboard for stories" (86). "Atheling" also praises his other self, Blish, for writing a story in which the "explanation of how psi powers might work differs completely from that proposed in his only other major flight on the subject . . . but what is more important, it also differs completely from any proposed by his editor (Campbell) up to that time" (89). Blish indicates that Campbell's obsession led some writers to find ways to subvert the theme even as they made use of it.

In a letter to Clifford Simak in 1953, Campbell took credit for ideas explored in two of the best-known superman stories published in his magazine:

> The impossibility of portraying the superman was behind the moves I made back in 1939 to get some superman stories of a new type written. There are two possible approaches to avoid the problem:
>
> 1. The approach typified by the play "The Women" which was all about men, yet had not one man on stage. I pointed out this proposition to Norvell Page; he wrote "But Without Horns" for me. In that one, if you recall, the superman was never on stage—only people who had met him and had been changed, or men who were fighting him.
>
> 2. The super-*man* can't be fully portrayed. But since ontogeny recapitulates phylogeny, a super-human must, during boyhood and adolescence, pass through the human levels; there will be a stage of his development when he is less than adult-human, another stage when he is equal to adult-human—and the final stage when he has passed beyond our comprehension.
>
> The situation can be handled, then, by established faith, trust, understanding, and sympathy with the *individual as a character* by portraying

him in his not-greater-than adult human stages—and allow the established
trust-and-belief to carry over to the later and super-human stage.

A. E. Van Vogt worked out "Slan" in response to that comment-discussion
from me. (Chapdelaine 178)

Thus not only did Campbell publish superman stories and favor writers
who could be relied on to keep offering new variations on the theme, but he
even invented many of the variations himself. Soon after Campbell began
editing *Astounding* in 1937, he stopped publishing fiction under his own
name, but he never stopped writing it. If fiction had credits like Hollywood
movies, much of the work published in *Astounding* would have to say something like "story by A. E. Van Vogt, screenplay by A. E. Van Vogt and John
W. Campbell, Jr., from an original idea by John W. Campbell, Jr."

Van Vogt was Campbell's most reliable producer of superman stories.
His superbeings range from telepathic slans of the 1940s to shape-shifting
Silkies two decades later. Both Van Vogt and Campbell were strongly influenced during this period by the psychological theory (not yet inflated into a
religion) of fellow SF writer L. Ron Hubbard. Hubbard's *dianetics* promised
that everyone who went through his process of psychic clearing could gain
extraordinary powers. The subsequent transformation of dianetics into sci-
entology indicates how close the idea of superman is to that of a god, and
indeed, the theme of the superman often metamorphosed after about 1960
into fictions about attaining godhood through technological or other means.
Frank Herbert's *Dune* (1965) illustrates the shift, with his hero Paul Atreides
beginning as a budding superman and ending as a reluctant messiah. This
variation on the theme remains popular in SF. For instance, much of the
work of Orson Scott Card, especially his *Wyrms* (1987), explores the borderline between the superhuman and the divine.

Campbell's promotion of the superman theme and his cheerleading for
Hubbard's schemes were both outgrowths of his interest in psychic powers. As
a graduate of Duke University, he was familiar with Joseph B. Rhine's experiments with extrasensory perception, but his later views departed from Rhine's
modest claims and careful scientific methodology, taking on an evangelical fer-
vor. Philip K. Dick later recalled the pressure Campbell exerted on writers:

> In the early Fifties much American science fiction dealt with human
> mutants and their glorious super-powers and super-faculties by which they
> would presently lead mankind to a higher state of existence, a sort of
> Promised Land. John W. Campbell, Jr., editor of *Analog*, demanded that the
> stories he bought deal with such wonderful mutants, and he also insisted
> that the mutants be shown as (1) good; and (2) firmly in charge. (411–12)

Dick's comments indicate that Campbell's fascination with such superbeings, a fascination which Campbell shared with the SF audience, was
rooted not only in his faith in psi, but also in his acceptance of a particular
model of human evolution. In this view, racial advances are triggered by

exceptional individuals who impose their wills on the lesser beings around them. Unlike Nietzsche, who imagined that the Overman would be unconcerned with the lives of lesser mortals, Campbell and his writers developed a scenario in which the superior being would naturally take charge, hauling mankind up behind him regardless of mankind's wishes (Frisby 107). This long-term benevolence often involves short-term cruelties, as in Heinlein's "Gulf," in which the supermen freely make decisions affecting common humanity, from the withholding of technology to selective executions of dangerous individuals.

From a political perspective, the superman scenario is the antithesis of utopia. In utopian fiction, progress is a communal process—the entire society evolves together. The mechanisms for improvement are generally institutions: schools, governments, families, political groups, media, and so on. Such institutions are irrelevant to the superman. In superman stories, the individual evolves apart from, or even in opposition to, his society.

Indeed, the greatest danger to the would-be superman is to be incorporated into society, to accept its morals and its ways of seeing. It is better to be marked, hunted, persecuted—as are Van Vogt's slans. Van Vogt's hero Jommy Cross ends in triumph, but he begins his journey as a frightened child, torn from his mother and hunted by killers. His plight is made worse by his ability to read the minds of his hunters: "The horror of the rapacious minds snatched after him as he fled with frightened strength along the narrow walk beside the apartment buildings" (11). Nor can he hide effectively: the same fringe of golden tendrils that gives him telepathic powers marks him to any observer as something other than fully human.

Yet Jommy Cross's trials not only give him strength but also encourage the reader to identify with a character who might otherwise be too powerful and too alien for sympathy. Van Vogt uses a number of narrative devices to transfer the reader's allegiance from humankind to his slan hero. The human characters are weak, savage, or venal. Jommy, on the other hand, is resourceful and unselfish, though he learns to be ruthless in order to survive.

More subtly, Van Vogt keeps the reader close to Jommy by manipulating point of view. Most of the narrative is filtered through Jommy's perceptions. He is our camera—or rather, since most of the imagery is not visual but tactile, he is our hand, our body. The first line of the book sets the pattern: "His mother's hand felt cold, clutching his" (5). Within the next couple of pages, he feels his mother's fear as "a quiet, swift pulsation," feels other people's thoughts as they "beat against his mind," senses a "steady wave of vagueness that washed from the crowds pressing all around," catches a ride on a passing car by catching its bumper with "abnormally strong fingers," and even feels, rather than seeing, the "intensity of [the] gazes" of passers-by (5–8). When he does see something, our awareness of the visual image is muted by words like "glimpse," "blur," and "looming." We are not allowed to sit back and be spectators: we must occupy an imaginative space inside Jommy's skin.

And we are invited to collaborate in saving that skin. Van Vogt structures the narrative as a series of puzzles that we are invited to solve along with the hero. How can he hide among humans long enough to grow into his powers? How can he turn an enemy into an ally? Where are his father's scientific papers hidden? How can he get into the heavily fortified palace of the planetary dictator? The story repeatedly poses such challenges and then, when they are solved, rewards both Jommy and the reader with new information about his origins. For a certain sort of reader, a scientifically-oriented reader who considers himself adept at tackling intellectual puzzles, this structure guarantees a powerful identification with the superman.

There is evidence that *Astounding*'s readers, who were used to being praised by their editor for being "technically minded people" (Tymn 66), did indeed find *Slan* unusually compelling Or perhaps that should be *interpelling*, playing on Louis Althusser's term for literature's power of interpellation, or hailing. Hailing goes beyond mere identification with a character. It is a process through which readers accept and internalize an identity constructed for them by the text. *Slan* uses every sort of narrative device to hail SF readers: inviting them to see themselves as more perceptive, more resourceful, and more isolated than non-fans. And readers responded. The phrase "Fans are slans" became a byword at SF conventions, and fans launched amateur magazines with names like *Slantasy* and *Slant* (James 136).

The reaction of the SF fans was also John W. Campbell's, who clearly ranked himself and his colleagues on the slan side. Writing to Isaac Asimov in 1958, he described the two of them as belonging to a group marked not only by mental superiority but also by visible indices of that intellectual difference: "But you and I *can* be spotted as Eggheads from at least as great a distance as a Negro can" (Chapdelaine 358). How? Not, as the term Egghead implies, by the sort of physical weakness and cranial hypertrophy described in Hamilton's "The Man Who Evolved," but by a characteristic dress, speech, facial expression, a particular degree of "neuromuscular coordination," and even an "aura" (358) that marks them as a breed apart, just as strongly as skin color would—or slan tendrils.

Though Campbell depicts members of the Egghead caste in terms of superior abilities, he reveals some insecurity by twice equating their distinctiveness with the signs of stigmatized minorities, with African-Americans in the above quotation and later with homosexuals:

> We're abnormally aware of *all* the things around us. The result is that we handle ourselves, our bodies, with an efficiency and economy of movement that the normal can't depend on himself to achieve.
>
> We, my friend, have gestures and body-postures that are as identifiable at long range as anything a fairy does. (358)

Like slan tendrils, these exterior signs of intellectual ability call forth fear and hatred from the "Normal," who, Campbell says, knows he cannot compete (359–60).

But the question arises: compete at what? The answer is built into the social Darwinian framework. The contest is the mating game. The goal is reproduction, making more copies of oneself. He who dies with the most boys wins. (Females, in the evolutionary narrative, do not reproduce themselves or their traits but only provide the means for superior males to do so.)

In *The Descent of Man,* Darwin emphasized sexual selection as a primary form of evolutionary pressure. He observed that while some characteristics seem to be passed on equally to all offspring, others only show up in one sex or the other. In his account of sexual difference, though, the characteristics that count the most are those associated with maleness, for he saw sexual selection as operating primarily to distinguish among male candidates for reproduction. He thought that masculine pursuits such as hunting required "the higher mental faculties, namely observation, reason, invention, or imagination," which would, through sexual selection, "be transmitted chiefly to the male offspring at the corresponding period of manhood" (Darwin 576).

Herbert Spencer, whose goal-directed account of evolution largely replaced Darwin's random one in the popular imagination, does allow for some specifically female traits, but those are developed in response to male behaviors:

In the course of the struggles for existence among wild tribes, those tribes survived in which the men were not only powerful and courageous, but aggressive, unscrupulous, intensely egoistic. Necessarily, then, the men of the conquering races which gave origin to the civilized races, were men in whom the brutal characteristics were dominant; and necessarily the women of such races, having to deal with brutal men, prospered in proportion as they possessed, or acquired, fit adjustments of nature. (Spencer 19–20)

These feminine "adjustments" included the ability and the psychological need to please their mates by means of disguising their own emotions, using indirect means to persuade, and intuiting the states of mind of others, especially men (20). Thus, evolution itself dictated that man should be aggressive, brutal, courageous, and powerful, while woman is cast as the Angel in the Cave. Even though this is supposed to be an account of human origins, it also clearly operates, in myth fashion, as a way of authorizing institutions and relationships in the present.

The assumptions built into this evolutionary narrative have been challenged almost from its first articulation. Antoinette Brown Blackwell, as early as 1875, objected to the tendency to interpret "fact by the accepted theory that the male is the representative type of the species—the female a modification preordained in the interest of reproduction, and in that interest only or chiefly" (Newman 1). More recently, archeological and ethnological evidence has called into question the belief in hunting by males as a primary food source and concomitantly as the sole arena for the development of "cooperation and sharing, communication, and the invention of tools, weapons, equipment, *and* art" (Bleier 122, 116). As Donna Haraway has demonstrated, all such origin narratives—including not only the theories but also the evidence, such as field observations of primates, on which they are based—inevitably inscribe the beliefs and identities of the observers, thereby representing those identities as natural (Haraway 4–5).

Despite these criticisms, the story told by Darwin and Spencer continues to exert its mythlike power on our interpretations of present conditions and events. More curiously, the evolutionary story even seems to constrain visions of the future, as in Van Vogt's superman stories.

What do Van Vogt's heroes do with their remarkable new powers? They compete with other males for access to females. In order to win his game, Jommy must rescue Kathleen Layton from human villains. One of these seeks to kill her, another to make her his mistress, but the two threats are curiously fused. The first attack on Kathleen is presented as if it were attempted rape rather than murder: "The man was inside her bedroom, and was at this very instant creeping on his knees toward her bed" (20). Kathleen telepathically feels the attacker's "gathering excitement" and fears that he will "rush her before she could move, pin her down under the blankets and have her at his mercy" (20). Despite her slan powers, Kathleen can only defend herself by appealing to her father, who keeps her safe until he can hand her over to Jommy.

Jommy, in contrast, can win any woman to his side, human or slan, through telepathic seduction:

> His mind concentrated. The coordinated power of his sense abruptly dissolved her facial expression into triumph and a genuine joy. Alertly, his brain pressed against her mind shield, probing at the tiny gaps, absorbing every leak of thought, analyzing every overtone, and second by second his puzzlement grew. Her smile flashed into soft laughter; and then her shield went down. Her mind lay before him, exposed to his free, untrammeled gaze. (171)

Jommy's ability psychically to penetrate women is embodied in the tendrils that also make him vulnerable to attack by rival males. These tendrils might not seem so blatantly sexual if the text did not reinforce their phallic associations. When Jommy reveals his tendrils to the first male slans he meets, who lack such visible marks of difference, he feels their revulsion:

> "God," the first one thought, "it's a snake!"
> And from the other came a thought utterly cold, utterly merciless: "Kill the damned thing!" (48)

Tendrils, in other words, make men react to Jommy as a dangerous rival. Exposing his tendrils—in essence, exposing himself—is read as a hostile act by males, a dangerous but seductive one by females. Metaphor transforms the tendrils into a snake, and that snake then becomes, by synecdoche, the whole person. To the tendrilless slans, Jommy *is*, rather than merely possessing, the power of the phallus.

In Jacques Lacan's revision of Freud, which treats the unconscious as a sign system, the phallus is not a male organ or male sexuality, but rather that which maleness confers by virtue of not being its opposite. The phallus, in this sense, is society's enforcement of the difference between masculinity and femininity. It assigns power and selfhood to males, passivity and indefiniteness to the female Other. The emphasis is on significance, rather than flesh.

The phallic power acquired by Jommy Cross accords best with a Lacanian reading, despite the blatant Freudian symbolism Van Vogt slips into the scene of discovery. When Jommy comes of age, he is finally able to "take possession of his father's secret" (57). That secret is a weapon, part of which is in physical form and part in the form of secret knowledge. However, the tangible portion of the inheritance, "a thick rod of metal" that can spew a "burst of virulent fire," is actually the lesser half (63). More important in the long run is the stack of papers containing "his father's mighty science" (53).

Once Jommy possesses those papers, he takes over his father's role as "the greatest living slan" (138). When he presents his discovery to Kathleen's father, he is rewarded with a set of fairy-tale gifts: entry into the true slan society; the hand of the ruler's daughter; and, replacing the childhood nickname of Jommy, his own true name, which is also his father's: "John Thomas Cross, I welcome you and your father's discovery" (184). As in Lacanian theory, the "name of the father" is what underlies the entire sign system and authorizes one's entry into the world of order and meaning.

Behind Jommy's father are other fathers, going back to the patriarch of all slans, Samuel Lann, or S. Lann, whose name they all bear. The slans trace their ancestry from Lann—not even the biological father of the first slans but merely their discoverer—rather than from the nameless mother who bore them. The male lineage is what counts, even if it is an intellectual rather than a genetic lineage. The father's name and the father's science constitute essential identity. Those enable Lann to mark the slans as his own children, thereby winning the evolutionary battle.

Yet in Lann's and Jommy's victories we see enacted a paradox that lies at the heart of the evolutionary narrative. The slans achieve victory by superior force in the name of superior intelligence. But how does a selection process that favors brute strength and aggressiveness produce what Spencer calls "the civilized races"? Who is the hero of the myth: the most aggressive male or the most perceptive, the strongest or the smartest, the paleolithic scientist or the captain of the tribal football team? The myth asserts that these are one and the same, but for the male reader of the myth—especially for the intellectual who is most likely to *be* reading the myth—there is always the fear that the story it tells is of someone else's triumph, and not one's own. Since the myth doesn't distinguish among different types of superiority, it implies that one ought to be superior in all things: brains, brawn, beauty, and boldness. If our distant fathers excelled in all of these, why can't we? And if we do not, will superior science suffice? What if, after all, Campbell's Egghead is not Van Vogt's slan?

Though the fairy-tale structure of *Slan* keeps these anxieties largely at bay (in a fairy tale, it is expected that the hero will begin as the most unprepossessing character), they begin to emerge in Van Vogt's later work. In *The World of Null-A,* for instance, the slan-like superman Gilbert Gosseyn believes it necessary at one point to kill himself so that his even more powerful clone can come on the scene. In order to overcome his superhuman will to live, Gosseyn creates a recording that will reprogram his unconscious mind while he sleeps. "I'm nobody," it tells him. "I'm not worth anything. Everybody hates me. What's the good of being alive? I'll never make anything of myself. No girl will ever marry me" (128). This recording is itself the textual unconscious: it says what the story denies, marks the gap that the text tries to smooth over.

Part of the collaborative development of the superman theme was the recognition and exploitation of its darker side, a task for which there were writers better suited than Van Vogt. Henry Kuttner's "The Piper's Son," for instance, includes an embedded narrative that can be read as a *Slan* parody: it is the story of the Green Man, "a figure of marvelous muscular development, handsome as a god" who defeats a series of opponents from rival races (179). A wish-fulfillment fantasy broadcast telepathically to younger members of a group of mutants, the Green Man's adventures are propaganda aimed at enticing young Baldies to see themselves as separate from and superior to non-telepathic humanity. Older Baldies have staked their fortunes on blending in with the existing human civilization. Baldies are not only telepathic but also marked, as their name suggests, by complete hairlessness. Although older Baldies typically try to "pass" by wearing wigs, the disguise is transparent, leaving them as the targets of abuse by normals and the objects of their children's scorn.

Kuttner's story enacts John W. Campbell's comments about Eggheads. The Baldies' eggy hairlessness, like that of Hamilton's Man Who Evolved, makes visible the more important difference inside their heads. Their wigs remind us of strategies adopted by the other groups to which Campbell compared Eggheads: the processed hairstyles of African-Americans (especially at the time Kuttner was writing) and the closeted behavior of gays.

Kuttner builds his story around questions of male identity expressed through various relationships: father to son, doctor to patient, Baldy to Normal. All involve issues of difference, power, and resentment. Kuttner's hero, Ed Burkhalter, proves remarkably adept at negotiating a path through these hazards without accepting repeated invitations to use physical violence or mental force. To do so, he must forego the sort of glory represented by the Green Man. In place of masculine honor, the story offers him the compensations of mutual respect, especially between him and his wife.

For this is a story in which sexual selection has already taken place. The story indicates that the Burkhalters have selected one another, rather than reenacting the evolutionary tale of battling males and a female prize passively awaiting the outcome. In this version of the contest, the Baldies have already won, for what ordinary man, not matter how strong or aggressive, could offer a woman anything better than this:

> His thought reached out before him into the low, double-winged house on the hillside, and interlocked with hers in a warm intimacy. It was something more than a kiss. And, as always, there was the exciting sense of expectancy, mounting and mounting, till the last door swung open and they touched physically. *This,* he thought, *is why I was born a Baldy; this is worth losing worlds for.* (199)

Kuttner does not go so far as to imagine a female superbeing. Ethel Burkhalter is even more closeted than Ed: "not even her husband had ever seen her unwigged" (198). Nor do we see her exercising any of her psychic strengths. Kuttner left it to his wife C. L. Moore to investigate the nature of superwoman, in stories that will be examined in the next chapter. Ethel plays little part in the story's action except to reinforce her husband's decisions, and yet her presence provides the necessary underpinning for Ed's rewriting of the masculine script. Lacking such support he might have turned out more like the self-doubting hero of Stanley Weinbaum's *The New Adam.*

In deliberately invoking and investigating, rather than covering up, the anxieties built into the theory of sexual selection, Kuttner may have been consciously following Weinbaum's example. Weinbaum's novel is in many ways the most interesting superman story to come out of the Campbell era, and that may be because it was actually written before the era began. Weinbaum died shortly before Campbell took up the reins at *Astounding,* but he left enough unpublished manuscripts for a posthumous career more distinguished than many SF writers' lifetime achievements. *The New Adam* was first published in 1939 in hardcover and then serialized in *Amazing Stories* four years later, after Campbell and Van Vogt had whetted fans' appetite for superman fiction. This combination of circumstances meant that the novel did not go through Campbell's editorial mills. It is more awkward in spots than anything Campbell would have published, but it is also edgier, more complex, and more direct in its challenge to SF conventions and attitudes.

Weinbaum's superman is clearly another Egghead. Edmond Hall is marked physically by his hands. Long and slender with an extra joint in each finger, they are variously described as "tentacles" (8) and "snakes" (53), suggesting that they stand for the same complex of meanings as Van Vogt's slan tentacles. Certainly they embody his extra abilities as well as the difference that makes him a childhood outcast. And by the same synecdoche that makes a slan a "snake," his fingers represent himself: abnormal, disturbing, but at the same time "unusually apt and delicate" (10).

High intelligence, introversion, delicacy of build and movement—these are not the attributes of the Spencerian brute but of the ninety-eight-pound weakling featured in the Charles Atlas ads on the back covers of SF magazines. They are also characteristics that can be read as code for homosexuality, and the text flirts with this meaning. Edmond is repeatedly referred to as "queer" in contexts that gradually shift the dominant meaning from "peculiar" to "sexually deviant." First, it's, "You'll bring him up queer unless you get him some friends" (9). Then, "Who's the queer boy friend, Vanny?" (47). And finally, in a failed encounter with a prostitute, "Well, for God's sake! Turned down! I never been so—Say, I know what's wrong with you! You must be queer!" (53). And, indeed, the strongest emotion portrayed in the first part of the book is Edmond's fascination/rivalry with his human rival Paul Varney.

Paul is the boy who first taunts him with the name "Snake-fingers" (12). Paul is handsome, athletic, and popular. He is even smart, apparently the best student in the class, for Edmond chooses not to display his intelligence. Furthermore, the first time we meet him, Paul already has a girlfriend: "Very grown up was Paul; he dated with little Evanne Martin in the fifth grade in Platonic imitation of his elders" (12). In order to prove himself Paul's evolutionary superior—and at the same time defuse the possibility of a sexual interest between the two males—Edmond must be able not only to outthink him, but to steal his girl.

Like Jommy Cross, Edmond finds that women can be his best allies against male rivals. He notes that "the few women I have encountered have not hated me so intensely" as the men, and decides that this is because "Men hate their masters; women love them" (60). Evanne, or Vanny, takes up his cause at first because she feels sorry for him and later because she is fascinated by his difference from the norm. She encourages him to challenge the alpha male: "Why don't you get mad at Paul once in a while? He rides you too much" (13). Edmond does get mad, but he never admits as much to himself. When he begins to pursue Vanny, he believes that he is merely investigating the human capacity for pleasure, just as he has already tested the satisfactions of power, wealth, and scientific inquiry, finding each of these to be mere "intellectual masturbation . . . in that I let the seeds of my thoughts die sterile" (75). The metaphor here reveals that Edmond's crisis is one of sexual identity, as well as intellect.

If he is to become the superman he believes himself to be, he must prove himself *to* Paul *through* Vanny. He must figure out how to construct a masculine persona even though he is "not a man such as Paul" (70). He cannot do so merely by reversing the previous dominance, for "Paul had nothing to give him worth the taking" (70). Instead, following a pattern identified by Eve Sedgwick as a central principle of nineteenth-century culture, an unstable homosocial relationship must be resolved by the exchange of a woman between the two men. That is why Edmond focuses his attentions on Vanny rather than on any other pretty girl, and why he announces to himself that "Paul must serve me here. . . . He shall procure me a woman" (76). Only after Paul does so, reluctantly reintroducing Vanny to Edmond, is Edmond able to declare to himself that "I am the Enemy, that which will destroy; I am the replacer of mankind, and the future incarnate" (72). He is ready to be the rider rather than the ridden.

From this point in the story, Edmond's focus shifts from Paul to Vanny. He plans a campaign to seduce her, making use of drink, dancing, Paul's jealousy, and, as the ultimate sexual lure, science fiction! It seems that Paul has been telling Vanny about his vision of the city of the future, but "being Paul, he is probably wrong" (95), says Edmond, who then proceeds to capture Vanny's imagination with his own description:

> He began to speak in a low monody that droned in Vanny's ears like a murmur of distant waters. Gradually the sense of them merged into a continuity, but the pictures they evoked lived on, grew into a sort of reality. She wondered momentarily at this phenomenon, then lost herself in the magic imagery; it did not occur to her that she was being lulled into a quasi-hypnotic state. (96)

While Vanny grows more and more pliant, Edmond conjures up pictures of an exotic metropolis, far in the future, where she is the famous Black Flame and he the mysterious Master of the world. Here Weinbaum seems to be indulging in self-parody, for he was the author of a novel about a far future city and a woman called the Black Flame. This is the Egghead's fondest dream: that the awkward, brainy guy can become superman—and win the girl—by inventing a really great science fiction story.

But Weinbaum ironizes the wish even while metafictionally fulfilling it. It doesn't matter, it turns out, what sort of tale Edmond spins for Vanny. The key is his storytelling style: "it mattered little what story he told if only it seemed real to his listener (97). By spinning a futuristic romance, he takes control of his listener's will. He is both slan and the creator of slan, seducing not through telepathic tendrils but via the invention of a narrative scenario.

Edmond's triumph brings about its own undoing, for Vanny, once possessed, ceases to be that which he sought to possess. She is no longer herself; more importantly, she is not Paul's and so no longer of interest. In the final section of Weinbaum's novel, Vanny finally emerges as an independent character, and as she does so, the evolutionary narrative breaks down. Interestingly, just as Vanny begins to become aware of both Edmond's nature and her own, a fourth major character appears, the superwoman that Edmond has previously denied could exist:

> "What restrains woman, the thing that prohibits the sex from greatness, is her physical organization."
>
> "You mean her more delicate make-up?"
>
> "I mean her ovaries. Whatever creative genius she has flows into them." (69)

This notion, that reproductive demands on females keep them from developing intellectual powers equal to those of males, is another part of Spencer's evolutionary narrative (Newman 6), and so it is entirely appropriate that a self-proclaimed evolutionary milestone like Edmond Hall should cite it. The novel, however, proclaims both Hall and Spencer wrong. Edmond's female counterpart does exist, and she is capable of creative activity. It turns out that Edmond already owns one of her paintings, in which he has recognized a sensibility akin to his own.

The superwoman, Sarah Maddox, is curiously there and not there in the text. She comes and goes mysteriously, perhaps by psychic projection; she is hardly described at all and when the text mentions her appearance it declares her nondescript (though we know she has Edmond's serpentine fingers). She defies categorization as either feminine or masculine (126); she shows no emotion, at least that Edmond is able to perceive; and she says almost nothing that is not an echo of some comment of Edmond's:

> "You are Sarah Maddox, then," he said. "I might have guessed."
>
> The woman smiled.
>
> "I have two minds," said Edmond, "or a dual mind, but not such as the beasts call a dual personality."
>
> "Yes," said Sarah.
>
> "I have known a City, not past or present, but a place where I am at one with life."
>
> "I know," said Sarah. (126)

Sarah's phantom presence changes the sexual equation in several ways. She becomes the foil for Vanny, her superhuman unresponsiveness causing Edmond to find more value in Vanny's humanity—and making him less sure of his own superiority over Paul. Sarah also seems to be more involved than he in the decision to have a superhuman child She chooses *him* to help *her* reproduce herself, reversing Darwin's model of sexual selection. Edmond eventually decides that she is truer to the new type than he is, because of his closer association with ordinary humans and their emotional entanglements. Even in that judgment, though, Weinbaum uses Sarah to destabilize gender, for the text provides clues that whenever Edmond reads Sarah's character, exercising the masculine prerogative of analyzing Woman, he reads her wrong.

At the end of the book, Edmond distributes himself. He gives Vanny back her own will, gives their child to Sarah, bequeaths the future to that child, gives his own death to Paul, and leaves his stories to the reader. With those acts of renunciation, he begins to form an identity that is his own and not what the evolutionary myth would make of him. Edmond refuses to become merely a more powerful version of an image that already exists: superman as man writ large. Weinbaum comments in his prologue that it is a mistake to impose such a restriction on the imagination: "this is the fallacy of Nietzsche, the fallacy of H. G. Wells. These, like others who deal with the matter, have believed that a man, a human being, raised to the nth degree, represents the superman" (5).

What Weinbaum does not point out is that these versions of the superman are not really whole beings raised in degree, but extrapolations from certain selected human characteristics and potentialities, and specifically those characteristics that have been assigned the meaning "masculine." Because, in the binary system of Darwinian evolution, "feminine" is defined as the absence of masculine traits, it is no wonder he cannot depict a super-woman: in the terms he sets up, that would amount to exaggerating a negative. But he does negate the exaggeration, leaving open the possibility of other directions for the imagination.

One of those directions was taken by a writer who might be said to mark the close of the Campbell era as Weinbaum marks its beginning. Philip K. Dick's story "The Golden Man" (1954) exactly follows the Campbellian rules quoted earlier: it describes a human mutation involving extrasensory powers; the mutant is most definitely in charge; and he is arguably innocent, if not exactly good. Dick, being Dick, finds ways to turn each of these specifications on its head. Dick was aware of the attractions of the psi-superman formula: "I think these people secretly imagined they were themselves early manifestations of these kindly, wise, super-intelligent *Übermenschen* who would guide the stupid—i.e. the rest of us—to the Promised Land" (412). So he set out to write a story that would lull readers into the same sort of identification before opening up a gulf under their feet.

The story closely follows the outlines of an earlier work for which Campbell claimed a share of the credit, Norvell Page's "But without Horns." In this novella, the viewpoint character is not the superman but his enemy. Campbell persuaded Page to leave his superman entirely offstage, so that he might be known only by his effects on other characters. We discover those effects gradually as they are uncovered by the FBI agent who pits himself against the superman, John Miller. This device allows Page to frame the narrative as a mystery, with the detective coming closer and closer to the unreachable center.

As Walter Kildering, the agent, pursues his prey, we see John Miller first as a criminal, responsible for murders and robberies. Then we discover that Miller can cause changes in behavior, so that no one opposing him is a trustworthy ally. Next we learn that he is a mutation, caused by his parents' work with radioactive ores; his siblings and all of his offspring to date have been physically monstrous, and we are invited to see Miller, too, as a monster of a different sort. Moving into Miller's home territory, Kildering discovers that Miller has made himself into a dictator, ruthless but surprisingly benevolent in certain respects: his city, like Mussolini's trains, runs efficiently. Even when he commits mass murder, he kills only the stupid, so he might be said to be benefitting the community as a whole (so long as the reader identifies with the survivors and not with the culled).

The next revelation is that Miller's powers have a sexual dimension. He has accumulated a harem of young women each of whom wishes to bear him a son—there is no mention of possible daughters (50). Miller's attraction is such that it makes good girls behave like loose women: we first see one of his kidnap victims buying perfume, the scent of which is "titillat[ing]" (46), to make herself more attractive to Miller. Finally, we discover that Miller has set himself up as a god to his followers. He can appear in angelic guise, combining the sexual and the divine in a way that even, intolerably, tempts Kildering:

> Walter Kildering, face down on the floor, could not tell whether he had fired that last, utterly necessary, shot. He could not tell because hot pincers were tearing at his brain. Because of the face amid the golden light. A beautiful face—hellishly beautiful— (79)

One might question whether the kind of identification talked about by Dick operates in this story. Surely Kildering, not Miller, is the reader's surrogate as well as the moral center of the story. The answer I believe, is that there is little difference between the two. The closer Kildering comes to Miller's presence, the more he comes to resemble his opponent. The tactics he is forced to adopt, including murder, are those of his enemy. One of his colleagues even comments that "Kildering isn't human. . . . He's damned near a superman himself, the way he stands it" (100). The reader is given a choice of identifying with the failed superman, Kildering, or with the successful one, Miller.

In a novel that is virtually a rewrite of Page's story, Frank Robinson's *The Power* (1956), this identification is made even more explicit. The hero, Bill Tanner, who has been fighting against a hidden superhuman opponent throughout the book finally discovers that he too is superman and immediately resolves to appropriate every one of his rival's prerogatives: "It was going to be fun to play God" (190).

Robinson presents this godhood in more explicitly sexual terms than did Page. The superman, Adam Hart, seems to be able to turn anyone around him into a sexual object. Tanner's severely asexual secretary, Patricia "Petey" Olson, is revealed to have another life as Adam Hart's kept woman. A key scene is Tanner's breaking into Petey's apartment to discover bottles of perfume, lace underwear, and silk sheets. Tanner's reaction, cuing the reader's, is a mixture of envy and fear, envy of Adam Hart's ability to transform the pseudo-man Petey into a responsive woman and fear that he could do the same to anyone else. (There is probably an element of dread in that envy, and more than a trace of desire in the fear.) The text drops a couple of clues about Hart's sexual omnivorousness: he left "half a dozen bastard children" in his hometown and also "experimented all over town—with everything and everybody" (78). The implication is that both Petey Olson and her brother John were among those experiments. Later Tanner's girlfriend Marge is added to their number. Will Tanner be next?

One of the ways writers try to convince us that their supermen are truly superior is to set up analogies: superman is to man as man is to X. Weinbaum filled the X in with "slave," Page with "dog," but in both texts there is another implied term: "woman." Robinson makes the analogy explicit: Tanner fears losing masculine difference, of becoming the feminine or feminized Other to Adam Hart's phallic will. His only recourse is to become that which he envies and fears.

Unlike Van Vogt or Page—or Campbell—Robinson makes the shift from simply using the scenario to investigating it. *The Power* is both an example of the superman myth and a critique of its appeal. Robinson is probably interested in distancing himself from the superman image partly because of postwar revelations about Nazi uses of the myth—it is not a coincidence that Adam Hart shares initials with Adolf Hitler. But his more critical stance may also have to do with the increasing sophistication of the genre: by 1956 Campbell no longer represented the advance guard of SF. Robinson's story was published by a major hardcover press rather than in an SF magazine, but even magazines like *Galaxy, The Magazine of Fantasy and Science Fiction,* and *If,* in which Dick published "The Golden Man," were open to greater psychological depth and a more complex attitude toward scientific ideas and science fictional tropes than were tolerated in *Astounding.*

Taking advantage of that openness, with "The Golden Man," Philip K. Dick wrote a story that talks back to "Slan" and "But without Horns" with an even greater degree of ironic self-awareness than did Robinson's novel. From the first paragraphs, we are in a world whose rich texture and emotional nuance implicitly criticize Van Vogt's futuristic fairyland or Page's cops-and-robbers movie set. Dick's world, unlike theirs, is full of different sorts of people: hairy-armed workmen, teenaged lovers, a "ratfaced cab driver," a tired woman shopper. In a greasy café, a traveling salesman flirts with a bored waitress and pulls out lewd photos to impress the locals.

But the photos are of a mutant—an eight-breasted woman from an internment camp near Denver—and the fat, ingratiating salesman is really a government agent seeking leads on other mutations caused by radioactivity from a recent war. Beneath its realistic surface, this is the familiar hunted-superman scenario, and Dick uses it to hail the reader just as Van Vogt did, just as Kuttner's story-within-a-story of the Green Man hailed its Baldy listeners. By the time the superman appears, we are ready to cast our lot with him rather than with the ordinary townspeople or the sleazy government hunter.

And we get our reward: the mutant, Cris Johnson, is grand, powerful, golden. He seems to be another glorified version of the Egghead, gazing beyond the concerns of the merely Normal:

> Remote, detached, aloof. Seeing past everyone and everything—that is, until all at once something clicked and he momentarily rephased, reentered their world briefly. (35)

He even shows the greater "efficiency and economy of movement" that Campbell attributed to his tribe:

> Cris said nothing. He bent slightly, a supple arc of his incredibly graceful body, then moved his arm in a blur of speed. (36)

Cris Johnson's name suggests that he is another version of the slan John T. Cross, combining great strength, agility, endurance, and uncanny knowledge of his opponents' weaknesses. He even has a version of slan tendrils—or the Egghead's aura—his skin and hair are gold, giving him the appearance of "a Roman monument that's been gilded" (41). As his beauty indicates, Cris's greatest weapon is sexual attractiveness. His appearance makes him the object of desire, a desire so intense it can only be spoken of in religious language, so that he becomes "a god come down to earth" (40). He is not only Jommy Cross, but also the figure who lurks behind that name: a Jesus Christ without the asceticism, Christ Belvedere.

Beneath the divine glow, like the "golden light" surrounding the "hellishly beautiful face" of Norvell Page's John Miller (79), lurks another version of Egghead wish-fulfillment: the smart guy who gets *all* the girls. But just as Dick metathesizes the name, he also inverts the meanings. The sting in the story is that Cris isn't smart. He speaks no language; doesn't even think as humans do; has an inexorable drive but no will behind it. He acts purely on instinct; his uncanny prescience is a reflex rather than a mark of higher intellect. He is irresistible to women because his appearance signals masculinity more perfectly than does any merely human male's body.

The Golden Man is everything that the collaborative superman story says he should be: resourceful, ruthless, masterful. He has Jommy Cross's power, John Miller's ability to cloud minds, Adam Hart's sexual predatoriness, and the Green Man's glamor. However, there is nothing underneath, no benevolent leadership, no new knowledge, no direction, no communication. He signifies *only* sexual difference, and therefore he has none of the qualities that actual men share with women, including empathy and self-doubt.

Dick shows us that all his predecessors were making the mistake identified by Weinbaum, of assuming a superhuman would play the game by human rules. Defining themselves in terms of above-average intelligence, they imagined a superman in terms of even greater intelligence. "So," says Weinbaum, "a Neanderthaler in his filthy cave, using his embryonic imagination, might have pictured his superman as a giant in strength and size, a mighty hunter, one whose meat-pot and belly is never empty" (5).

The Golden Man neatly sidesteps Campbell's rules, at the same time taking the evolutionary masterplot to its logical limit. As one of Dick's characters points out, "Superior survival doesn't mean superior man. If there were another world-wide flood, only fish would survive. If there were another ice age, maybe nothing but polar bears would be left" (48). The greatest irony in Dick's story is that Cris Johnson is not a fish or a polar bear, but a man-shaped void. In becoming what the evolutionary scenario says he should be—powerful, handsome, ruthless, and completely self-centered—he has sacrificed every faculty that might benefit others: "He doesn't build anything or utilize anything outside himself" (48).

If sexual difference is both the mechanism of evolution and its goal, then continued evolution can only result in difference with nothing to differ from: masculinity with the humanity distilled out. The alternative is to imagine a different evolutionary scenario, one in which, for instance, women and men, like Kuttner's unglamorous but companionable Baldies, might choose one another and scale the evolutionary ladder together.

CHAPTER

WONDER WOMEN

Between the Campbell tradition and comic books, we have a pretty good idea of what a superman might be like: muscular, handsome, keen-eyed, gifted with extraordinary senses and superior intellect, able to out-fight or outwit any opponent. But what about his female counterpart?

Curious things happen when *Homo superior* undergoes a sex change. Despite the fact that A. E. Van Vogt, Henry Kuttner, and Stanley Weinbaum were working with the premise of a racial advance, a new breed of human-ity, they seemed to find it difficult to imagine feminine counterparts for their super heroes. Van Vogt gives his female slan, Kathleen Layton, the same powers as his male hero, but constructs a narrative in which she is unable to make effective use of them. Kuttner offers a glimpse of a new kind of marriage between psychically gifted superbeings, but when his attention turns to the wife in the relationship, she turns out not to be superwoman but merely Mrs. Superman. Weinbaum's *The New Adam* first denies the possibility of such a being and then, when the plot requires her, portrays her as a set of absences.

Part of the trouble is that the master evolutionary narrative which generates the notion of a super male offers no extrapolative path toward superwoman. Exaggerate the traits that the megatext associates with masculinity and you get the stronger, smarter, faster, more aggressive, more inventive superman of SF tradition. Exaggerate the feminine traits and you get someone who erases herself from the story. The female function, according to Darwin and Spencer, is to follow, to accommodate, to receive, to deny self. Extrapolating from these traits calls up a picture of someone who has no self. Where, one wonders, did she go?

She did leave a few traces behind her in the early magazines. Stanley Weinbaum offered a more substantial version of the superwoman in a story called "The Adaptive Ultimate" (1935). In this story we actually get to see the superwoman evolve from a "drab, ugly, uneducated girl" (46) into a force that threatens to take over the world. This woman, Kyra Zelas, first appears as a tuberculosis case, someone so close to death—and so unimportant—that she can serve as guinea pig for an experimental technique developed by young Dr. Daniel Scott.

In the figure of Kyra, Weinbaum suggests not only gender issues but also those of class and race. The language used to describe her continually pushes her into the margins of society. She has "dark, cropped, oily hair," and her face is "flat and unattractive" (44). She wears an ill-fitting and "worn black suit" and does "piece work in some sweatshop" (46). Her name is ethnically marked, in contrast to the Western European, hence non-ethnic, names of Drs. Scott and Bach. Her name and her sweatshop job suggest that she is a recent immigrant. Poor, ignorant, foreign, and female: she could hardly be more strongly Other.

And, of course, the Other is dangerous. Dan Scott's mentor, Dr. Herman Bach, sums up the danger very early in the story: despite her plainness "there's something appealing about her. She adapts quickly" (46). Kyra is a danger even before she is given the fruit fly hormones that turn her into a superwoman. She adapts. And she attracts. Had she not contracted TB, one senses, she might have found her way out of the slums on her own. Like other immigrants, she might have ended up owning the shop, marrying up, or even going to Hollywood to become a star. If this last seems far-fetched, consider the description of Kyra after her treatment, when the "something appealing about her" has bloomed into an eerie glamor:

> Something strangely different about her appearance; surely her worn black suit no longer hung so loosely about her. What he could see of her figure seemed—well, magnificent.
> "Take off your hat, Miss Zelas," squeaked the attorney.
> Scott gasped. Radiant as aluminum glowed the mass of hair she revealed! (48)

Scott's treatment has done little for her appearance that a Hollywood makeover could not do, including the new Kyra's chameleon-like ability to go from blonde to brunette and from "alabaster pale" (48) to "creamy tan, the skin of one exposed to long hours of sunlight" (50).

But her appearance is not the only thing that has changed. The hormonal treatment gives Kyra the ability to adapt to anything in her surroundings. Sunlight makes her tan, instantly. Wounds heal in seconds. She can metabolize poisons into harmless substances. And the key component in her environment, the most dangerous thing she must adapt to, is men. It is men who have the money, the prerogatives, the decision-making ability that she has always lacked. She adapts, accordingly, by becoming what men desire.

Dan Scott is only the first to fall in love with Kyra. On trial for murder (a murder she actually did commit), she charms judge and jury into setting her free. As Weinberg has Dan comment, "faced with danger there in the courtroom, faced by a jury and judge who were men, she adapted to that! She met that danger, not only by changed appearance, but by a beauty so great, that she couldn't have been convicted!" (53) She is actually exhibiting the same willingness to please that Herbert Spencer saw as women's evolutionary role, but when the motivation behind that willingness is self-advancement, it becomes, from the masculine point of view, a deadly duplicity. Her beauty is a way of manipulating men, as is her capacity for lying with absolute sincerity: "Her silver eyes looked steadily into his from a face like that of a marble angel. 'I swear it,' she murmured. 'By anything you name, I swear it, Dan'" (59). Since she has no stake in the masculine power structure, she has no compunctions about defying it; none of its laws and none of its (paternal) names have any hold over her.

Soon she becomes the companion of an influential politician, and then, using his connections, she emerges as a Washington power-broker aspiring to world domination. At that point, the logic of the plot requires that she be stopped, and so Scott and Bach work out a scheme to undo the transformation, turning her back into the plain seamstress. To the infatuated Dan, however, she remains "Kyra the magnificent" (70). To the reader, likewise, the impression that lingers is of the amoral, unearthly siren that she has been. She is all the more memorable because she is essentially unreadable. We don't know what she thinks, what she wants, except power, and she seems to want power only to gain autonomy:

> "Dan, I have learned something. What one needs in this world is power. As long as there are people in the world with more power than I, I run afoul of them. They keep trying to punish me with their laws—and why? Their laws are not for me." (59)

The implied male reader is left wondering, like Sigmund Freud, just what it is that women like Kyra want. Perhaps, like another enigmatic blonde, she just wants to be left alone. Or maybe, like the fisherman's wife of the fairy tale, she wants to be God. We know that she rejects middle-class morality (either because she is now beyond it or because of her origins as an outsider). We know she cares nothing for institutions or for other individuals. We know that her own charms are a matter of indifference to her, except as a means to ends she might desire. Her femininity is a mask, and as Joan Riviere noted in 1929, "the conception of womanliness as a mask" leads men to suspect "some hidden danger" (43).

Riviere's Freudian training gave her little help in identifying what might be under the mask. Her analysis refers to Oedipus, castration, stolen masculinity—in other words, the standard masculine personality profile that Freudians applied to women as well as men. If the mask of womanliness hides nothing but male anxiety, then it is entirely appropriate that Weinbaum describes Kyra as all glittering surface. The male observer cannot see beneath the reflective aluminum hair, marble skin, and silver eyes—can only see himself contorted in the reflection. Dan's question, "Well, actually, how far can a woman go?" (61), is one that had no answer, at least not in 1935.

Weinbaum's version of the superwoman launched one tradition of SF superwoman stories. In it, the male writer depicts a superhuman femme fatale, the object of equal parts fear and fascination. The transformation of plain Kyra into super Kyra can be read as a metaphor for the glamour that desire casts over its target. The metaphor reveals, as well, the anxiety that accompanies such an investment of libido. The brighter the sheen of desire, the less we actually perceive of Kyra the woman. So long as the writer is looking at superwoman from outside that reflective screen, from the perspective of the male observer, she remains a wonder and a fearsome mystery.

The first depictions of superwomen are, not surprisingly, by men. Not only were an overwhelming majority of SF writers in the early years male, but the act of defining has itself traditionally been decreed a masculine prerogative, as in the Adamic myth. What is a woman; what is true womanhood; what do women want? Until quite recently, men would not have thought of asking women to answer these questions any more than one would have asked a cat to define cathood. Even when more women did begin to write science fiction, the language and tropes they had to work with were primarily those developed by men. To write about superwoman from a feminine point of view, it was necessary simultaneously to incorporate and to erase existing images such as that of Weinbaum's Adaptive Ultimate. The process necessitated re-imagining both narrative conventions and the voice that uttered them. In order to speak of superwoman from a woman's point of view, it was necessary to create a feminine register with which to speak of her. The process has taken decades and has involved the work of scores of writers, both male and female (for the gender of the written register is not wholly dependent on the sex of the writer).

Kyra herself is already a rewriting, with some feminist implications, of the well-known super-temptress created in 1886 by H. Rider Haggard: Ayesha or She Who Must Be Obeyed. In Haggard's *She* (strictly speaking a lost-race fantasy rather than a work of SF), the wicked demigoddess who gives the work its title embodies a whole gamut of male responses to female power, from awe to lust to revulsion. It is no wonder that she, or rather She, has been subjected to psychological examination by everyone from Freud and Jung to Sandra Gilbert and Susan Gubar. She is the perfect projection of what Jung called the anima: in contrast with the actual women that men (as James Tiptree, Jr., pointed out in a classic story) don't see, the anima is the phantom woman men *do* see—and desire and fear.

The enduring popularity of Haggard's novel and of the many imitations it spawned indicates that he did not so much invent as discover She. She already existed in the male psyche, whether planted there by biology, as Jung believed, or by language and culture. (Speaking of language, Haggard's novel is undoubtedly responsible not only for dozens of later jungle queens but also for a grammatical irregularity rampant among fantasy writers—the She Who syndrome, in which capitalized pronouns imperiously remain in the nominative case regardless of their role in a sentence. We never hear about anyone worshiping Her Who Formed the Universe, though that would be the grammatical norm.)

A slightly different version of the male-generated superwoman downplays the terrifying mystery of the anima and emphasizes her physical strength and attractiveness. In the 1980s, she appeared regularly on book covers as a leather-clad warrior-babe in sunglasses. This character's fighting skills are rarely accompanied by any particular force of character. Like the woman guards who regularly attacked James Bond in the movies, she donates her formidable prowess to some powerful masculine chief. Even Molly Millions, the artificially enhanced battler of William Gibson's "Johnny Mnemonic," plays a surprisingly small part in determining the course of the stories. She serves more as ornament and as backup for the hero than as a motivating force in her own right.

Like Her Who Sprang from the imagination of Haggard, and like the Amazons of legend and of fantasy novels derived from Robert E. Howard and Edgar Rice Burroughs, these cyber-amazons tell more about male desire and dread than about female identity. The Amazon motif may, however, play a double role, functioning one way for male fans and quite differently for female writers and readers. In the 1930s and '40s, C. L. Moore and Leigh Brackett created amazon characters who actually had inner lives and personal histories, while still providing desirable images for adolescent readers—desirable not just for male teenagers, either, as evidenced by the lesbian subtext of a 1990s incarnation of the Amazon image, television's *Xena*. Like the muscle man of sports magazines, the Amazon provides a safe (i.e., not overtly sexual) context for admiring sleek and powerful bodies of one's own sex, even for essentially heterosexual adolescents.

Moore and Brackett opened the way for a whole feminist subgenre in the '70s and '80s, represented most notably by the Free Amazons of Marion Zimmer Bradley's novels, who form a separate and independent society within the largely male-dominated world of Darkover. Bradley's Free Amazons, though, are not particularly aggressive or powerful (and they don't wear leather jumpsuits). Most of them do not even have the psychic gifts that characterize

Darkover's aristocracy. They are more closely linked with the feminist utopian tradition than with the idea of a superwoman.

There is one famous Amazon, though, who is clearly a superwoman, and who represented something more to female readers than her creator may have intended. Wonder Woman was invented in 1941 by a psychologist, William Moulton Marston, who conceived of the character as a way of harnessing what he believed to be the fundamental psychological drives of dominance and submission in the service of feminine liberation (Bunn 107). Marston's conception of Wonder Woman is an impossibly mixed signal, combining an all-female utopia called Paradise Island, a pantheon of goddesses, frequent scenes of bondage and threatened torture, and a costume for the heroine that simultaneously fetishizes her and frees her limbs for fighting and flight.

It is hardly surprising that readers took a contradictory set of messages from Marston's creation. Where Richard Reynolds sees in Wonder Woman "a frank appeal to male fantasies of sexual domination" (34), Lillian S. Robinson attests to her importance as "the apotheosis of the female hero" (101) in the era of anti-feminist retrenchment that followed World War II. Perhaps Wonder Woman's appeal lies in that ambiguity. Certainly Marston knew he was creating something that might function differently for different readers. For boys, who might otherwise reject a female hero as "girl stuff" (Marston 42), he threw in plenty of violence and a half-clad star. For girls, who might not be inclined to pick up a superhero comic book, he provided his leading character with a unique combination of freedom and security: Wonder Woman can roam around the world in her invisible airplane and subdue the roughest of male roughnecks with her golden lasso, but she knows that she can always go home to Paradise Island, ruled by benevolent Mom.

Cobbling together ancient legends, futuristic technology, and a coherent if peculiar psychological theory, Marston managed to create something from a culturally-defined nothing, to amend the big blind spot within the superman megatext. He succeeded because he saw his task as one of identifying and supplementing not one but two kinds of absence. On one hand, he pointed out the usual female character's lack of "masculine" characteristics: "And that's the point; not even girls want to be girls so long as our feminine archetype lacks force, strength, power" (Marston 42). But, on the other hand, he saw the male hero as equally wanting in "feminine" features: "It seemed to me, from a psychological angle, that the comics' worst offense was their blood-curdling masculinity. A male hero, at best, lacks the qualities of maternal love and tenderness which are as essential to a normal child as the breath of life" (42).

How can a positive female image be created out of two sorts of negative? Part of the answer lies in the concreteness of the comic book illustration: Wonder Woman must exist because we can see her. She is there on the page, unarguably and attractively feminine in appearance, undeniably powerful in her actions. Another part is Marston's use of traditional motifs, such as the island of women, names like Hippolyte and Diana, and even the golden lasso, which suggests the magical girdle Hercules stole from the Amazon queen (as well as functioning like the lie detector Marston helped to invent).

But perhaps most importantly, Wonder Woman is not postulated as a lone challenger to the human norm, the way most early supermen were imagined. The new race of higher beings already exists in secret; she is only its emissary to humanity. Wonder Woman's strength and agility, her superior technology, her defiance of conventional female roles—all these stem from her membership in a superior society of women, any member of which would become a Wonder in the eyes of the outside world. Membership in this community not only gives Wonder Woman her powers, but it also obliges her to serve the needs of the other Paradise Islanders, especially the need to keep the island safe and secret. In America, one of her first acts is to assemble a band of college coeds (led by the formidable Etta Candy) into a substitute Amazon cohort (Marston, *Sensation* 40). This aspect of the superwoman, her placement within a structure of social relationships and obligations, becomes a recurring and central theme in many later treatments of the type.

Marston seems to have conceived of his hero in terms of conventional gender attributes. Her popularity, he said, derived from "the wonder which is really woman's when she adds masculine strength to feminine tenderness and allure" (Marston, "Why" 43). But at least some readers of the comic came away with a sense that hers was not masculine but feminine strength. In a self-sufficient community of Amazons, what qualities are masculine or feminine? Likewise, whatever "feminine love allure" Wonder Woman might possess (44), she already had it before leaving the island, and it had less to do with her short skirts and flowing black hair than with athletic prowess and confidence. Her allure *is* her strength, says Marston:

> Well, asserted my masculine authorities, if a woman hero were stronger than a man, she would be even less appealing. Boys wouldn't stand for *that*; they'd resent the strong gal's superiority. No, I maintained, men actually submit to women now, they do it on the sly with a sheepish grin because they're ashamed of being ruled by weaklings. Give them an alluring woman stronger than themselves to submit to and they'll be *proud* to become her willing slaves! ("Why" 43)

From a male perspective, then, Marston sees Wonder Woman as not so different from Rider Haggard's She or Weinbaum's Kyra Zelas. The combination of power and desirability is still alarming, still a threat to masculine control. But Marston considers the threat to be part of the attraction, a little extra sexual voltage to mix with the "love appeal of a true woman" (44) and thereby draw male readers into his vision of a feminist utopia.

Female readers got the point without the sexual bribe. For Lillian S. Robinson, the wonder of Wonder Woman is her twofold power. As the amazonian warrior who is also heir to a peaceful and independent matriarchy, she possesses two wonder-generating powers: first, the strength that represents "exceptional power *for a woman*" (Robinson 101) and, second, the power unique *to* women, namely the ability to reproduce and maintain the human species. And if she can combine these two apparently incompatible kinds of wonder, what else can a woman be? For the generation that grew up on Wonder Woman, that question would become, not Freud's insoluble riddle, but a challenge to the imagination.

Another of the keys to Marston's success in creating Wonder Woman is that she is forever poised on the brink of full maturity. Our first glimpse of her, in the initial Wonder Woman comic, is as a sort of Head Girl among the younger amazons. Even in the later episodes, she remains the dutiful (though occasionally resentful) daughter to the more alarming Queen Hippolyte.

In contrast with the mature superwoman, whom even Marston associated with sexual threat, the superior girl-child is often portrayed with tenderness and sympathy by male writers. If powerful potential lovers tend to be seen by men as dangerous, daughters or daughter-substitutes are viewed as manageable extensions of themselves into the female world. In science fiction, young girls, even super ones, frequently combine the charm of an Alice in Wonderland with the spunk of Dorothy Gale. Unlike sons, who are potential rivals, daughters can surpass their Daddies without doing too much damage to male egos.

Mark Clifton's 1952 story "Star, Bright," tells of a child who, at age three, constructs a mathematical paradox, a Moebius strip, and seems to be aware of its peculiar properties. As her father watches, little Star carefully cuts a band of paper, gives it the half twist that makes it defy topological expectations, and picks up a crayon to trace the line that proves its one-sidedness. Clifton uses the scene not only to demonstrate Star's remarkable intelligence but also to convey the delicate negotiations between daughter and father. He wants her to surpass him but at the same time wishes to keep the upper hand. She relies on him for guidance even while she tries to keep him from knowing how far beyond him she has already gone.

> "That's called the Moebius strip, Star," I interrupted her thoughts.
>
> She came out of her reverie with a start. I didn't like the quick way her eyes sought mine—almost furtively, as though she had been caught doing something bad.
>
> "Somebody already make it?" she disappointedly asked. (72)

As Star grows, and it becomes clear that her intelligence is "beyond all measurement" (74), her father is put in an unaccustomed position. As he reminds himself,

> Nobody knows better than you the futility of trying to compete out of your class. How many students, workers, and employers have tried to compete with you? You've watched them and pitied them, comparing them to a donkey trying to run the Kentucky Derby.
>
> How does it feel to be in the place of the donkey for a change? (74)

To Star, her father is neither Bright, like her and, later, her friend Robert; nor Stupid, like the other children and her schoolteacher. He is an in-betweener, a Tween. Four-year-old Star confesses that "I made those names up when I was little" (76). Tweens may be genius-level by human standards, but they can hardly compete with superhumans.

Star and Robert, it turns out, can speak to each other telepathically, read a book without opening it, and, eventually, transport themselves to any time or place they can imagine. The narrator can learn to do each of those things, but slowly, painfully, with much guidance from the children. By the end of the story, however, the superbright children have figured out how to leave the ordinary historical continuum—described in the story as another Moebius strip—entirely. Star's father may not be able to follow. He is, after all, not quite superman himself.

The story ends inconclusively. The narrator disappears, leaving a manu-script for his friend Jim (another Tween). Was he able to make the leap to join his daughter and her friend? What sort of world was Star able to imagine her-self into? What sort of maturity could follow such a childhood? Clifton's wist-ful story leaves the reader still wondering: the answers are "anybody's guess" (96). Super girl can only grow up by disappearing from view. Male writers seem to be able to follow daughter characters just over the line into adoles-cence, as in James Schmitz's stories of Telzey Amberdon from the 1960s. Beyond the point at which Daddy's little girl becomes her own woman, she vanishes into mystery.

It is, after all, no easy feat for a writer of either sex to create a fictional super woman when Western culture offers no satisfactory definition of *woman.* Just about the same time the pulp magazines were institutional-izing the SF code in the form of tropes like the superman story, Simone de Beauvoir and her successors began to question the ability of any code created in a patriarchy to convey women's identities, viewpoints, and experiences. From Beauvoir's *The Second Sex* (1949) to Luce Irigaray's "This Sex Which Is Not One" (1977), feminist philosophers looked for woman-centered texts, terms, and ideas but found only silence, disorder, or distorted reflections of the masculine.

Beauvoir explains that it is impossible to say what a woman is outside of the cultural construction of the feminine, for culture has no outside: "it must be repeated once more that in human society nothing is natural and that woman, like much else, is a product elaborated by civilization" (681). Part of women's cultural role has been to play the Other that allows men to see themselves as the norm. If one is not the speaker, the definer, then one is left with no position except that of the Other. If there is no feminine *I,* there can only be *She.* But the Other is, like Haggard's She, a dangerous, alien, funda-mentally unknowable being. How is a woman to explain herself in terms of not-Self? It is no wonder that writers, both male and female, have expounded on the mystery of the feminine:

> To say that woman is mystery is to say, not that she is silent, but that her language is not understood; she is there, but hidden behind veils; she exists beyond these uncertain appearances. What is she? Angel, demon, one inspired, an actress? It may be supposed either that there are answers to these questions which are impossible to discover, or, rather, that no answer is adequate because a fundamental ambiguity marks the feminine being; and perhaps in her heart she is even for herself quite indefinable: a sphinx. (Beauvoir 264)

So it is only natural that Weinbaum's superwoman, Kyra Zelas, is portrayed in terms of illusion, ambiguity, unreadable surface. These are historically the characteristics—or rather the noncharacteristics—of womanhood itself. To exaggerate them is only to create a deeper mystery.

Yet one SF writer of Beauvoir's generation found in the trope of the superbeing a way to posit a female self. Asking, like Weinbaum, how far a woman could go, Catherine Lucille Moore offered several striking images of powerful women. In three stories in particular, Moore explores the idea of the superwoman, each time taking the feminine character farther from the role of seductive, unreadable Other. Moore's superwoman stories transform images from the pulp SF tradition into feminist metaphors anticipating those of Beauvoir, Cixous, and Irigaray.

Moore's first version of the superwoman was written in a register that was readable at the time as masculine, especially when reinforced by a male viewpoint character and an unmarked byline: Moore always published under masculine pen names or as "C.L." rather than Catherine. In her first published story, "Shambleau" (1933), Moore used many of the same images Stanley Weinbaum had used to describe his Adaptive Ultimate. Drawing on popular adventure formulas, she describes a meeting between her recurring space hero, Northwest Smith, and a glamorous but deadly siren. The Shambleau of the title is a scarlet-haired alien who combines irresistible allure with a sort of psychic vampirism that nearly finishes off Northwest Smith. But the Shambleau is not, any more than Kyra Zelas, unambiguously evil.

Reporting the thoughts of Northwest Smith, Moore vividly expresses male horror at female sexuality, blatantly symbolized in her Medusa-like hair:

> the unspeakable tangle of it—twisting, writhing, obscenely scarlet—hung to her waist and beyond, and still lengthened, an endless mass of crawling horror that until now, somehow, impossibly, had been hidden under the tight-bound turban. It was like a nest of blind, restless red worms . . . it was—it was like naked entrails endowed with an unnatural aliveness, terrible beyond words. (18–19)

Yet if one filters out the male paranoia, the seductive, devouring Shambleau could also be a portrait of female power and independence: a girl (she looks very young) on her own using whatever means she possesses to get by in a hostile universe. We get just a glimpse into the Shambleau's thoughts when Smith asks what language she speaks:

> She lifted her head and met his eyes squarely, and there was in hers a subtle amusement—he could have sworn it.
>
> "Some day I—speak to you in—my own language," she promised, and the pink tongue flicked out over her lips swiftly, hungrily. (7)

The Shambleau's glint of amusement at the thought of her own transgressive language hints at a more explosive sort of mirth, the sort that Hélène Cixous called the laugh of the Medusa. The Medusa is, like the Shambleau, a representation of female autonomy. Despite men's fears, says Cixous, "she's not deadly. She's beautiful and she's laughing" (255). If that statement is only ambiguously applicable to the Shambleau, it is indisputably true of Moore's next superwoman, who utters the indomitable, disruptive laugh of Cixous's new woman.

In Moore's 1944 story "No Woman Born," male fear is not gone, but it is no longer allowed so fully to determine the reader's response. The nonborn woman of this tale is Dierdre, once the most famous actress in the world. A theater fire has left her barely alive; an experimental operation has given her an artificial body of metallic segments. She is in some ways the opposite of the Shambleau: inorganic, instead of moistly fleshy; hairless; expressionless; more autonomous than predatory. But, like the Shambleau and Kyra Zelas, the new Dierdre is on her own in a world of aliens, and her success seems to depend on her ability to impersonate men's desires.

We hear about Dierdre before we see her. The male viewpoint character is already composing her story as one of irretrievable loss, of past perfections commemorated in the past perfect verbs of his soliloquy:

> She had been the loveliest creature whose image ever moved along the airways. John Harris, who was once her manager, remembered doggedly how beautiful she had been as he rose in the silent elevator toward where Dierdre sat waiting for him.
>
> Since the theater fire that had destroyed her a year ago, he had never been quite able to let himself remember her beauty clearly, except when some old poster, half in tatters, flaunted her face at him, or a maudlin memorial program flashed her image unexpectedly across the television screen. (236)

But Dierdre refuses to stay a pleasantly melancholy memory. She returns, in a new and considerably more powerful guise.

The new Dierdre is a cyborg. Her rescued brain is now housed in a gleaming body that simultaneously is and is not human. Eavesdropping on John Harris's impressions, first we hear her voice that "for one dreadful moment" is "the voice of an automaton that sounded in the room, metallic, without inflection" and then immediately corrects itself to "the old, familiar, sweet huskiness he had not hoped to hear again" (241). Next we see her, only we don't. Instead, we get an image, conjured up from Harris's memories, of the old Dierdre: "tall, golden, swaying a little with her wonder dancer's poise, the lovely, imperfect features lighted by the glow that made them beautiful" (241).

By the time the "real" Dierdre appears on the page, we have already met her several times in Harris's imagination: as nostalgic memory, as ambulatory answering machine, as seductive whisperer, as dancer transcending her own imperfection, as "lurching robot" (241). We are primed, at this point, not to accept Dierdre as any one thing, any simple truth. She is human; she is a machine; she is still herself; she is her scientist-creator; she is whatever the perceiver assembles; she is what she herself wills. What the narrative accepts as the final truth is Dierdre's own claim, "It's me, John darling. It really is, you know" (242). Harris thinks he knows what that means. Dierdre knows he doesn't.

Dierdre's new body is described as sculpture, an elegant abstraction from the human form. Her face is an eyeless mask, through which Dierdre must try to convey a full range of emotional expressions. But, says the story, so is any human face a mask:

Figure 3. Woman Wondering. The cyborg Dierdre, from C. L. Moore's "No Woman Born" (1944), as depicted by Greg and Tim Hildebrandt for the cover of *The Best of C. L. Moore.*

eyes, even human eyes, are as a matter of fact enigmatic enough. They have no expression except what the lids impart; they take all animation from the features. . . . it is the position in the face, not the feature itself, which we are accustomed to accept as the seat of the soul. Dierdre's mask was in that proper place; it was easy to accept it as a mask over eyes. (243–44)

Dierdre's comments on her condition indicate that she is several steps ahead of Harris in exploring the paradox of herself. "Luckily," she says, "I never was beautiful" (247). Her beauty, her vitality, her femininity, were all carefully prepared performances. The dangerous secret that Joan Riviere hinted at in her 1929 paper was that *all* womanliness (and, by extension, all manliness?) is a masquerade:

The reader may now ask how I define womanliness or where I draw the line between genuine womanliness and the 'masquerade'. My suggestion is not, however, that there is any such difference; whether radical or superficial, they are the same thing. (38)

Dierdre has always used her body to create an illusion, whether on stage or off: "I've always had . . . well, power over my audiences. Any good performer knows when he's got it" (253). All that is new about her manufactured body is that the limits are gone.

While the men around her are thinking of what she has lost, she speculates about possibilities. She demonstrates her new strength and speed, but the observers cannot quite comprehend, or even say, what they have seen: "Not like anything that those who use our language had ever seen before, or created words to express. The mind saw, but without perceiving" (282). She is outside the symbol system now, and that makes her either a superwoman or nothing at all. In mathematical terms, she has become woman times X; if the value assigned to woman is zero, she remains a zero, but if not, she may well approach infinity.

Malzer, the engineer who built her new body, can see only nullity, absence. "She's lost everything that made her essentially what the public wanted," he says, and he defines that "everything" in explicitly sexual terms (258). "Remember Abelard?" he asks. "She isn't female any more" (258). (Making comparison to the castrated Abelard is an interesting lapse: his female partner Heloise was not unsexed. Who's afraid of what here?)

Malzer understands Dierdre's value in terms of her ability to please, to entertain, to charm—all grounded not in her intentions or knowledge but in biology. "One of the strongest stimuli to a woman of her type was the knowledge of sex competition. You know how she sparkled when a man came into the room? All that's gone, and it was an essential" (259).

But Dierdre knows exactly how and why that sparkle was manufactured; she can always make more. She proves it by making an absurd gesture seem so normal that neither man notices its absurdity: she picks up a cigarette and mimes smoking it. To Harris, "there was something about her just now more convincingly human than anything he had noticed before" (280). Dierdre's response to their acquiescence is laughter:

> She was looking at Maltzer. He, too, watched, spell-bound in spite of himself, not dissenting. She glanced from one to the other. Then she put back her head and laughter came welling and choking from her in a great, full-throated tide. She shook in the strength of it. Harris could almost see her round throat pulsing with the sweet low-pitched waves of laughter that were shaking her. Honest mirth, with a little derision in it.
>
> Then she lifted one arm and tossed her cigarette into the empty fireplace. (280)

Her laughter signifies the opposite of absence. It is the abundant, explosive laughter of Hélène Cixous's Medusa, the woman released from patriarchal bounds. Like Shambleau, Moore's earlier sketch of Medusa, Dierdre is amused by the men for whom she performs. Her amusement is no longer Shambleau's surreptitious glance, but a "full-throated" public statement. Unlike Shambleau, she is free to choose whether or not to maintain the disguise of vulnerable, desirable femininity.

Dierdre deliberately lets that pose slip for a moment when Maltzer tries to blackmail her emotionally by attempting suicide. She lets him know that she is no longer what he believes her to be, neither the machine he manufactured nor the woman she had been:

> "Do you still think of me as delicate?" she demanded. "Do you know I carried you here at arm's length halfway across the room? Do you realize you weigh *nothing* to me? I could—" she glanced around the room and gestured with sudden, rather appalling violence—"tear this building down," she said quietly. "I could tear my way through these walls, I think. I've found no limit yet to the strength I can put forth if I try." (284)

Dierdre is not only Cixous's laughing Medusa; she is also the cyborg Donna Haraway has proposed as an ironic inversion of "the central myths of origin of Western culture" (175). Origin stories, says Haraway, depend on a "myth of original unity, fullness, bliss and terror, represented by the phallic mother from whom all humans must separate, the task of individual development and of history" (151). The original Medusa myth, like "Shambleau," ends in the defeat of the powerful, serpent-tressed female by the male hero, who attains his mature identity by suppressing her. But according to Haraway, the story of a cyborg assumes no original wholeness, no fortunate fall, no natural order of things that always, somehow, ends up elevating the signs of masculinity at the expense of the feminine. "Every story that begins with original innocence and privileges the return to wholeness," she says, ends up assigning to women:

less selfhood, weaker individuation, more fusion to the oral, to Mother, less at stake in masculine autonomy. But there is another route to having less at stake in masculine autonomy, a route that does not pass through Woman, Primitive, Zero, the Mirror Stage and its imaginary. It passes through women and other present-tense, illegitimate cyborgs, not of Woman born, who refuse the ideological resources of victimization so as to have a real life. (177)

Haraway's cyborg is so close to C. L. Moore's vision that I am always surprised, upon rereading the essay, that Haraway doesn't cite "No Woman Born," though Jane Donawerth has made the link (61–63). A cyborg like Dierdre transcends the dualisms of Western culture by denying "natural" boundaries like those which separate human from machine, organic from inanimate, feminine from masculine. By the end of Moore's story, she, like Haraway, has redefined qualities such as strength, autonomy, and curiosity as feminine by de-naturalizing the feminine.

The cyborg Dierdre cannot be stopped, as Kyra Zelas was, by her male creators, nor will she allow herself to be delimited by either their desire or their pity. She is not sure, however, where the route she has taken will ultimately lead. What does she herself desire? Having stepped out of the symbolic order, what sorts of utterance can she construct for herself? The story leaves the question unresolved, and ends with her asking it of herself, for there is no one else of her kind to ask:

> "I wonder," she repeated, the distant taint of metal already in her voice. (288)

C. L. Moore wondered still further in a version of the superwoman story called "The Children's Hour." This story, also from 1944, was published under the pseudonym Lawrence O'Donnell, which means that it was, like all her later work, written in collaboration with her husband Henry Kuttner. The style and theme of the story, however, indicate more of Moore than of Kuttner, and the O'Donnell by-line was often used to mark work that was chiefly hers (Tuck 3:543).

As in "No Woman Born," we see the superwoman in "The Children's Hour" through the eyes of a (merely human) male admirer. Indeed, this story seems for much of its length to be *his* story: a romantic tale of love found and lost, of a captive maiden and a heroic attempt to rescue her. Only gradually do we realize that Lessing, the lover, represents only a brief episode in the development of Clarissa, and that his understanding of her and of their time together is both fragmentary and distorted. The real Clarissa comes across only in glimpses in mirrors and through cracks in the narrative.

At the beginning, she has vanished even from Lessing's memory. When conscious, he is aware of no gaps in his recall; however, under hypnosis, he discovers that he has lost three months of his life. Clues begin to emerge: an unrecognized face, a shadow, lines from a poem, a walk in a park. These all resolve into an image of Clarissa. Clarissa seems to be an ordinary young girl, pretty, a bit sheltered, perhaps all the more desirable for being kept inaccessible by her shadowy guardian aunt. Lessing's recovered memories are charming but unremarkable except in the way the remembered images are invested with a sense of heightened color and clarity, a glamour that Clarissa seemed to cast on the world around her.

Then Lessing stumbles across discrepancies in the sequence of events. First, the aunt who seems to him to be the villain in the piece turns out never to have been on stage:

> She had stood before the mirrors, hadn't she, looking down? Had she? What were her outlines against the light? She had no outlines. She had never existed. (260)

Next, Lessing begins to remember moments of strangeness, like the time Clarissa disappeared from a potentially traumatic scene:

> He knew he had seen the circle of shaken air ring her luminously about, like a circle in water from a dropped stone. It was very like the spreading rings in water, except that these rings did not expand but contracted. And as they contracted, Clarissa moved farther away. She was drawn down a rapidly diminishing tunnel of shining circles, with the park distorted in focus beyond them. (261)

Other moments are mysteriously rewritten in mid-scene, leading Lessing to surmise that there was a purpose, a plan, a Writer intervening in Clarissa's life—and that Writer must be a rival, a masculine god preparing Clarissa for eventual marriage. A glimpse of Clarissa in a haze or shower of gold confirms his suspicions: she is another Danaë being courted by some alien, super-human Zeus. The aunt is His agent, Clarissa's grim duenna, making sure no one like Lessing can get too close.

Acting on this suspicion, Lessing convinces Clarissa to run away with him, but the flight ends in defeat. Scenes shift, streets twist, the shower of light returns, and finally,

> The dazzle of her eyes and her smile was a little blinding, and that haze still diffused all his efforts to focus upon her face. But he could see enough. They were exactly where they had started, at the curb before her apartment house.
> "Good night," said Clarissa again, and the door closed behind her. (276)

Lessing has lost. Someone—he thinks it is the Aunt—makes him forget, takes Clarissa away for good, sends him back to his normal life. The God has won.

But there is no divine rival. At this point in the story, Lessing's reconstruction of events falls apart, and another interpretation emerges. This version is based not on a classical (that is, patriarchal) myth but on a fairy tale

Clarissa remembers being told by her Aunt (an old Un-wives' Tale), about a little girl born in a kingdom of blind people. The little girl has never opened her eyes, not knowing that she herself is not blind. One day the girl hears a voice telling her that she does not belong among the sightless ones:

> "you are a king's daughter, born among these humble people as our king's children sometimes are. . . . The day will come when you open your eyes and see." (279)

Putting this tale together with the things Lessing has told her, Clarissa offers another explanation of her situation. She is the king's daughter, not of Lessing's kind at all. She is a cuckoo hatched in a human nest, an emerging superbeing. The narrator depicts Clarissa's dawning self-awareness in one of the story's many references to Lewis Carroll's *Through the Looking-Glass:*

> Alice, walking with the Fawn in the enchanted woods where nothing has a name, walking in friendship with her arm about the Fawn's neck. And the Fawn's words when they came to the edge of the woods and memory returned to them both. How it started away from her, shaking off the arm, wildness returning to the eyes that had looked as serenely into Alice's as Clarissa's had looked into his. *"Why—I'm a Fawn,"* it said in astonishment. *"And you're a Human Child!"* (279)

But Clarissa is both the Fawn and Alice, watching in wild surmise as the vistas of a Wonderland open out before her, and Lessing is hardly there at all.

In this version of the events, the Aunt is not Clarissa's jailor but her Red Queen-ish mentor. Lessing is not the rescuing hero but a mere Lessoning: the romantic love he offers is something she needs to experience once and then transcend. And Clarissa is the center of it all, not the captive princess but the hero of her own wonder tale.

The outcome of that tale remains undefined by the end of the story, as is Clarissa's superhuman nature. We know only that she, like the tale, is complex and open-ended, a many-dimensional being with analogues on innumerable other worlds. The Clarissa Lessing has met is merely:

> one out of a possible infinity of facets. Upon each face of that unimaginable geometric shape, a form of Clarissa moved and had independent being, and gradually developed. Learned and was taught. Reached out toward the center of the geometric shape that was—or one day would be— the complete Clarissa. One day, when the last mirrorfacet sent inward to the center its matured reflection of the whole, when the many Clarissas, so to speak, clasped hands with themselves and fused into perfection. (286–87)

This version of superwoman is a vision of woman herself as something not singular, not restricted to a unitary meaning or state of being. It is, again, reminiscent of the project undertaken by feminist philosophers, to overturn the dualisms that make women no more than a point of reference for men, an Other to be defined against.

The philosophical statement closest in spirit to Moore's vision of Clarissa is Luce Irigaray's "This Sex Which Is Not One" (1977)—not that Moore and Kuttner's original readers would have seen the story as anything resembling Irigaray's psychoanalytical-philosophical treatise. If one were to reprint "The Children's Hour" in an anthology of Golden Age superman stories, it would look much like its neighbors. If the story had been included in Lester del Rey's collection of *The Best of C. L. Moore,* it would blend right in with other Moore-ish tales of psychic powers and thwarted love, like her 1936 reincarnation story "Tryst in Time."

But if "The Children's Hour" were included in a volume of feminist fables like those of Cixous, Irigaray, and Haraway, another dimension of Moore and Kuttner's narrative would emerge. Images like Clarissa's mirrored chamber, plot elements such as her unexpected appearances in alien scenes where she plays parts quite unlike her usual ingenue role—these fall into place as an exploration of feminine power and identity paralleling those of the French philosophers, especially Irigaray. Choosing between these two readings of the story depends largely on whose voice one hears in it. Is it the masculine register C. L. Moore learned from reading the pulps, or is it the emerging voice of Catherine Lucille Moore?

Irigaray characterizes women as belonging to the "sex which is not one," because the Freudian paradigm for gender allows for only one pattern of sexual development: the masculine. But she reformulates the meaning of "not one" from "less than" to "greater than." *Woman* is not one thing but many, just as women's sexuality is not identifiable in terms of a single phallic integer— or the lack of that phallus—but instead is distributed among several reproductive organs and erogenous zones. Among the latter, Irigaray calls attention to the lips of the vulva, "which embrace continually. Thus, within herself she is already two—but not divisible into ones—who stimulate each other" ("This" 100).

Here Irigaray is using the inevitable Freudian synecdoche: letting the (private) part stand for the whole person. Her essay dwells on exactly the aspect of feminine identity Moore could not talk about in a Campbell-era SF story: sexuality. Science fiction discourse in the 1940s could accept Lewis Carroll's looking-glass but not Irigaray's speculum. Yet Moore's image of Clarissa infinitely reflected in her "dark room full of mirrors" (278) is an image of sexuality as well as Carrollian transformation. "The Children's Hour" is from first to last a story of desire. As the story progresses, this desire gradually alters, not its object, but its subject. The center of gravity shifts from Lessing as lover to Clarissa as self-desiring self-discoverer. Her passage to adulthood is marked by growing awareness of her own multiplicity and her own desirability.

Reading Moore's wonder woman through the lens of feminist philosophy, we see that indeed, "her sexuality, always at least double, is in fact *plural,*" for

" 'She' is indefinitely other in herself" ("This" 102–03). Clarissa's "(re)discovery of herself can only signify the possibility of not sacrificing any of her pleasures to another, of not identifying with anyone in particular, of never being simply one" (104). It may be said that Clarissa "experiences pleasure almost everywhere" (103), if we bear in mind that the "everywhere" is not just every part of the body, as Irigaray intends, but every image of herself scattered across the universe. Indeed, Clarissa herself "is a sort of universe in expansion for which no limits could be fixed and which, for all that, would not be incoherency" (104).

Irigary describes feminine self-discovery in terms that uncannily echo images used by Moore:

> That "elsewhere" of feminine pleasure can be found only at the price of *crossing back through the mirror that subtends all speculation.* . . . A playful crossing, and an unsettling one, which would allow woman to rediscover the place of her "self-affection." Of her "god," we might say. ("Power" 77)

Clarissa's immersion in the shower of light is an erotic joining with the divine, not with the seductive Zeus but with her Other selves, her own reflections. The singular, solitary Lessing can only turn away from this ecstatic vision to the simple voyeuristic pleasures of "a good floorshow" (287). At the end of the story, his memory is once again blocked, not by the aunt (who may be, indeed, only another of Clarissa's aspects) but by his own defenses. Men are blind, says the story, because they cannot bear to see such wonder.

Moore's three editions of the wonder woman, with help from Marston's cartoon goddess, opened up the field of the superman story to women. Before 1944 there were no more than a handful of stories depicting female superbeings, most of them by men and most viewing the prospect with great trepidation. After the mid-40s, women writers tackled the theme with increasing assurance. Echoing Moore and Marston, they depict the wonder woman as self-pleasuring Medusa, as emissary from an Amazonian utopia, as cyborg, or as networked multiple being.

However, Moore's successors rarely approach her tone of rapturous discovery. For writers in the later '40s and '50s, it was not so easy to imagine women's freedom as expanding. "The Children's Hour" and "No Woman Born" both emerged from the heady days of the end of World War II, when many American women were experiencing unprecedented freedom both on the job and in their personal lives. Dierdre the cyborg, one might say, is Rosie the Riveted.

In direct contrast, Judith Merril's "That Only a Mother," from 1948, so precisely expresses the post-war reimposition of restrictions that few commentators seem to notice that it, too, is a version of the superwoman story. Margaret, the viewpoint character of the story, has a job, at least at first, but what one remembers from the story is Margaret at home, in the hermetic circle of mother and child. Margaret's infant daughter is a superbeing. She speaks at five months, sings at seven, is described as having a "four-year-old mind" in a "ten-month-old body" (213). Margaret and baby Henrietta together create a miniature utopia in the nursery: their conversation as Margaret bathes her daughter is a scene of innocently erotic bliss: rosy-pink, steamy, and sweet-smelling.

Into this domestic Eden comes Margaret's husband Hank, home on leave. He seems completely indifferent to his daughter's extraordinary capabilities; he is aware only that she is physically deformed. The same radioactivity that triggered Henrietta's superhuman intellectual development has left her without arms or legs, a fact Margaret seems to have completely blocked from consciousness. Margaret's "beautiful daughter" is, to Hank, something subhuman, a worm or "sinuous, limbless" snake (216). She is Medusa shrunk to one of her own serpents, her dangerous power reduced to infantile impotence.

Like other fathers that Margaret is vaguely aware of hearing about on the news, Hank will respond by committing infanticide. Which has disturbed him more: his daughter's physical strangeness or the mental superiority that has resulted in such close communion with Margaret? "Only a mother" could fail to see the wrongness in the child, but only in the name of a Father could someone deny her humanity. "Oh, God, dear God" says Hank as he begins to strangle his daughter (216). And Margaret is as helpless to intervene as Henrietta is to save herself, for she is "only a mother."

In superwoman stories from the 1950s and early '60s, a recurring pattern among women writers is to posit communities of mutants in which the males are assigned most of the privileges of superhumanity while the females get the burdens. Such is the case in Wilmar Shiras's *Children of the Atom* (1953), Phyllis Gotlieb's *Sunburst* (1964), and most explicitly, Zenna Henderson's "Gilead" (1954).

Henderson's is one of a series of stories about the People, a race of psychically gifted exiles from a destroyed world hiding on earth. "Gilead" concerns two children who are half alien and half human and in whom the talents of the People emerge imperfectly and unpredictably. Peter, the elder sibling, gets racial memory and wingless flight. Bethie, his younger sister, gets the ability to weave light into pretty patterns along with a cripplingly powerful sensitivity to other people's pain. "Oh Bethie," sympathizes her mother; "all the burdens and none of the blessings!" (47). Bethie is not only given a raw deal with regard to the distribution of abilities, but she is also placed in the conventionally feminine position of empathizer and comforter. Eventually, when she learns to control her talent, she does becomes a healer and a valuable addition to the community of People, but her ability is still defined in terms of service to others, rather than any special prerogatives.

In other Henderson stories, female characters are similarly burdened with an extra dose of responsibility and a more limited range of movement than the men. Yet by the time the later People stories were written, things had begun to even up. In the "Interlude" stories which Henderson used in 1961 to gather a number of stories into a linked collection called *Pilgrimage,* we see women of the People in several positions of authority: Karen, the Sorter; Valency, the Old One; and Bethie, now a Healer. These women fly, communicate telepathically, make decisions for the group, and intervene to save the life of a suicidal human named Lea. They are still represented in conventionally feminine roles and with a suggestion of the extra sense of obligation that keeps working women doing more housework than their male partners. Nonetheless, the division between feminine "burdens" and masculine "blessings" is beginning to erode.

In the later People stories, the Canyon where most of them live begins to resemble a feminized utopia: that is, a community operating largely on the feminine-coded virtues of empathy, mutual obligation, family tradition, and compromise. Not all the leaders are women, but the most prominent men are those who have been initiated into such social patterns under the tutelage of a woman, usually one of Henderson's many schoolteacher characters (Henderson was herself a schoolteacher). The world these women and men have created is one of hard work and strange delights. Suicidal Lea once convinced herself that there was "for me no wonder more . . . Except to wonder where my wonder went, And why my wonder all is spent" ("Interlude: Lea 1" 5), yet eventually she acknowledges that even lacking the superhuman powers of Karen, Valency, and the others, she can partake in the wonder of their world.

But the world of the Canyon is as insulated in its way as the nursery of "That Only a Mother." Both are utopian, but neither has the power to impose its vision on the masculine-dominated world outside. The women in science fiction stories of the postwar period, like many women outside of fiction, were still struggling to define themselves against a whole slew of institutional norms. Taking up positions of power within those institutions seemed both impossible and a betrayal of their integrity. Perhaps for that reason, few new variations on the superwoman theme appeared even during the feminist revival of the 1970s.

That decade was one of significant achievement for women writing SF, as demonstrated in the rich assortment of fictions collected within Pamela Sargent's pathbreaking *Women of Wonder* anthologies. But those writers were busy exploring other tropes and images, from Joan Vinge's alien ethnographies to Tiptree's devastating investigations of biological determinism. In their stories there were powerful women, women as aliens, women confronting technology, female cyborgs, and many voyages to feminist utopias. But women writers did not return to the superhuman until a woman of wonder could also be a woman in charge.

The newer form of superwoman story revives C. L. Moore's ecstatic vision but deepens and darkens it. Writers whose reality includes women Prime Ministers, Supreme Court Justices, Secretaries of State, and Presidents (of Iceland, anyway) continue to depict their wonder women as cyborgs and laughing Medusas and multi-faceted, mirror-entranced paradoxes. Now, however, those paradoxical women are engaged in transforming not only themselves but also the worlds they live in. And that task requires them to give up some of the indeterminacy of Moore's Clarissa and the autonomy of her Dierdre. They must commit themselves, stake out their territory and defend it against threats, and acknowledge the sacrifices they have demanded of their followers and the harm they have done to opponents and bystanders.

This is the direction taken in two ambitious superwoman sagas of the 1980s and '90s: Octavia Butler's Xenogenesis trilogy and Nancy Kress's Beggars in Spain novels. In these dense and subtle narratives about power, identity, and community, Butler and Kress carry forward the tradition of earlier wonder women.

Before Butler published the Xenogenesis novels, she wrote a set of books about psychically gifted mutants, the Patternists, in which she began to examine the themes of power and difference that dominate the later trilogy. The first Patternist story, *Patternmaster* (1976), is set in a future ruled by rival male leaders; women don't play a big role. The second novel, *Mind of My Mind* (1977), does have a female protagonist and begins to invoke more typical superwoman features, such as her multiplicity. The protagonist, Mary, deliberately allocates her own strength among her linked family of telepathic misfits. It is this apparent weakness, her lack of a clear and powerful center, that allows Mary to defeat the male ruler Doro.

As Butler delves deeper into her imagined world in the novels, she also moves back in time. The last book in the series, *Wild Seed* (1980), which examines the earliest origins of the Patternists, is also the volume most clearly linked with the tradition of wonder women. Its protagonist, Anyanwu, is a healer and shapeshifter born in pre-diaspora Africa; the novel follows her to America. Anyanwu becomes a semi-mythical figure to her many descendents, an Eve at war with the Adamic father-Creator Doro. Butler invokes two sorts of origin myth—the Biblical creation and the evolutionary account of human origins—and undermines gender assumptions in both.

In *Dawn,* the first book of the Xenogenesis trilogy, she further questions origin myths by telling the story of Lilith Iyapo, whose very name signals her role as challenger of Biblical norms and hierarchies. Like Adam's legendary first wife, this Lilith is disobedient, disruptive, and unnatural. She is not even fully human. She has been revived from a devastated earth by an alien race and re-engineered into something partly human, partly technological: a cyborg of sorts, though Oankali technology is itself organic. She is an instrument for the alien Oankali, who hope to create a race of human-Oankali hybrids.

At first Lilith finds the thought repulsive. She imagines her descendents as "Medusa children. Snakes for hair. Nests of night crawlers for eyes and ears" (45). But eventually she decides that this unnatural cross is humanity's best hope. Her own artificial body gives her the strength not only to survive but to lead her people into a new way of life, one for which no mythic narrative has prepared them.

Butler's cyborg, like Haraway's, rejects origin myth in favor of new directions. Lilith makes unprecedented choices for all of humanity and is frequently blamed for her choices. Writing in a confidently feminine register, Butler wastes little time in wondering what a woman is or what she wants: the question is what she will do.

Nancy Kress's superbeings are, like Butler's, deliberately manufactured, through technological intervention into the human genome. However, the manipulators in this case are human. By removing the need for sleep, they have unwittingly created a master race. The Sleepless turn out to be extraordinarily intelligent, inventive, well-adjusted, perhaps even immortal. They are even happier than ordinary people: Leisha Camden, the central character of *Beggars in Spain,* seems to have been born joyful, and every discovery she makes adds to her pleasure: "The day she realized the golden flow was light she laughed out loud with the sheer joy of discovery" (19). Like C. L. Moore's Clarissa, she is a child of wonder, bathed in a golden glow that is not the gift of a god but of her own seemingly boundless capacities.

But Leisha is not content to live in solitary bliss; she is another doer. She wants the whole world to be as joyful as she, including both the entire community of the Sleepless and the hostile and self-destructive population of Sleepers (which is to say, the rest of us). Working toward this goal, she makes mistakes—important mistakes, because she herself is important.

As the story progresses, the Sleepless are revealed as less the inevitable successors to humanity than an odd evolutionary by-way. Nor are they the only possible variety of super-being. Other engineered types begin to appear, each with a different set of strengths and the weaknesses inherent within those strengths. Superwoman, suggests Kress, still belongs to "the sex which is not one," not even one form of superiority. In the later books, Leisha's initial utopian vision recedes until the very idea of evolutionary progress is questioned. The wonder woman is no longer innocent; she has fallen into history.

Though Kress's and Butler's versions of the superhuman are movers and shakers, rather than victims or seducers, still they represent a natural outgrowth of the earlier ideas of Moore, Marston, Merril, and even Weinbaum. No longer is the female superbeing an absence multiplied by a void; no longer need she be governed by cultural narratives that equate her with evil or unnature. She exists now as an SF trope alongside the alien, the robot, and the super man. Like them, she can now play many parts and take on many meanings, even contradictory ones. She can be employed not only by women writers but also by those men who have learned from the tradition of Moore and her successors: examples include Theodore Sturgeon, Samuel R. Delany, and John Varley.

And, like any sign in a living language, the super woman continues to evolve and to differentiate. She is no longer Haggard's "She" but "They." Just as the once-common term *woman,* as in "the Woman Question," has been replaced by references to individual women, and just as it seems more natural to speak of multiple feminisms rather than a single philosophy of feminism, the comic-book Wonder Woman has given way to a host of wonder women. They may be noble, sinister, laughing, or sober, but they are never merely weaker versions of the Campbell-era superman. They represent an alternative vision of humanity's future, in which evolutionary leaps are the result, not of Darwinian competition, but of negotiated cooperation within communities of women or of women and men together. In the most ecstatic expressions of the trope, this integration becomes a merging of many unlike selves into a wondrous new being, something that can only be glimpsed, like Moore's mature Clarissa, darkly, as in a mirror.

CHAPTER

WOMEN ALONE, MEN ALONE

Reuben, Reuben, I been thinkin'
What a grand place this would be
If the boys were all transported
Far beyond the northern sea.

Traditional song

One way to find out just how men and women really differ might be to catch them by themselves. Look at the way women behave when there are no men around to bluster or be wrapped around little fingers. Watch the men when no women can rescue them from their own messes or hold them back from adventure. Men are most manly, according to this theory, in combat or in the locker room. Essential womanliness can be found in the nursery, the sewing room, the ladies' lunch.

The theory has obvious weaknesses, of course. First, it's impossible to isolate the sexes thoroughly enough to demonstrate such absolutes of feminine or masculine behavior. Second, the traditional examples are skewed. Masculinity might be one thing on the battlefield, but it is something different in a choir of Benedictine monks. A definition of femininity based on separation would have to include not only the coffee klatsch but also the reunion of barnstorming aviatrixes. Women's groups now include feminist political caucuses, rugby teams, and assembly lines in Asian shoe factories. Men are less often alone now than in the days when whaling ships and Congress were equally woman-free, but there are still Lion's Club meetings, Black Muslim marches, and gay leather bars. A theory based on sexual separation should take all of these into account.

Within science fiction, separation by gender has been the basis of a fascinating series of thought experiments. The best known of these are the feminist utopias of the 1970s, the decade when women writers of SF ceased to seem exceptional. Utopian fiction was generally considered a dead genre by the early '60s, having petered out with Edward Bellamy and his commentators three quarters of a century earlier. Discredited by the totalitarian turn of real-world utopian experiments in China, Germany, and the Soviet Union, the fictional utopia had been replaced by dystopia, it was said. Rationally regulated societies could only be portrayed as earthly hells like Huxley's *Brave New World.* Implied in this judgment was the belief that existing social systems, messy as they were, were better than anything that could come from social engineering.

This consensus broke down when women began to ask, better for whom? A number of writers began to toy with the idea that a world constructed on feminist principles, whatever its flaws, could hardly fail to improve things for most women. For many of these writers, such a world was imaginable only in terms of sexual separatism; for others, it involved reinventing female and male identities and interactions. The pattern of the feminist utopia did not spring into existence all at once, but only emerged gradually through the combined efforts of writers and critics. Once the category existed, though, it gathered to itself earlier texts and also stimulated newer variations on its themes, in the collaborative mode characteristic of SF tropes.

Perhaps the agglutinative origins of the form can best be seen in a year-by-year summary of the decade of its emergence. Some of the titles listed here now belong among the "usual suspects" of utopian studies. They would not, however, have become standard examples, nor would there be a labeled category for them to exemplify, if there had not been a concurrent and corresponding growth of feminist scholarship, providing a context in which to value the fictional texts.

1969

The feminist '70s may be said to have begun in 1969, making it a decade-plus-one, or baker's decade. 1969 saw the appearance of two novels that differed dramatically from one another and from earlier models of utopian narrative. The first of these, Ursula K. Le Guin's *The Left Hand of Darkness* is not, strictly speaking, a feminist utopia, since it does not portray a utopian state, nor are any female characters present. Rather, it is a thought-experiment in gender, imagining a world without sexual difference. Nonetheless, the implications are both feminist and utopian: a world in which no one is expected to be either masculine or feminine automatically erases so many forms of injustice that its societies, no matter how inefficient or authoritarian, seemed a major improvement from the perspective of many women readers (and not a few men).

The other novel of 1969 is Monique Wittig's *Les Guérillères*. Part manifesto, part prose poem, Wittig's text imagines a group of women warriors sometimes battling against, sometimes freed from, patriarchal restraints. Their struggles will change or have changed the world (sequence in the book is deliberately disrupted) so completely that a new language is necessary to describe it. Wittig's text is more overtly utopian than Le Guin's but it does not offer as many details about the way the society will operate nor enough narrative continuity to give a sense of life in the blueprint.

1970

The following year, Joanna Russ published her second novel, *And Chaos Died,* a book that mainly concerned the transformation of a male hero into a psychic superman but also involved a planet (reminiscent of the world of James Schmitz's 1966 *The Witches of Karres*) that secretly houses a utopia run along pacifist, ecological, and egalitarian principles.

1971

Wittig's novel was published in English in 1971, in a translation by David Le Vay. The same year, Russ, stimulated by Le Guin's *The Left Hand of Darkness* ("Afterword" to "When It Changed" 280), finished a book that combined satire, metafiction, and feminist utopia. It was not published until four years later under the title *The Female Man* (*To Write* 133). She also voiced some of the novel's concerns in an essay called "The Image of Women in Science Fiction," published in a fanzine called *Red Clay Reader* and reprinted the following year in an anthology of *Images of Women in Fiction: Feminist Perspectives.* This anthology also contained Russ's classic "What Can a Heroine Do? Or Why Women Can't Write."

The former essay complained that SF had squandered its capacity for questioning social norms by portraying future societies in which spaceship crews were always "red-blooded, crewcut, woman-hungry men, rather like the cast of *South Pacific* before the nurses arrive" (85), while women were stuck in "Galactic suburbia" (88). In the latter essay, she imagines things otherwise: what if, she proposes, our supply of cultural narratives included such alternatives as "Two strong women battle for supremacy in the early West" or "A young girl in Minnesota finds her womanhood by killing a bear" (3)? *The Female Man* was to include, as one of its utopian premises, just such a bear-hunt.

Also in 1971, Dorothy Bryant published *The Comforter,* later retitled *The Kin of Ata Are Waiting for You.* Bryant's novel is more fantasy than SF, more arcadia than utopia, but it does portray a society based on principles often identified with women: kinship, pacifism, and unselfish love.

1972

The first public glimpse of Russ's separatist utopia was a story called "When It Changed." In it, the women of a world called Whileaway confront the return of men to their stable, varied, pragmatic society. The men assume that they will be welcomed, even if the welcome must be imposed by force. The women see the return of an old tyranny.

Russ's story might have been a direct response to the stories reprinted by Sam Moskowitz in his historical anthology *When Women Rule,* which appeared the same year. (Russ went on to examine five examples from the volume in an essay called "*Amor Vincit Foeminam:* The Battle of the Sexes in Science Fiction," published in 1980.) The matriarchies imagined by Moskowitz's authors (all male) are, as Pamela Sargent points out, "more a reflection of the fears or wishes of their authors than serious extrapolation" ("Introduction," *Women* xlix). Nonetheless, their republication in this volume contributed to a growing awareness of the usefulness of SF tropes in exploring gender roles. More importantly, they made people want to argue.

1972 also marked the publication of the first academic essay on women in science fiction, Beverly Friend's "Virgin Territory: Women and Sex in Science Fiction." The subtitle is indicative of the traditional treatments of gender in the genre: in early SF, women *are* sex; men are people. Despite the scarcity of stories in which women are neither gadgets in disguise nor mere prizes for the male heroes, Friend saw potential for better writing about women in two trends: the emergence of more women writers and the trope of the all-female society. Even though most treatments of the trope to date had been written by men and nearly all depicted the women's world as a grimly repressive state needing men's intervention, Friend noted the possibility of a more thoughtful examination of gender, and in later revisions of the article she was able to point to Russ's "When It Changed" as an example.

1973

Lyman Tower Sargent started the investigation, long delayed, of women's roles in classic utopian literature with an essay titled "Women in Utopia," published in *Comparative Literature Studies.* The same year, though, the journal *Studies in the Literary Imagination* failed to include gender as one of the significant "Aspects of Utopian Fiction" covered in a special issue on the subject. Nor were any women writers discussed, except for a brief mention of Le Guin by SF scholar David Ketterer (Ketterer 99).

1974

When Pamela Sargent released the first of three anthologies of *Women of Wonder* in 1974, she reminded readers of the major contributions to SF of writers such as Judith Merril and Katherine MacLean. In her introduction she invited readers and writers to follow their lead in subjecting gender roles to the same sort of examination that SF had traditionally given to problems in planetology or time-travel paradoxes. Like Beverly Friend, Sargent saw unexploited possibilities in the single-sex societies imagined by writers like John Wyndham and Poul Anderson. She too saw those glimmerings being realized in Russ's fiction.

Two texts from 1974 provided new grist for the mills of both feminist scholars and utopianists. Having already produced one of the decade's first gender explorations in *The Left Hand of Darkness,* Ursula K. Le Guin declared her utopian sympathies openly, if ambiguously, in *The Dispossessed.* Subtitled *An Ambiguous Utopia,* this novel posits twin worlds, one wealthy and sophisticated but full of injustice, the other harsh and uniform but idealistic and egalitarian. Neither world is entirely feminist, but rugged Anarres is run on the anarchistic principles of the woman philosopher Odo. Hence, occupations like child-rearing and physics have been largely freed of gender associations.

In contrast, Suzy McKee Charnas's *Walk to the End of the World* extrapolates from the most extreme patriarchal models of gender difference. Charnas turns many of the conventions of the SF genre upside down in a story that begins like a standard masculine coming-of-age and ends up as a narrative of female escape. In this book, Charnas highlights the dystopian implications of a male-dominated society; her look at the female counterpart was to come four years later.

1975

In 1975, Lyman Tower Sargent continued his examination of women's roles in utopian fiction in "An Ambiguous Legacy: The Role and Position of Women in the English Eutopia." The questions Sargent raised, about why utopian thinkers failed to address women's roles and rights, were answered in various ways by three other works appearing the same year: Naomi Mitchison's *Solution Three,* a new edition (the first since its 1890 publication) of Mary Bradley Lane's *Mizora,* and Russ's *The Female Man.*

All three novels involve some separation of the sexes. In Mitchison's imagined future, conflict and overpopulation have both been attributed to heterosexual contact. Redirecting desire toward members of one's own sex and replacing sexual reproduction with cloning have led to an era of peace and plenty—but also to new problems stemming from lack of diversity and from mistreatment of heterosexual deviants. Unlike many earlier thought-experiments, *Solution Three* does not propose going back to a heterosexual norm but onward to a more flexible version, Solution Four.

Lane's utopia was originally produced as part of the nineteenth century debate over women's rights. Rediscovered, along with many other works by women writers, during the feminist revival of the 1970s, it took on new meaning as evidence of a female tradition of speculative and utopian thought.

Even though Lane incorporated racist ideas and dodged issues of sexuality, her assertion of women's strength and independence helped offset SF's misogynist tradition and offered an important reading context for newer experiments like *The Female Man.*

In Russ's novel, the futuristic world of Whileaway is not invaded by men as it is in the story "When It Changed." Rather, *it* invades the male-dominated present by sending back an emissary, Janet Evason. The visitor-from-utopia is an effective twist on the utopian trope, used earlier by William Dean Howells, among others; in Russ's hands it offers opportunity for a variety of satirical takes on gender roles, from the he-mannish stupidity of military leaders and politicians to the bizarre rituals governing dating.

Janet Evason's story is only one strand of this complex and still-challenging book. Another concerns an alternative universe in which men and women not only form separate societies, but wage war on one another. Russ's Manland is pure patriarchal dystopia: all violence and sexual posturing, with brothels full of men altered to look like caricatures of women. Abuses within the woman's land are not so obvious, but it too is dystopian in its violence and its dehumanization of the male Other. One of Russ's characters suggests that this female version of dystopia is a necessary step on the road toward green and pleasant Whileaway.

1976

Like Russ, Marge Piercy, in *Woman on the Edge of Time* combines glimpses of alternative futures, both utopian and dystopian, with an indictment of present-day gender politics. Because Piercy had already established a reputation outside of SF circles, her book received more attention from feminist critics, though Russ's is the more complex treatment of issues. Piercy's ideal state involves de-emphasizing sex roles: men nurse babies, women make art; both feel free to form sexual attachments with members of either sex. The androgynous society of Mattapoisett contrasts sharply with a militaristic, male-dominated alternative future that is trying to come into existence in its place. The seeds of both futures exist in the present, from which a woman named Connie Ramos is journeying back and forth in time. Connie, considered valueless by her society because she is female, Hispanic, poor, and emotionally vulnerable, is nonetheless one of the keys that will decide which future comes into being.

Another story from 1976 likewise uses the device of futuristic visions, although in a manner more sardonic than Piercy's. Raccoona Sheldon's story "Your Faces, O My Sisters, Your Faces Filled of Light," published in an anthology called *Aurora: Beyond Equality,* describes a young woman journeying simultaneously across two landscapes. One is a pastoral, all-female utopia; the other, dangerous, cynical contemporary America. Unfortunately, the welcoming community of women exists only in the mind of the young courier; all others see her as delusional and defenseless, and the story ends in a grim act of violence at the hands of the male gang that she sees as a group of sisters.

In the same anthology there appeared an equally powerful piece of utopian fiction by James Tiptree, Jr. Tiptree's "Houston, Houston, Do You Read?" makes an effective companion piece to "Your Faces, O My Sisters," because it posits a future in which the female utopia has actually come to pass. While the perspective and the storytelling voice in "Your Faces" are strongly feminine, in "Houston, Houston" both are convincingly masculine. The thematic similarities between the two stories are easier to explain than the stylistic differences, for James Tiptree, Jr., and Raccoona Sheldon were soon to be revealed as pen names for the same writer, Alice Sheldon.

"Houston, Houston" follows the thoughts of one of three male astronauts transported from the present. This point of view temporarily disguises the fact that the view of reality they have brought with them, in which women are sub-servient and male sexuality is venerated, is as delusional in the new social context as the fantasy world of the courier in "Your Faces." We see the feminist world only indirectly, as the viewpoint character becomes aware of such details as the existence of lines of clone-sisters and the identity of the apparently male "Andy" on board the rescuing spaceship as another female who has had andro-gen treatments to increase "his" strength. With these adaptations, the women have effectively eliminated any need for men, and they reluctantly decide the astronauts are too dangerous to retain, even as curiosities.

A fourth influential story from 1976 came from a rather unlikely source. Marion Zimmer Bradley had been publishing stories about a world called Darkover since the early 1960s. Darkover is a fantasy world thinly disguised as SF, combining romantic backdrops, Medieval costumes, swordplay, and magical jewels redefined as telepathically-produced "matrixes." Darkovan society is decidedly un-feminist: its aristocratic clans are governed by male leaders and its women are confined in castles or cloistered in matrix-working Towers. Yet for her tenth Darkover novel, *The Shattered Chain,* Bradley invented a new institution that transformed the imaginary world and intro-duced many fans of the series (who were not necessarily reading Shulamith Firestone or Kate Millett) to feminist ideas. The Free Amazons of Darkover form a community within the larger community, a utopia that exists wher-ever its members might gather. Free Amazons work at any occupation they choose, they cast off clan rivalries and traditional marriage vows, and they form a society of equals loyal to one another and to their calling.

1977

In 1977, the feminist journal *Frontiers* devoted an issue to "Fantasy and Futures." One of the entries was Carol Pearson's "Women's Fantasies and Fem-inist Utopias," revised as "Coming Home: Four Feminist Utopias and Patriar-chal Experience" in 1981. Unlike earlier scholars, Pearson was not reduced to talking about the dearth of believable women characters and the misogyny that emerges when SF writers imagine matriarchy. Rather, she was able to point to several recent or rediscovered instances of women writers developing feminist ideas into full-blown utopian fictions. There were enough examples for her to begin identifying common threads among the imagined societies, such as organization along familial patterns rather than formal institutional lines (65).

1978

In 1978, Suzy McKee Charnas published *Motherlines,* a companion piece to an earlier work, the sequel to her novel *Walk to the End of the World.* Like Tiptree/Sheldon, she described a female society of clone sisters: the "Motherlines" that give the book its title. Charnas describes her initial reluctance to omit men from the narrative: "I was terrified to discover that leaving men out altogether was going to be 'right' for the new book" ("A Woman Appeared" 105). Once she accepted the artistic necessity of this decision, however, she found that, like Darwin's finches, women were perfectly capable of adapting to fill any niche: "with the spectrum of human behavior in my story no longer split into male roles (everything active, intelligent, brave and muscular) and feminine roles (everything passive, intuitive, shrinking and soft), my emerging women had natural access to the entire range of human behavior" (106–07).

1979

1979 saw the appearance of Sally Miller Gearhart's *The Wanderground,* a lyrical set of sketches and tales, some published previously, about a tribe of women who have reclaimed their lives and the natural world from patriarchal abuses. Most men are confined to the city, which is also the only place where guns and machines still work. The lives of the hill women are portrayed positively, in terms of psychic attunement to nature and sexual attachment to one another. However, as Jennifer Burwell has pointed out, their society is founded on a sense of outrage (Burwell 68). Its central ritual is the telepathic sharing of memories of rape, to keep alive the anger that fuels their vigilance against the men of the city. Could their utopia exist, one wonders, without the "remember guides" who "call up and re-play, for those who did not know it, all or any part of the hill women's violent backgrounds . . . 'Lest we forget how we came here.' " (24)?

To complete the decade, 1979 was also the year when Charlotte Perkins Gilman's *Herland* was finally published in book form, after being hidden away in Gilman's magazine *The Forerunner* since its serialization in 1915. Like Lane's *Mizora,* Gilman's is a separatist utopia. Both books smack a bit of the hygienic; they are full of what Ursula K. Le Guin has called "smartass utopians. Always so much healthier and saner and sounder and fitter and kinder and tougher and wiser and righter than me and my family and friends." (*Always Coming Home* 316). Gilman's women, like Lane's, are sexless: their erotic impulses are channeled entirely into motherhood, at least until men arrive on the scene.

However, *Herland* is ultimately a much more useful precursor than *Mizora.* It incorporates insights from Gilman's studies of history and economics as well as her feminism; it cleverly undercuts readers' assumptions by building them into the narrative in the viewpoints of three callow male explorers; and it anticipates many of its successors' solutions to the problems of patriarchy.

By the end of the 1970s, then, the feminist utopia was well established, with a respectable genealogy, a canon of standard examples, a reverse canon of opposing works by anti-feminist men (some as recent as Edmund Cooper's *Gender Genocide,* from 1972), and a set of shared assumptions, if not about the nature of the ideal society, at least about the terms in which the debate might continue.

And the debate has continued, in the form of additional rediscoveries, reaching back to Katharine Burdekin's 1937 *Swastika Night* and even to Margaret Cavendish's 1668 *The Blazing World;* further critical and bibliographic work by Marleen Barr, Lynn F. Williams, and others; and more works of thoughtful fiction, written by women like Pamela Sargent, Joan Slonczewski, Suzette Haden Elgin, Sheri S. Tepper, Margaret Atwood, and Nicola Griffith—and a few feminist-influenced men, notably Geoff Ryman, John Varley, and Samuel R. Delany.

The standard historical account of the field is a two-stage evolution: first, male writers invented the repressive matriarchy, then women responded with portraits of more attractive female-dominated societies. Many of these feminist utopias, in fact, are portrayed within the texts as having emerged from struggles against male-dominated dystopias, thereby reenacting the genre's history. This model certainly accounts for most of the fiction from 1969 and later, and it corresponds with common views of male and female behavior. As Gwyneth Jones says in a review of a recent version of the separatist utopia, "We have often been told by feminist writers that women, freed from male constraint, are not perfect but 'only human,' " so that we can expect from them a system that at least respects human imperfections, while "men, in similar isolation, are something else; and something worse" (13).

Existing social systems too often wink at or applaud the abuse of women by men. If the sexes were only separated, it is easy to imagine that mistreatment would vanish from the women's world and be redirected inward in the men's. And men do often construct for themselves systems based on aggression and abasement, a statement that holds true not only of men in places like prisons, says Jones, "but relatively true in any all-male situation, whether it's around the water-cooler at the office, or in an elite public-I-mean-private boys' boarding school" (13).

So it seems obvious that all-male worlds should be dystopias and all-female ones at least evolving toward utopia. Yet this formulation leaves out a number of complications. It does not explain the process by which writers could take something as anti-feminist as the "When Women Rule" trope and transform it into feminist utopia. It doesn't explain how one could apply the utopian ideal to the real world, barring the invention of a male-killing plague virus. And it doesn't reflect the fact that fictional all-male societies before the 1970s were not usually dystopian at all, but scenes of conviviality and cooperation.

Examples of this last paradigm go back at least to Herman Melville's "The Paradise of Bachelors," the companion piece to his dystopian "The Tartarus of Maids" (published together in 1855). While the women toil in an infernal factory, the men take their indolent pleasures—including the pleasure of one another's company—in a city club. While Melville uses the male utopia to make a point about injustice, other writers invoked the same image without irony. Arthur B. Evans describes the many enclosed societies of Jules Verne, such as the miniature world aboard the Captain Nemo's submarine, as "vehicular utopias." Their utopian qualities come not only from the labor-saving gadgets with which the vehicles are equipped, but also from their insulation from any form of "ideological contamination" (Evans 5). The men aboard are sheltered from contact with anyone unlike themselves, which is to say anyone who isn't middle-class, rational—and male.

The science fiction of the early twentieth century abounds in echoes of Verne's vehicular utopias; however, maintaining that ideal required a certain degree of unselfconsciousness about class, gender, and sexuality. Once writers like Russ and Charnas began to call attention to those issues, the cozy male world became problematic. Notwithstanding this later loss of confidence, the truism about the dystopian quality of all-male world turns out, like most truisms, to be only true-ish.

In order to take such complications into account, I need to define some terms more precisely. Etymologically, "utopia," Thomas More's "no place," means any fiction whose social setting is presented as a plausible and radically new alternative to existing cultures. Utopias need not solve all social problems; they may be good, bad, or merely so different from existing systems as to offer a critical perspective. Within this larger category, we can distinguish between positive and negative formulations by calling the former *eutopia,* "the good place," and the latter *dystopia,* "the bad place." Fictional societies that fall between these two poles can be called "ambiguous" or, in Tom Moylan's terminology, "critical" utopias (10).

The heading of feminist utopias includes both those composed of female citizens only, like Russ's Whileaway and Gilman's Herland, and those of mixed sex in which the social organization derives from women's modes of thought and interaction: for instance, Piercy's eutopian Mattapoisett or the dystopian world of Cooper's *Gender Genocide.* The contrasting masculist utopia can consist either of men alone or of men plus women whose presence and influence are suppressed, as in Katherine Burdekin's *Swastika*

Night. Classic social nightmares like *1984* are both male-dominated and misogynistic and could be analyzed as masculist utopias.

My justification for lumping single-sex utopias with those in which the population is mixed but the balance of power tipped one way or the other is that the excluded sex is never completely excluded. There may be no men in Whileaway, but men are present throughout *The Female Man* (at least for real-world readers) in the form of the unlamented past, the pressure no longer felt, the horrible example, the stolen prerogative. There seem to be no women in the masculist society portrayed in Lois McMaster Bujold's *Ethan of Athos,* but the book's protagonist discovers that his whole world depends on the effaced, radically reduced women who are the unacknowledged mothers of all. There is a spot of yin in the most scrupulously yang of utopias, and vice versa.

Also present in every utopian text are echoes of its predecessors. Robin Roberts points out that Gilman's and other early feminist utopias—or rather eutopias—were a dialectical response to a long tradition of presenting female power in terms of hive-like rigidity and irrationality. A typical hive world is described in Wallace G. West's "The Last Man" (1929), in which citizens of an all-female society are described as having evolved into "narrowflanked, flat-breasted workers . . . with dull curiosity on their soulless faces" (1030). The editorial comment on the story proclaims that it is "founded upon an excellent scientific basis" (1030). The dystopian vision, she says, can give rise to the eutopian without necessarily changing any element. Both views "share the same tropes," she says, but "differ dramatically in their interpretation and use of the paradigm of female ruler." The feminist eutopia "valorizes reproduction, depicts mothering as a justification for female rule, and looks toward idyllic futures brought about by the adoption of feminine values" (68). Earlier dystopian fictions had portrayed the same pattern but called it anything but idyllic. The relationship between the two is, then, not one of simple contradiction but of reversing values while retaining the basic configuration.

Taking a metaphor from art criticism, one might call this the intaglio effect. Intaglio is low-relief sculpture in reverse; instead of carving away background to leave the figure, as in a cameo, the most prominent features are sculpted most deeply. The effect is an optical illusion in which the eye translates concave into convex. However, if you put a regular cameo next to an intaglio, under the same light, highlights and shadows will be eerily reversed.

Suzy McKee Charnas's *Walk to the End of the World* generates just such an intaglio effect. Charnas portrays a horrible society: a band of survivors from an ecological and military holocaust have instituted a system that privileges older white males by exterminating all other races and most animal and plant species, enslaving women, and keeping even their sons in a permanent state of smoldering rebellion. The novel isn't obviously feminist at first; the viewpoint characters in the early chapters are young men, and the story seems to be about their struggle for justice. Charnas plays on common themes of male-centered SF: the young misunderstood genius, the uncovering of hidden

In the text at the bottom of the illustration: "Unwittingly he had leaned farther and farther over the railing of the balcony. Now, without warning, its ancient moorings parted and a large section of the balustrade tottered slowly outward and fell."

1031

Figure 4. In the Hive. Frank R. Paul's illustration for Wallace G. West's "The Last Man" (1929) suggests the worker-bee uniformity ascribed by male writers to all-female societies, although Paul did not follow the text's warning that such female workers would be "flat-breasted."

truths about the world, jockeying for status in a quasi-military organization, conflicts between social convention and science, and fights that result in apparent enemies becoming allies. She even throws in a son's quest to find an absent father.

There are no named women characters in the first section of the book. After a brief historical prologue, the only female presence is an occasional glimpse of or derogatory reference to "fems." Fems are workers, drudges, sometimes "hags." It is not clear until much later that fems are human at all. Not until the narrative adopts the viewpoint of the fem Alldera, about two-thirds of the way through, does it begin to be evident that the story is not a conventional masculine quest but a story of feminine escape from an intolerable system.

The elements that make up Charnas's masculist dystopia include a set of powerful institutions—clans, military companies, guilds, a school that is also a mechanism for culling unsuitable boys, and a priesthood—all governed along strictly hierarchical lines, like ranks within a Masonic order. The laws authorizing these institutions are enforced by scarcity and threats; moreover, they are revered as if they were both divine and natural laws. The system is reinforced by an ancestor cult that includes reciting the names of long-dead iconic figures—the Chants Commemorative.

This society is maintained by an invisible labor force of slaves, the fems. The role of women in producing offspring is diminished and disparaged: boys are taken from their mothers as soon as possible and the goal of education is to eliminate the womanly taint resulting from imprisonment in the womb. Women are so abject that any contact with them, including sexual contact, is humiliating. Both desire and loyalty are properly directed only toward one's equals, which means male members of one's age cadre. Sex is described as a power struggle, compulsive and violent like sex in the cat world. Indeed, a particularly enticing male character is described in explicitly feline terms: "heavy-muscled, smooth-moving, a tawny-colored night-slinker, a prowling predator with a broad, blunt-nosed face and a wide-curling mouth . . ." (9–10).

With sexual desire thus separated from reproduction, and both from females, reproduction can be redefined as recruitment: new citizens are not born of women but selected and trained by men. At the end of the process of recruitment, the ordinary citizen becomes a Senior, holding the power of life and death over others and in possession of such ancient knowledge as has survived.

When I first read *Walk to the End of the World,* I found this whole pattern naggingly familiar, but I didn't identify the source of that familiarity because of the intaglio effect. I could not pin it down until I began to describe the social structure to myself as neutrally as possible, without the emotional charge given it by Charnas's narrative. Then pieces of the pattern began to be recognizable as echoes of earlier SF works. There was some of Kipling's comradery in it, an echo of Verne's utopian vehicles, a hint of Doc Smith's cadre of Lensmen, and a whole lot of Heinlein. That was the clue: somewhere in Heinlein there was a story in which a society much like Charnas' Hold-fast was portrayed as a eutopia. The story turned out to be the 1948 juvenile novel *Space Cadet*.

Space Cadet is vintage Heinlein: smoothly written, tightly paced, subtle in its introduction of futuristic wonders, and flattering to the reader who identifies with its idealistic hero. I had never thought of it as a utopia, but its coming-of-age theme turns out to be a dandy disguise for the stranger-tours-ideal-society structure of the classic utopian novel.

So what sort of society is it that Heinlein's young hero Matthew Dodson is inducted into? It is, first and foremost, hierarchical. The Patrol is, after all, a military institution, modeled on the Air Force with which it shares the Colorado setting of its Academy. It is all-male, unlike Heinlein's later *Starship Troopers*. It is selective—the first and most effective section of the novel concerns Matt's successful negotiation of the rigorous weeding-out process. It is an institution to which members are expected to commit not only their professional efforts but also their personal loyalties and their spirituality. Heinlein's description of Patrol rituals makes it clear that it is not merely a branch of the military but also a cult, complete with icons such as heroic dead whose names are chanted at the end of each roll call. And, like most cults, this one is jealous of prior loyalties. Paralleling Matt's induction into the traditions of the Patrol is his gradual detachment from home and family.

One of the most uncomfortable scenes is Matt's first visit home after his initial training. He discovers that home now seems small and tasteless, old friends are now strangers, and his family is unable to understand his new life. His mother, in particular, shows herself to be out of touch with everything he has learned to value: she doesn't understand astrophysics or maneuvering in free fall and she refuses even to think about the orbiting bombs maintained by the Patrol as a deterrent to earthly conflict. Matt's father, only slightly more aware of the Patrol's high calling, explains privately to Matt that "Women get worked up so easily" (123).

Other women in the story don't come off much better than Mrs. Dodson. Matt's old girlfriend Marianne is dismissed after he discovers that she "was the sort of girl who never would get clearly fixed in her mind the distinction between a planet and a star" (117). Matt's roommate Tex must abandon his collection of photos, his "harem," when the cadets take off for space: they, and by implication the women they portray, are excess baggage (52). Women in Heinlein's version of space stay in the background: the "decorative young lady," for instance, who sorts out candidates arriving at the Academy (11), and the unseen "feminine voice" that talks the shuttle in for a landing at Terra Station (90). These anonymous functionaries stand for the many workers who provide earthside support for the Patrol station, which is obviously not self-sufficient.

Though the novel frequently pays lip-service to women's "decorative" qualities, any actual or intended sexual encounter with females results in humiliation. On leave at Terra Station, the cadets try to pick up a scantily dressed shopper who promptly puts them in their place. (She is a sketch for a number of later Heinlein characters who look like *Playboy* models but talk like senior officers—baritone bimbos all).

When the cadets set out in search of more suitable female company, the ringleader Tex ends up drunk and vomiting, and on the return trip his box of souvenir candy depressurizes—his chocolate cherries burst embarrassingly all over his uniform. So much for (symbolic) sex. No wonder, as Matt muses, "most Patrol officers do not marry until their mid-thirties, after retirement" (117).

But lack of heterosexual activity doesn't necessarily mean absence of desire. Matt's intense interest in the uniform and physique of an older cadet contrasts with his indifference toward Marianne: "The cadet did not hold himself erectly; he crouched the merest trifle, knees relaxed and springy, hands ready to grasp. His feet glided softly over the floor. The effect was catlike, easy grace . . ." (13). Matt, says the text, "wanted very much to look like him" (13).

This is a safe sort of desire because there is no way for it to become overt. Heinlein's Patrolmen are happily celibate, channeling all their sexual energies into sports, bomb-tending, soul-stirring ceremonies, and close relationships with their buddies—there is a lot of negotiating for the right roommates. This is, after all, a book for boys, so the cadets are portrayed as sexually immature despite their ages. Rather than displaying the catlike grace that attracts Matt, his peers look like "a basket of kittens" (58). Sex, like alcohol, is for some unspecified time in the future. After the humiliating encounter on Terra Station, the boys decide to wait to try out the pleasures of drinking in a setting free of feminine influence:

> "Maybe some day," says Matt, "I'll get you to chaperone me and find out what happens. But not in public."
> "It's a date."
> "Say," demanded Pete, "what goes on here?" (98).

That, I think, is a very intriguing question.

The system Heinlein outlines is aimed at creating and perpetuating an elite brotherhood, a corps of officers armed with arcane knowledge and bound together by ties of loyalty, desire, deprivation, and shared responsibility. Careful selection and rigorous training render each member of the Patrol fit to make life-or-death decisions over the rest of humanity.

The entire system depends on the benevolence of its elders and the wisdom of its laws. If, as has been suggested, successful utopias must either be ruled by angels or populated by saints (Russell 62), the masculist pattern opts for angels—for coercive government by incorruptible rulers rather than self-control by virtuous citizens. A character in the story even compares the typical Patrolman with his orbiting bomb to "an archangel, charging around the sky and brandishing a flaming sword" (105). But not all angels are benevolent and not all laws are wise. The rulers of Charnas' Holdfast are no less righteous in their own eyes than Heinlein's officers, but they are fallen angels nonetheless.

This list doesn't exhaust the parallels between Heinlein's utopia and Charnas's intaglio version of it. Both are ritualized, hierarchical, homosocial, legalistic, misogynistic utopias. It is just that everything good for you, in one model, is bad for you in the other. But Charnas's dystopia is more than just a critique of the attitudes Heinlein stands for. It is also the first step toward creating an alternative social vision. The intaglio effect is not the only way in which one utopia can generate another. *Walk to the End of the World* was followed by Charnas's feminist utopia, *Motherlines* (1978), which demonstrates a different generative process.

The society of Riding Women that Charnas portrays in *Motherlines* is related to that of Holdfast, not as a reverse rendering of the same values but as a manifestation of everything left out of the first book. Utopias are, among other things, filtering mechanisms. They filter out anything incompatible with the author's intention: everything that might adulterate the prescription or weaken the warning. A lot of things got caught in the filter when Holdfast—and Heinlein's Patrol—were created. Among them are female agency, kinship ties, links with nature, freedom of movement, freedom of conscience, diversity among women's personalities, noncompetitive sexuality, female desire, childbearing, and social change. There are other things missing as well—the class of excluded things is always potentially endless—but these are the ones that the text implies and then denies. Heterosexual love is missing as well but is outside the bounds of the fictional universe. It's irrelevant, as are aliens and spaceships. They were never there even as implied contrasts or excluded options.

What Charnas does in *Motherlines* is to look in the filter for all the odds and ends left out of the earlier novel, tip them out into a fictive Petri dish, and "culture" them. That is to say, she makes a culture out of them, grows an entire social system from ideas Holdfasters have rejected. In place of their top-down system, the Riding Women illustrate the power of non-institutionalized forms of social control, especially sexual bonding, shared responsibility for children, and the authority of custom and oral tradition. On the scale of angelic rulers versus saintly citizens, this is a utopia of saints, but their sainthood is relative and grounded in ethnographic and sociological observation. The result is a eutopia more fully imagined than the dystopia it critiques, a compelling narrative in an appealing world. Whereas *Walk* and *Space Cadet* illustrate the intaglio effect, *Motherlines* shows how utopias may be related another way, through the filtration effect.

The dialectical nature of utopian thought means that no single text can be the final word on the subject. Filtration and intaglio may be used in turn to generate new utopias from ideas embodied in *Motherlines;* moreover, these are not the only devices available. A writer can, for instance, portray the same society with the same scale of values but put it in a new frame that dramatically alters its implications. Nicola Griffith's *Ammonite* (1992) takes place on a world that closely resembles the land of the Riding Women, but reframes a number of key concepts. Instead of a post-apocalyptic future, this is an alien planet; the role of patriarchal Other is played by a corporate structure rather than a fortress full of bickering men; women play villains as well as heroes; the mechanism that has allowed women to live and reproduce without men is not an exercise of mental power but an alien virus (the same virus that killed off the men—two boons from one bug). These are changes that not only alter the internal dynamic of the story but also reflect the reframing effect of a decade of struggle and adaptation within feminism itself.

Several feminist utopias use the filtration effect to generate masculist dystopias within the same narrative. Manland, in Russ's *The Female Man* is a filtered version of the utopian Whileaway. In Sheri S. Tepper's *The Gate to Women's Country* (1988), warrior garrisons are deliberately created to hold the residue—both cultural and human—filtered out of the eutopian women's towns.

These masculist dystopias, in turn, can be subjected to reframing or reversal by intaglio effect. Ursula Le Guin's "The Matter of Seggri" (1994) puts the men into an enclosure and leaves the women outside. A series of off-world observers describe the men of the planet Seggri variously, depending on their own assumptions about gender. Either they are privileged lords waited on by female drudges or sexual slaves for the free women. Only in the last section of the story do we get a look at life inside the male preserves, and it is a life from which the male narrator of that section is desperately grateful to escape.

Eleanor Arnason's *Ring of Swords* (1993) supposes that even a warrior society can be based on principles other than female subjection and armed hostility among males. The men of her society of *hwarhath* are in some ways caricatures of masculine-coded traits: militaristic, restless, arrogant. But they are also subtle, adaptable, loyal to their clans, respectful of the women clan leaders back on the home world, and capable of forming deep and lasting sexual attachments to one another.

One of Arnason's innovations in this novel is to look at the male utopia from around a corner, as it were. Her main viewpoint characters are not *hwarhath* males or females, nor even ethnologists sent out to study them, as in Le Guin's "Seggri." Instead, we get to know the masculine utopia first through the eyes of a human woman who is observing a human man who has been adopted into it. We get *her* take on *his* understanding of the culture in which he is a partial participant—and his sense of the alien ways is filtered in turn through the perceptions of his *hwarhath* lover and other contacts within the society, who do not necessarily agree on the way their culture works. These multiple screens allow Arnason to present the same set of traditions and behaviors simultaneously as paranoid and honorable, aristocratic and egalitarian, violent and restrained, rigid and cautiously flexible. Half eutopia and half dystopia, the novel doubles as an alien thought-experiment and a portrait of human masculinities, which, it implies, are likewise manifold and contradictory.

As depicted in *Ring of Swords* and in several short stories and an as-yet-unpublished sequel called *Hearth World, hwarhath* women and men have their own customs, social structures, even favored art forms. The men like hero plays and prose romances, while the women prefer decorative arts and animal plays. Men seem to favor high-tech solutions to problems (and live in space, where such solutions are necessary), while women prefer the simplest devices that will get the job done, like trains and trolley cars. The men, who are in a sense permanent exiles, form passionate and lasting romantic attachments with one another, while the women, more anchored to place and family, tend toward shorter, more casual liaisons or "long-term long-distance romances where the two lovers visit back and forth, but are more often apart than together" ("The Lovers" 38).

The rigid separation between the sexes among the *hwarhath* is reminiscent of many Mediterranean cultures, from ancient Athens to present-day Sicily or Tunisia. Outsiders, with some justification, view these cultures as oppressive of women, but a view from outside can overlook the measure of autonomy and influence afforded to women in such a system. Arnason's thought experiment brings out separatism's potential for equalizing gender relations. The *hwarhath* system eliminates not only the abuse of women by men but also overpopulation, child neglect, homophobia, environmental degradation, and male restlessness. Women gain power and security; men gain, among other things, freedom from the need to define themselves as un-womanly.

But there are trade-offs. *Hwarhath* women do not travel freely; *hwarhath* men have essentially relinquished their home world. While each gender role offers more variety than human codes typically offer, the limits are more absolute. And heterosexuality is not even a marginalized option. We meet a few such deviants among the *hwarhath,* but they do not play the exception-that-proves-the-rule, as homosexuals do in many earthly societies. No gender safety valve exists among the *hwarhath.* There is no place for the woman warrior or the male homebody. For such a person, eutopia must quickly become dystopia.

By contrast, Lois McMaster Bujold, in *Ethan of Athos* (1986), suggests that a world of men might be structured along the lines of a feminist utopia, with an emphasis on child-rearing, kinship, and pair-bonding rather than on military prowess and rank. Bujold's novel may be an intaglio version of A. Bertram Chandler's *Spartan Planet* (1969), which portrays an all-male dystopia of hypermasculine soldiers and effeminate nurses (it is implied that all sexual pairings include one of each type: butch and femme). In Chandler's novel, the masculist society depends on deception: the planet's true history is suppressed, the need to import ova to maintain the population is disguised, and the existence of a few women prostitutes is a secret known only to the doctors who make up the planet's elite. Once the soldier protagonist comes into contact with an off-world woman, he immediately throws off all conditioning and reverts to heterosexuality.

In Bujold's revision of Chandler's scenario, sexual separation has freed the male colonists of Athos, like the warriors of the *hwarhath,* from the need to prove their rejection of femininity. Thereby men are authorized to demonstrate a full range of personality types and interests, rather than dividing into butch and femme camps. There are men of Athos who, if they were not so xenophobic, would be perfectly comfortable living among Arnason's *hwarhath.* They would certainly approve of *hwarhath* sexual arrangements, for the world of Athos was settled by men so virulently misogynistic that they consider any contact, especially sexual congress, with women to be corrupting. There are other Athosians, though, including the title character, who would like nothing better than to find a good man, settle down, and begin raising children. Venturing off planet, the unusually open-minded Ethan even finds it possible to form a friendship with a woman. Unlike Chandler's hero, though, he has no sudden inclination to change his sexual orientation.

Bujold's recognition of difference within—rather than between—genders may represent an evolutionary advance in the masculist utopia, a stage reached slightly earlier by feminist utopias. Whereas Gilman's Herlanders all seem pretty much alike, the world of Griffith's *Ammonite* is populated by farmers, warriors, mystics, artisans, traitors, boors, scholars: in other words, a full range of female persons. In earlier separatist utopias, the assumption had been that men and women would differ most sharply in isolation from one another, while more recent versions show them converging.

The feminist-influenced masculist eutopia has, so far, only come from women writers such as Bujold and Arnason. If you map out recent utopias by subject and writer, you find feminist eutopias by women, feminist dystopias by men, masculist dystopias by women, and a great gap where you might expect masculist eutopias by men. There are several possible reasons for the silence of male writers on the subject:

First, men have less reason than women to question cultural assumptions about gender because those assumptions generally give males more prerogatives and more power—why should men want to exclude the very people who make their lives easier?

Second, reimagining men in terms of personal ties and social obligations requires separating those ideas from the category of woman, or in other words, having already worked through feminist principles.

Third, the writer must be familiar enough with domestic economy and child raising to give those activities a central place in the social system, rather than leaving them invisibly offstage. A Vernian vehicular utopia may be a pleasant place to live, but it cannot sustain itself without replenishing its supplies and membership from outside.

The fourth hurdle, though, may be the most difficult for many writers to get over: in Heinlein's day sexual arrangements could be left undefined, but a contemporary blueprint for masculist eutopia has to consider possible sexual ties between males.

Sex, it turns out, is not only a means of reproduction but also a mechanism for resolving conflicts and creating communal bonds. Recent studies of species like dolphins and bonobos have challenged an older model of sex as a limited commodity embodied in females and competed for by males. In those species, sexual contacts of all sorts and between individuals of any sex serve to defuse aggression and encourage cooperation within the group. Most feminist utopias since the 1970s echo (or anticipate) this perspective on sex. Desire between utopian women serves as a sign of female self-affirmation and self-sufficiency and integrates the outsider or misfit into the utopian system.

By contrast, male homosexuality in utopia, if acknowledged at all, is represented in terms of dominance and humiliation. Within older SF in general, only a few stories by gay male or gay-friendly writers like Edgar Pangborn, Marion Zimmer Bradley, and Theodore Sturgeon challenge this perspective. Bradley's 1963 story "Another Rib," written with John Jay Wells, is one of the first SF stories to posit not only a version of gay marriage but also male motherhood. When I read this story (alerted by Lynn Williams's bibliography on gender and utopia), I thought I had finally found the rare all-male eutopia by a male writer—until I discovered that John Jay Wells was a pseudonym for Juanita Coulson.

More typically, SF stories that portray groups of men alone adopt a "Don't Ask, Don't Tell" policy with regard to sexual activity. Philip Wylie's 1951 novel *The Disappearance* is typical in this regard, though it challenges many other SF norms. Wylie's novel is a double dystopia, half feminist and half masculist. Its premise is that humanity suddenly splits into two separate realities: a world without women and one without men. In the women's world, lack of technical expertise and leadership experience lead to one sort of apocalypse, while the men engineer their own downfall through war and tyranny.

The book sometimes seems to be making claims about biological determinism, as when the narrator describes rising hostility in the male world in terms of "Temper that rose from an absolute and insatiate hunger, an utter frustration, and an inner loneliness . . . temper which made the presence of men, and of only men, a constant source of bursts of violence" (197). At other points, though, the text decries the cultural bias underlying sexual divisions that have left half of humanity unprepared for leadership and the other half incapable of harmony.

Though Wylie attempts to keep both strands of his narrative parallel, the men's world seems ruled primarily by instinct, while flaws in the women's world are attributed to cultural conditioning and are thus easier to overcome. Nowhere is this distinction more evident than in the treatment of sexuality after the Disappearance. Wylie's Freudianism doesn't let him ignore the possibility of homosexuality in a single-sex world. But in the women's world, women begin fairly quickly to form attachments modeled after schoolgirl crushes. The female protagonist, Paula, seriously considers having an affair with her attractive neighbor Kate. Wylie's psychoanalytic perspective interprets the attraction in terms of Paula's hitherto concealed masculine streak, which she renounces as soon as she becomes conscious of it: once again, "She was satisfied to be a woman" (326).

In the men's world, though, homosexuality is entirely defined in terms of female-substitutes: pre-Disappearance stag movies, life-size "Miss America" dolls, and female impersonators. Paula's husband Bill is never tempted by these ersatz women; the possibility is never even raised that he might be more interested in his wife's onetime lover: handsome, accommodating, perennial bachelor Teddy Barker. Yet Teddy shows up in just those sections of Bill's narrative that parallel Paula's flirtation with Kate. The closest thing to an acknowledgement of attraction between the two men is a conversation about Teddy's affair with Bill's wife, after which Bill:

> did not think: this man stole the affections of my wife, or, this man has shared my wife, or, here is a man by whom I have been made cuckold. He thought: This is our friend.
> He walked halfway home with Teddy. (211)

In SF of the 1950s, a man could only walk halfway home with Teddy. Wylie's men, even more than his women, were locked into conventional behaviors and acceptable character variations. Acceptable behavior included violence but not acknowledged sexual desire toward other men; tyranny but not interpersonal negotiation; death, as Leslie Fiedler pointed out in the same decade, but not love. Hence, though both worlds devolve into dystopia, the men's world becomes more immediately and more thoroughly dystopian than the women's.

The depiction of male homosexuality in *The Disappearance* both dates the book and calls into question many of its assumptions about sexual difference. In the decades since its publication, several different models of homosexuality have emerged, from the bisexual ideal of glamour rock to the macho-man promiscuity of early gay liberation to the post-AIDS emphasis on stable partnerships. None of this variety is even hinted at in *The Disappearance*. The thought of multiple versions of homosexuality does not appear in SF until Samuel Delany's *Stars in My Pocket Like Grains of Sand* (1984), Geoff Ryman's *The Child Garden* (1989), and John Varley's *Steel Beach* (1992). The societies imagined within these novels are given a tinge of utopia by the open-endedness of gender coding within both homosexual and heterosexual relationships.

Bujold's and Arnason's utopias likewise invoke multiple versions of gay identity as a means of shaking up gender norms and conventional social structures such as the family. Other texts, in turn, examine what might happen if one particular model of homosexuality were to replace heterosexual norms. Lucy Sussex's "My Lady Tongue," and Geoff Ryman's "O Happy

Day!" both demonstrate the need to resist enforced notions of gender even in the guise of utopian reform, while Karen Joy Fowler's "Game Night at the Fox and Goose" asks whether utopia can cope with the intricacies and ambivalences of human desire.

In Sussex's story, a young woman growing up in a feminist enclave is thrown together with a man who does not fit the masculine image she has learned. As the story's title hints, the two, like Shakespeare's Beatrice and Benedict, fight their way to friendship and then to love. At least he falls in love. She, unlike her predecessors in a host of male fantasies, is not overwhelmed by the first male she sees. Instead, she elects to return to the women's utopia, though with the knowledge that things are more complicated than she has been led to believe. She goes back, but we are invited to believe she will always be a questioner, keeping the female haven from becoming too rigid.

Ryman depicts a harsh revolutionary society in which heterosexual men are sent to extermination camps and homosexuals are tolerated so long as they collaborate with the unseen female overseers. The narrator attempts to rescue one prisoner, Royce, by pretending they are lovers, but Royce offends the camp bully, who rapes him, leading to reprisals from the overseers. It is a terrible scenario but there is nothing in it that is not implicit somewhere among feminist utopias. The narrator wonders where to assign blame: previous injustices toward women, male proclivity for hierarchy and sexual violence, or the revolutionary higher-ups who have created a situation in which there is no decent way to act. Where is the place for a man who identifies neither with the patriarchal system nor the dystopian rule that has replaced it?

Fowler's protagonist has just been abandoned by a married lover. In the Fox and Goose bar, she is approached by a tall, unusually confident woman who tells her about an alternative reality in which women have rebelled against male duplicity and abuse. "Is it better there?" asks Alice. "Better for whom?" the woman responds (240). Alice decides to accompany the woman to her home universe (via the women's restroom in the bar), only to find that she has been deceived, again, by a man. He has disguised himself to fetch her to be the "small thing" that can "tip the balance" between women and men in his world (241). Why Alice? The story does not exactly say, except that we know she likes men, is heterosexual, is vulnerable (and pregnant), and tends to blame herself in bad situations. Is she destined, simply by her sexuality, to betray the feminist society?

Focusing on misfits in utopia, these three stories examine generalizations about gender proposed by previous utopias. These stories ask whether any single system can account for the varieties of experience and inclination found among actual women and men. Other stories exploring the same question have been discussed by Wendy Pearson, Veronica Hollinger, and Ann Weinstone in a special issue of *Science-Fiction Studies* devoted to the relationship between SF and queer theory.

So how do women behave when they are left alone? What would men be without women? Do masculist texts represent natural, hard-wired, instinctual masculinity? Which of the feminist utopias most truly expresses women's needs and desires? The dialectical nature of utopia indicates that no answer to these questions can be complete or final. A central premise of utopian thought is that the cluster of attitudes and behaviors that we call "human nature" is not fixed but can be altered by indoctrination and by social systems that favor certain behaviors over others.

As history keeps reformulating the issues, writers keep reframing, filtering, and inverting the utopian systems that embody them. The latest take on gender and utopia seems to be that gender itself can become a dystopian system. Forcing all members of either sex into a single pattern will inevitably result in dystopia, while the most positive visions of society are those in which women and men are similarly free to defy norms.

So the single-sex utopia, paradoxically, ends up asserting a peculiar sort of continuity between genders. In most of these utopias, differences are not flattened out but redistributed, so that the sex one belongs to no longer determines the sex one is attracted to, or the role one plays in battle, or one's ability to care for offspring. Men alone may turn out to be more like women than we thought, and women more like men. Such redistribution alters the meanings not only of masculinity and femininity, but also of possible overlap between them, and thus invites new readings of androgyny and of the text that signaled the beginning of the utopian revival, Le Guin's *The Left Hand of Darkness*.

CHAPTER

ANDROGYNY AS DIFFERENCE

A major task of the feminist revival of the 1960s and 1970s was a search for new tools for investigating and challenging gender assumptions. Before one could reinvent society along more equitable lines, one had to figure out a way to pry apart some of the apparently inseparable components of gender. But how could, say, the ability to repair a car be peeled off from the bundle of traits labeled "masculine" and reassigned to the category "feminine"? How could a woman rid herself of the obligations to be nurturing, enticing, and deferential?

The tool seized on by many feminist women and men was androgyny. If gender distinctions were unfair, why not simply do away with them? Androgyny was not only transgressive, but trendy as well. London designers of the '60s started dressing their male and female models identically; men's hair grew longer and women's shorter; mascaraed and glittering pop stars like David Bowie and Mick Jagger glamorized gender indeterminacy; films like *Teorema* (1968), *Performance* (1970), and *Cabaret* (1972) suggested that desire could transcend assigned sexual roles. At the same time, androgyny was endorsed by one of the most influential feminist critics, Carolyn Heilbrun, who established its honorable intellectual lineage running through Plato, Shakespeare, Coleridge, Jung, and Virginia Woolf.

Heilbrun defined androgyny in her 1973 manifesto, *Toward a Recognition of Androgyny,* as "a condition under which the characteristics of the sexes, and the human impulses expressed by men and women, are not rigidly assigned" (x). She, like Woolf, saw this condition as both a desirable goal and an unacknowledged reality: most people already have more androgynous traits than their social roles allow them to express. Hence a society that learned to recognize and encourage fluid gender identities would be one in which lives would be more satisfying and psyches more integrated.

But how could this condition be achieved in a world where sexual differentiation is enforced with the special vigilance reserved for instilling what a culture believes to be natural? How could an androgynous identity even be represented when everything from public restrooms to personal pronouns insists on one's choosing sides? In Woolf's *A Room of One's Own,* her best effort at depicting the androgynous ideal was the image of two people getting into the back of a cab, an image more suggestive of inner conflict than of harmony or integration. Woolf better embodied the concept of androgyny when she turned to fantasy in her novel *Orlando,* but the book that, for many readers, most effectively fleshed out Heilbrun's and Woolf's intentions was Ursula K. Le Guin's 1969 science fiction novel, *The Left Hand of Darkness.*

The Left Hand of Darkness was immediately recognized by SF fans and critics as a classic within the field, a book that fulfilled SF's longstanding promise to generate stories both intellectually challenging and aesthetically rich. In it, Le Guin describes an alien world with a carefully worked out geography, climate, and ecology. So had many SF novelists before. But few writers before Le Guin added to this base layer upon layer of cultural detail: myths, manners, kinship customs, architectural styles, rituals both sacred and domestic, and epochs of historical change and continuity. In *The Left Hand,* each of these overlays offers a different context for, and arrangement of, a set of symbolic images—hearths, fields of ice, brothers, betrayers, shadows, light—images that then work themselves into the book's plot and help it carry out its work of investigating the paradox of gender.

The people of Gethen, Le Guin's imagined world, are particularly well suited for revealing that paradox, the polar opposition that is at the same time a complementarity. They offer a challenge to the notion of gender by having none. Gethenians spend most of their time in a state of sexual latency; when they become sexually active they may in a given cycle manifest as male or female. Any Gethenian is equally capable of bearing or fathering children. Any might become the object of desire; any might pursue. No social role is off limits for any Gethenian: priest, landlady, prime minister. On Gethen it is possible to say, "The King was pregnant." (69). There is no contradiction between the vulnerability of pregnancy and the arrogance of kinghood, no moiety of humanity debarred from one or the other.

The primary narrator of *The Left Hand* is not Gethenian but Terran. He is one of us, our surrogate in the text. Genly Ai, a man of good will but not

particularly acute perceptions, is able to articulate all the reader's objections—
*These people are freaks, How can I trust a woman who is also a man, Where do I
fit into all this?*—and thereby defuse them. If the controlling consciousness of
the book had been either a Gethenian or a female Terran, the book would
probably not have been so well received by the largely male SF readership (and
literary establishment) of 1969. But it would have been noticed by SF-reading
women, who had been looking for challenges to assumptions about their sex
and finding a few inklings in the work of Miriam Allen de Ford, Marion
Zimmer Bradley, Andre Norton, and other women active earlier in the decade.

Feminist readers do not all embrace science fiction. Susanna Sturgis has
noted the reluctance of many women readers to pick up SF novels (104). They
assume that the mode itself is difficult, even hostile to their sex. They will read
Joanna Russ's essays but not her fiction, will praise Octavia Butler only for
her historical novel *Kindred* (1979), will treasure Karen Joy Fowler's *Sarah
Canary* (1991) but react with shock at the suggestion that it might be science
fiction. Carolyn Heilbrun confessed in 1984 that she hadn't been able to fin-
ish either *The Left Hand of Darkness* or Russ's *The Female Man* (Barr 47).

But other women readers did find Le Guin's fiction user-friendly (it
helped that she showed herself proficient in a number of modes, from picture
book to postmodern historical fable). Word of mouth, along with academic
accolades, helped make *The Left Hand* a break-out book. It is now found on
reading lists for courses in women's studies as well as science fiction—and it
is likely to be the book of which students will confide (with an air of giving
the teacher a great gift) that "I think I'll keep this one, rather than sell it back
to the bookstore."

So *The Left Hand* has become part of the feminist canon—although
within that canon, unfortunately, it is sometimes reduced to a few memorable
quotations about gender, with the more obviously science fictional elements
discreetly ignored. Along with attention, furthermore, has come controversy.
Two objections have been raised against the book: first, that it does not go
far enough in its depiction of androgyny; and, second, that androgyny itself
is, rather than a liberating vision, a betrayal of feminist aims.

As evidence for the former objection, critics cite Le Guin's use of masculine pronouns for the Gethenians, the dominance of the masculine narrator
over the entire text, and the preponderance of masculine traits for the sup-
posedly gender-free characters. The second major character, besides Genly Ai,
is the Gethenian Therem Harth rem ir Estraven. "He" is a politician, an aris-
tocrat, an intriguer; we see Estraven negotiating with diplomats and pulling a
sledge across a glacier but we don't see "him" cleaning house or tending to
"his" child.

Whereas many early male readers (including me) found the book pro-
foundly challenging to their notions of sexual difference and social organization, some women readers testify that they found it unconvincing. One article
gives it limited approval as "feminism for men" (Barrow and Barrow 83).

"Is it possible," asks another critic, "to make the leap from biology to metaphor when characterization suggests androgynes—discounting when they are 'males' and 'females' engaged in sex—are not men/women but merely men?" (Rhodes 117). Still another reader complains that "One does not see Estraven . . . in any role that we automatically perceive as 'female': and therefore, we tend to see him as a man" ("Is Gender" 15).

This last reader is Le Guin herself, acknowledging the failure of the text to remake the world as fully as it promised. Though she has resisted the temptation to alter the original text of the novel, Le Guin has reframed it in a number of ways. She revised the short story "Winter's King," her first fictional glimpse of the planet, to make all the pronouns referring to Gethenians feminine. She wrote the essay quoted above, "Is Gender Necessary" not once but twice: in 1976 acknowledging some of the problems but defending her linguistic choices, and then in 1987 republishing the same essay with interlinear comments critiquing her own defense. Her final comments from the 1987 version sum up both sides of the controversy:

> I now see it thus: Men were inclined to be satisfied with the book, which allowed them a safe trip into androgyny and back, from a conventionally male viewpoint. But many women wanted it to go further, to dare more, to explore androgyny from a woman's point of view as well as a man's. In fact, it does so, in that it was written by a woman. But this is admitted directly only in the chapter "The Question of Sex," the only voice of a woman in the book. I think women were justified in asking more courage of me and a more rigorous thinking-through of implications. (16)

Readers who wish to see how Le Guin might have conceived her androgynes differently can find a sample in a more recent visit to their world, "Coming of Age in Karhide" (1996), a story that, like the revised essay, doesn't rewrite so much as show what is missing between the lines of the earlier text. In this case, the missing information includes what it is like to become a sexually adult Gethenian, how domestic arrangements might work in an androgynous society, what Gethenian bodies look and feel like, how homosexual desire could fit into the rather rigid sexual arrangements of Gethenians, and generally, what the "woman" side of a "manwoman" might be.

But none of these reframings would satisfy those whose complaint is not that *The Left Hand* is insufficiently androgynous, but that androgyny as such is inimical to feminism. This argument, which is directed more often at Heilbrun and her followers than at Le Guin's novel, asserts that androgyny denies the primacy of bodily experience and defuses the political urgency felt by women as a social class (Elshtain 149, 154). To critics of the androgynous vision, the integration of masculine and feminine into a single self is another, sneakier way to eliminate the feminine:

> Revolutionary theories of the androgyne worked out by men—even when those men ally themselves with the feminist cause—time and

again have a vision of the first sort of androgyny, the masculine completed by the feminine, but not of the second, the feminine completed by the masculine. In fact, these theories in utter and almost laughable unconsciousness simply take for granted woman's inferiority; it is impossible for the female vessel to contain masculine intelligence and spirituality, while it is not only possible but natural for the masculine vessel to be filled and fulfilled by feminine emotion and physicality. (Gelpi 151–52)

The only good androgyne, in other words, is a male androgyne—a case which can be easily documented by glancing at Jung's writing on the topic. Furthermore, a careful reading of the language in which androgyny is described by Jung and others reveals that the blending of traits, rather than eliminating gender differentiation, has the effect of fixing those traits in position (Secor 166). How can you say you are mingling the masculine and the feminine unless you are sure you know what it is to be feminine or masculine?

A final complaint is that the term "androgyny" refers to nothing real. It's a myth, "a purely imaginative construct, unusually malleable because it corresponds to nothing we commonly observe in our experience." (Harris 173). This last objection, however, holds the key to rethinking androgyny and its value in setting up feminist thought experiments like Le Guin's. If androgyny is a "condition," as Heilbrun posited, then it can be something either to be aimed for or avoided. But how can one achieve a myth, or avoid one? It is only possible to be "Against Androgyny," as Jean Bethke Elshtain proclaims herself, if androgyny is a real thing in the first place. There's no sense in being "Against Unicorns."

Androgyny is not a condition. It is a sign. Francette Pateau calls it "the impossible referent" (63). Nothing in itself, it is only a place-marker standing for other things. At various times, in various hands, androgyny has stood for wholeness, narcissism, fashion, bisexuality, heterosexual marriage, liberation of women, decadence, the balance between yin and yang, and, yes, appropriation of women's prerogatives by men.

As a sign, moreover, androgyny can only be represented by other signs. Woolf's *Orlando* uses one character's transformation from male to female as a marker of androgyny. More common ways of indicating androgyny include unisex clothing and the adoption, by one sex, of behaviors associated with the other. I have been calling Le Guin's Gethenians androgynes, as do most commentators, but they are really something else: ambisexuals, a form of hermaphrodite. Their bodies are a combination of male and female. The text invites us to take this physical condition as shorthand for a complex psychological and social alteration that we term androgyny. The meaning slips from sign to sign without our noticing. But we should notice, for the real usefulness of the term is in that slippage. What can't be pinned down to a single meaning can be redirected indefinitely, can continue to challenge assumptions about meaning and identity.

Le Guin told us early on that androgyny on Gethen was not to be taken literally: "Yes," she said in the introduction to the 1976 edition of the novel, "it begins by announcing that it's set in the 'Ekumenical Year 1490–97' but surely you don't *believe* that?" (ix). Don't confuse the signifier with the signified, she is saying:

> Yes, indeed the people in it are androgynous, but that doesn't mean that I'm predicting that in a millennium or so we will all be androgynous, or announcing that I think we damned well ought to be androgynous. I'm merely observing, in the peculiar, devious, and though-experimental manner proper to science fiction, that if you look at us at certain odd times of day in certain weathers, we already are. (ix)

What Le Guin has done is to use the techniques of fiction to call up a set of images that stand for other images that stand for ideas that stand for other ideas. As Gertrude Stein might say, there is no there there. There is only the act of signifying, of making meaning, of encouraging us to look and think in new ways. The text *performs* androgyny, or invites the reader to perform it, and it is not the same performance for any two readers or even any two readings by the same observer.

What the sign means, then, depends on who says it and who hears it. Even within the novel, androgyny is not the same thing when uttered by Genly Ai as it is in the single chapter in the voice of the female observer Ong Tot Oppong—whose observations, brief as they are, provide most of the frequently quoted lines from the book, such as "They do not see one another as men or women. This is almost impossible for our imagination to accept. What is the first question we ask about a newborn baby?" (66). The male narrator Genly talks more, but the female speaks more forcefully.

Androgyny is thus not merely a signifier; it belongs to a special class of signifiers that linguists call shifters. Shifters are words like "I" and "you," "here" and "there," "then" and "now": words that have their meaning only in relation to the speaker, the listener, and their current condition. The word "I" means nothing except the act of acknowledging that "I" am speaking and being heard by "you." Now I fall silent and "I" becomes your act of responding. But they are not the same "I": each is imbued with a different voice, a different set of memories, a different degree of authority. An utterance like "I don't think you should do that" might be read as a veiled threat or a querulous complaint, depending on the listener's sense of the speaker's power—which is in turn related to the gender and the ideas about gender of both speaker and listener. Similarly, androgyny, which incorporates ideas about power and desire, becomes a different signifier when viewed from a position of greater or lesser control over either of those qualities.

Think of some of the ways in which androgyny can be signified, and how its meaning can change according to the identity of the person sending the message. One such vehicle is cross-dressing. Put a woman in a man's suit, and you have an image of androgyny that is exotic, alluring, a little naughty, but from a patriarchal perspective, safe. You have Marlene Dietrich, glamorous in a tuxedo. But put a man in a woman's dress, and you have— well, if rumor is to be believed, you have J. Edgar Hoover. You have an image that is comical, oversized, gross, embarrassing—the kind of cross-dressing that is the origin, in fact, of the word *travesty,* a cognate of *transvestite.* In movies and theater, men in drag often stand for decadence and indulgence, like the vast actor Divine in the early films of John Waters. Women in drag are trim and spunky heroines like Shakespeare's Rosalind. In each case, the sign is, or rather stands for, androgyny, but the significance is utterly altered.

The difference is not merely a difference in body shape and size. Masculine and feminine are not interchangeable counters in the game of gender: the polarity is also a hierarchy. To move from feminine to masculine is to move up the ladder of status and power. To shift from masculine to feminine is to lose both rank and purity, for femaleness is nearly always coded as something messier and darker and more dangerous, as well as weaker, than maleness. The unconscious masculine view of androgyny is an image of something taken away—and not just for Freudian reasons—while the feminine perspective sees Value Added.

In *The Left Hand of Darkness,* the male speaker Genly expresses some of the anxiety that accompanies the masculine viewpoint on androgyny, but what comes through more strongly in the text is a sense of utopian possibility. Even in a world as bleak as wintry Gethen, and a story as harrowing as Genly and Estraven's tale of exile, endurance, and sacrifice, the glimpse of androgynous life is still exhilarating. As Investigator Ong Tot Oppong says, consider a world without war, without rape, without dualism, where "anyone can turn his hand to anything" (65). Consider a world where "one is respected and judged only as a human being" (66). Though Ong says of the latter that "It is an appalling experience," (66) do we believe her? Could any woman from our world make that statement without being disingenuous?

So the sign androgyny in *The Left Hand,* though it is presented complexly, obliquely, and in textual fragments; though uttered by a writer who in 1969 was only beginning to learn "to write like a woman" (in Joanna Russ's phrase)—still that sign is essentially the feminine form of the shifting signifier. As expressed in the text, it stands for justice, harmony, and the marriage of opposing forces. But in order to demonstrate that the sign is indeed a shifter, and not merely that Le Guin is allied philosophically with Heilbrun, we need to examine the same sign as uttered by a male writer.

The Left Hand of Darkness is not the first major SF text to portray a society of androgynes. Theodore Sturgeon's 1960 novel *Venus Plus X* is more explicitly a utopian fiction than Le Guin's. It recounts the visit of a man from our time (i.e., 1960) to a futuristic society inhabited by the peaceable, graceful, sophisticated Ledom. Like Genly Ai, Charlie Johns, the visitor to utopia, expresses the reader's doubts and anxieties:

> Then, just as they approached a side wall, he saw something that so dum[b]founded him he barely noticed the experience of being flipped two hundred feet up like a squirted fruit-seed; he stood numb with astonishment, letting himself be pushed here, led there, while his whole sense of values somersaulted.
>
> Two of the men who strolled past him in the central court were pregnant. There was no mistaking it. (17)

Charlie's shock at what looks like male pregnancy is supposed to echo the reader's. Like Genly, Charlie is irrational and opinionated enough to serve as foil to the more reasonable utopians, while being just good-hearted enough to let the reader identify with his confusion. Charlie misses obvious clues, reacts defensively, imposes structures from his own society on that of the Ledom; nonetheless, by the end of his utopian tour, he is ready to "sign" on to their world. "I think you're the most remarkable thing ever to hit this old planet, you Ledom" (135), he says, finally ready to see the Ledom as what their name, spelled backward, implies they might be: a model for humanity of a new and improved sort.

Sturgeon does not try to work out all the practical details of his utopia in the way that, say, Edward Bellamy does. What we see of the lives of the Ledom is a bit of architecture, some handicrafts à la William Morris, a little group singing, troupes of happy children, a few high tech gadgets. The descriptions of the utopian world need not be more elaborate, because they function primarily by contrast. The adventures of Charlie among the Ledom make up only half the narrative: alternating chapters describe the lives of ordinary suburban Americans of the late fifties, lives that seem increasingly dystopian as the contrast sharpens.

The environment from which Charlie Johns has escaped is still being experienced by his counterpart Herb Raile, along with Raile's wife Jeanette, daughter Karen, and son Davy. Their way of life is one in which gender roles are being tacitly renegotiated. In a series of vignettes, Sturgeon shows Herb and Jeanette sometimes upholding traditional sexual divisions, sometimes unconsciously defying them, and, occasionally, voicing doubts about the way things have always been. Herb doesn't want to be like his neighbor Smitty, who tells crudely anti-woman jokes, challenges Herb to answer who's the boss in his house, and wonders how kids are going to know which parent is the father. On the other hand, Herb is reluctant to give up masculine prerogatives, and he does not have a clear sense of what sort of man he would rather be. He finds great satisfaction in being with his children and muses on how undervalued father love is in comparison with maternal care, but he unconsciously differentiates between his treatment of his daughter and son, to the latter's great distress. He is disturbed by the trend toward androgyny among pop stars but fails to note the degree to which advertising has altered his own taste in clothing and personal hygiene.

Herb's wife is not nearly so concerned about the changes. "I told you before," she says to Herb, "we're a new kind of people now. We're inventing a new kind of people that isn't all bollixed up with Daddy out drunk and Mommy with the iceman. We're going to bring out a whole fat crop of people who like what they have and don't spend their lives getting even with somebody" (66). Jeanette's only problem is figuring out how to interact with men on a nonsexual level, or in other words, thinking of herself as other than the object of desire for males:

> "Now how can you like a man without wanting him?" she demands of herself aloud.
>
> There is no answer. It is an article of faith with her. If you like a man, it has to be because you want him. Whoever heard of it any other way? (101)

The entire novel is structured like a set of questions and answers: the questions coming from Herb and Jeanette and the answers from the Ledom. Whoever heard of nonsexual friendship between people? The Ledom have. Who is the boss in your household? Whoever is better at it, both parents or either in turn. Who are the new kind of people? Androgynes.

But these are not necessarily comfortable answers. They have to do with giving up large chunks of one's self-image and with accepting a certain utopian blandness and conformity. Even while Herb moves toward vague inklings of the Ledom way of life, and Charlie toward overt approval, there are countercurrents in the book. In the present-day segments, the feminization of American men is represented through images of weakness and vanity. Herb washes dishes with special hand-softening detergent, Smitty wears a new line of silky bikini underwear, and both use cosmetic products thinly disguised by brand-names like "Old Buccaneer." In the meantime, the women are buying desert boots.

Though Herb, who has been reading Margaret Mead and Philip Wylie, has begun to recognize the many ways his society has always suppressed women, he is disturbed by what he sees as a reversal:

> did men make women inferior for the same reason they tried to dominate the outsider? Which is cause, which effect?
>
> And—isn't it just self-preservation? Wouldn't women dominate men if they had the chance?
>
> Aren't they trying it right now?
>
> Haven't they already done it, here on Begonia Drive? (115)

Somehow, a meditation on justice segues into masculine paranoia. When Charlie Johns learns the full story of the Ledom, his reaction is even more violently paranoid.

The Ledom, it turns out, are not a mutation, nor are they humanity's distant destiny. Their society exists just a little ways into the future, in a hidden valley, and their hermaphroditic bodies are created surgically from ordinary human infants. An appalled Charlie imagines the procedure: "knives and needles stitching a manmade and inhuman newness into the bodies of babes" (149). The revealing word here is *into:* it is an artificial uterus that is being grafted *into* the hypothetical male baby. If Charlie were visualizing girl babies, the graft would presumably be *onto.* Still more anxiety is unleashed when Charlie imagines sex among the Ledom, which he sees in terms "of man with grafted uterus coupling with man with grafted uterus" (148). Suddenly there is no feminine component to androgyny, only an operation producing weakened, desexed, and perverted males.

At this point we learn that Charlie Johns does not really exist. The individual we have called Charlie is really a "Control Natural," an unaltered male kept among the Ledom as a test subject. He has been temporarily imprinted with the memories of a real outsider male to see if the time has come for the Ledom to reveal themselves to the rest of humanity, who are by this time blowing themselves up in territorial wars. "Charlie's" reactions indicate that the time is not yet ripe, or, from another perspective, they reveal that human males are not fit citizens of utopia. The price for entering Eden is an operation that is clearly, in Charlie's mind, a form of castration.

So we have two similar SF thought experiments about gender, constructed by two writers with similar beliefs about the arbitrariness and injustice of traditional sex roles, that in the end generate radically different messages about the erasure of gender difference. In *The Left Hand of Darkness,* androgyny is additive, a change that eliminates a number of social evils and culminates in the joining of two characters, Genly Ai and Estraven, in a telepathic merging that is described in the book as closer than sexual union: "I felt his sleep as if it were my own: the empathic bond was there, and once more I bespoke him, sleepily, by his name—'Therem!' " (176). Though they don't consummate their relationship physically, Genly and Estraven have become lovers. Estraven even hears Genly's mindspeech in the voice of his own dead partner. This is a marriage—another traditional emblem of androgyny—in which two individuals, their differences intact, each androgynous enough to find common ground, are joined into a greater whole. This sort of marriage between unlike equals is a recurring theme in Le Guin's work (Barrow and Barrow 83), though expressed through many signs besides the androgyne.

By contrast, in *Venus Plus X,* androgyny is subtractive, despite the book's title. The Ledom are not Venus plus X—femaleness plus an unknown extra—but rather Mars minus Y. They are men without the marks of maleness. And the emotional charge of the book is anxiety, the anxiety raised by a choice between losing one's sexual identity and being expelled from Paradise. Charlie enters into no psychic marriage with one of the Ledom, though he does find a female counterpart, another Natural (a term suggesting mental deficiency as well as unaltered sexuality) who has been concealed by her Ledom parent. The two Naturals, thrown together by circumstance rather than meeting as true and equal lovers, will never receive the full benefit of androgyny. They will be allowed, as a sort of consolation prize, to live together at the fringes of Ledom society. This is marriage as compensation, rather than as androgynous fulfillment.

These two versions of the sign are so different that it would be useful to have different names to distinguish the masculine from the feminine utterances. Luckily, such a word already lurks in the unabridged dictionary. Take the components of *androgyny,* break them apart and reassemble them, and you have *gynandry,* which is defined by Webster's Third New International Dictionary as "hermaphroditism, intersexuality; specifically the condition of the pseudohermaphroditic female in which the external genitalia simulate those of the male." This is a definition that fits the mood of *Venus Plus X* to a T. It is obscure, vaguely medical, and doubly marked by falseness, being both pseudo and a simulation. Furthermore, the compound word already existed in Greek, and meant "of doubtful sex." By contrast, Webster's defines *androgyny* as "having the characteristics of both sexes, being at once male and female," a definition that expresses no doubts, ascribing to its combination of *andros* and *gyne,* man and woman, no taint of artificiality or medical abnormality. *Androgyny* is plenitude; *gynandry* anxiety. Yet both are the same sign, shifted between female speaker and male. Le Guin imagines androgynes, one might say, while Sturgeon depicts gynanders.

Does the pattern extend beyond these two novels? Are there other SF texts in which the writer's sex affects the meaning of the sign? This question gets a little tricky, since, as I said before, there is no direct way to represent androgyny: it is a sign that must be indicated by other signs, which may involve bodies, dress, thought, or behavior.

Even though both *Venus Plus X* and *The Left Hand of Darkness* portray androgyny through the physical hermaphroditism of their imagined races, even that physical condition differs. Le Guin describes Gethenian sexuality not primarily in terms of organs but of responses: a Gethenian in the active sexual phase of *kemmer* responds to her/his sexual partner by taking on whatever features complement those of the lover. Sturgeon, though, talks about anatomy: twin uteri on either side of a new sort of "intromittent organ," all characterized by "reorganization of the nervous plexi, at least two new sets of sphincter muscles, and an elaborate redistribution of such functions as those of Bartholie's and Cowper's glands" (69). We don't see Gethenian bodies nude (Gethen is a very cold place), but the existence of "kemmer houses" indicates that they are open about displaying their bodies to one another. The Ledom rarely bother to cover their genitals because they are already obscured by a convenient built-in G-string of silky hair. In the one case, the obviousness of Gethenian response makes genital display unnecessary; in the other, Ledom anatomy makes the genital region effectively a blank. The two novels give different meaning even to the natural indices of sexual difference.

The two patterns do indeed extend to SF works by other writers. The genital blankness hinted at by Sturgeon is made even more explicit in a short story by Samuel Delany called "Aye, and Gomorrah . . ." (1967). Delany's story focuses on a group of space explorers whose work requires that they be neutered at puberty: gonads would be damaged by the radiation of outer space. These spacers are, as one character says, "creatures not even androgynous" (381) but entirely sexless. Yet their lack of sexual characteristics can be another way of signaling androgyny, or rather gynandry. What is the gender of someone without sex? That depends, says the story, on what sort of desire they inspire in others. Let masculinity be defined as the ability to attract those who desire men. The spacer narrator is therefore masculine because "You look as though you may once have been a man," even though "You have nothing for me now," says the young gay man in Paris (377). The same narrator also signifies femininity but not feminine fulfillment:

Figure 5. "Are There Two Sexes, and If So, Which?" Artist Georgie L. Schnobrich takes an alien perspective on androgyny in an illustration from the reissued *Khatru Symposium* (1993), the famous and fascinating discussion of women in science fiction in which Joanna Russ and other women writers argue with James Tiptree, Jr., still (in the first, 1975, edition) believed to be a man.

She smiled and patted the sunburst that hung from my belt buckle. "Sorry. But you have nothing that . . . would be useful to me. It is too bad, for you look like you were once a woman, no? And I like women, too. . . ." (378)

This is a version of gender-blurring marked by absence, negation, frustration. Whereas the androgyne can potentially meet the desires of either a man or a woman, including, as Delany reminds us here, those of homosexual men and women, the gynandrous spacer can only find a mate among those whose fetish is for lack of response. The story calls these spacer-groupies *frelks*. For frelks, the spacers' lack of sexuality, combined with their ability to function in freefall—they defy both planetary and human attraction—makes them the ideal sexual focus. One frelk apologizes,

"You don't choose your perversions. *You* have no perversions at all. *You're* free of the whole business. I love you for that, spacer. My love starts with the fear of love. Isn't that beautiful?" (382)

It isn't clear precisely what frelks *do* with spacers, although this frelk mentions the spacers' "childish, violent substitutes for love" (382), so there is a hint of sadomasochism. At the end of the story, the spacers return to space, having exploited, or been exploited by, or failed to connect with, frelks. No one is satisfied; no one changed by a meeting with the complementary Other; no one seems particularly happy with his/her/its own identity, though no one makes a move to change that identity. The implication is that gender itself is problematic: even new gender identities and their corresponding desires will not lead to wholeness but to further fragmentation of society and the psyche. Frelks and spacers, the story implies, are no better and no worse than homosexuals, heterosexuals, females, or males: gender is an illusion cast by desire and desire is that which, by definition, cannot be fulfilled. Delany's version of gynandry, like Sturgeon's, offers a strong critique of gender without proposing a solution to its dilemmas.

In Alan Brennert's "The Third Sex" (1989), the story's narrator is of equally "doubtful sex" (in Webster's terms), having been born without primary sexual characteristics:

I reached down under my pajamas and touched the smooth, unbroken skin between my thighs, and dreamed of the day—Daddy never mentioned it but I knew it had to come—when my own penis or vagina would start to grow. But somehow it never did. (53)

Here again, gynandry is represented as absence and as unfulfilled desire. This narrator, Pat, periodically tries on different gender identities during adolescence, but both are masquerades, ultimately unsatisfying. Nor are sexual contacts with either boys or girls rewarding. Pat's first petting session ends with the partner's violent rejection:

He stopped and drew back, eyes wide with shock and disbelief. "What—" he started to say, and by then I knew I'd made a mistake, a bad one; but some part of me tried to pretend it would all be all right, and I reached out to him, imploring, "Please . . . Davy, please—" There was fear, now, in his eyes, but I didn't want to see it. (55)

Brennert makes it clear that Pat's condition is indeed a sign for gynandry—though the story uses the more familiar term *androgyny*. "It's called—androgyny, isn't it?" asks Pat. But at the same time, Brennert also indicates the shiftiness, the sign-ishness, of the sign. "I looked it up. But that's just something out of mythology, isn't it?" (57).

A doctor consulted by Pat offers to disambiguate the sign of Pat's gender: "Now, as to sex organs, we can make a surgical incision in your—please tell me if this is getting too clinical—in your groin; then place a sort of plastic sac just inside the skin, and fashion a vagina and clitoris out of skin taken from elsewhere on your body" (58). Though Pat is briefly tempted, the operation begins to seem "less like a deliverance than a . . . a mutilation" (60). Better no sex organs at all than a plastic sac.

Pat does eventually find a sort of sexual identity as a facilitator between male and female. Meeting up with the Davy of the earlier disastrous sexual experiment, Pat is drawn both to Davy and his wife Lyn, who are having trouble communicating and conceiving a child. Pat discovers an ability to translate Lyn's comments for Davy's comprehension and vice versa. When the three of them end up in bed together, Pat similarly mediates between the sexual needs of the others: ". . . men and women had had such difficulty understanding one another, seeing the other's side . . . as though something were—missing, somehow. A balance; a harmonizing element; the third side of a triangle" (70). Pat too achieves a sort of non-genital pleasure in their joint lovemaking. Unlike Delany's and Sturgeon's gynanders, Pat finds a happy ending. But the lingering tone of the story is still one of absence and anxiety. The problem is more convincing than the solution:

There *was* no purpose. There *was* no identity. I was neither man nor woman, yin nor yang; I was the line, the invisible, impossible-to-measure demarcation *between* yin and yang, as impossible to define as the smallest possible fraction, as elusive as the value of *pi*. I was neither, I was no one, I was nothing. (62)

By contrast, Marion Zimmer Bradley's *The World Wreckers* (1971) and *Darkover Landfall* (1972), which were probably written in response to Le Guin's novel, suggest androgyny as the potential end to isolation and to doubts about identity. Set within her already well-developed fictional world of Darkover, these novels introduce the idea of an alien race, the *chieri*, as the source of the Darkovans' psychic abilities.

Both novels, one set at the beginning of Darkover's history and the other centuries later at its near-apocalypse, center around relationships between human and *chieri*. The first meeting, in *Darkover Landfall,* plays out like an old ballad: one of the survivors of a crashed Terran vessel meets an elflike being in the forest and ends up pregnant. Her daughter, half human and half alien, is the first of a line of Darkovan telepaths. The *chieri* is first glimpsed by a Terran man and described, from his perspective, in feminine terms: "a fair face, long colorless hair waving around her eyes, a voice too sweet, too heartwrenchingly sweet to be human, and hair turned to silver by the sun slanting through the trees" (53). When a woman scientist meets the alien, though, she sees "the beautiful one, the beautiful one. I thought at first it was a woman, like a bird singing, and his eyes . . . his eyes . . ." (58). It isn't yet clear whether there is one alien or two—one of each sex, one *for* each sex, like incubus and succubus of legend.

Judy, the human lover, even speculates on which legend or ballad best fits her vision:

> Had it been something like this, then, those old Earth-legends of a wanderer lured away by the fairy-folk, the poet who had cried out in his enchantment:
>
>> I met a Lady in the wood,
>> A fairy's child
>> Her hair was long, her foot was light
>> And her eyes were wild. . . .
>
> Was it like that? Or was it—*And the Son of God looked on the daughters of men, and behold they were fair. . . .* (91–92)

Only later, and ambiguously, is it established that there is just one *chieri* and that its sex is indeterminate: "For an instant a calm beautiful face, neither male nor female, swam in his mind" (143).

In *The World Wreckers,* though, one of the *chieri* is examined scientifically (literally examined, by a physician), and the sexual meeting of human and ambisexual happens on stage, in close focus. In this case, the human mate is a man, and he does express some anxiety about being attracted to someone who is half male, but when they finally make love,

> There was no great strangeness and nothing repellant. At the front of the slit, retracted now like a small folded bud, the male organ, smaller now than a human baby's, although when David, telling himself that he must somehow come to terms with the male in Keral, touched it gently, Keral murmured softly with pleasure. Behind it, deepening in color and faintly swelling, was the female organ, and David, losing his detachment, trembled slightly as he felt the slow throb under his hand. (165–66)

The impression here is not of wrongness or lack, but of fullness and multiplicity. Along with the sexual contact comes a telepathic touch like that experienced by Estraven and Genly Ai. Furthermore, the *chieri* are revealed to be our progenitors, humanity's older and wiser self. Androgyny may be that toward which we are evolving.

Octavia Butler's Xenogenesis trilogy (1987–89) uses a slightly different sign to stand for androgyny. As in Brennert's story, it is a third sex that interacts with both male and female. Unlike Brennert's Pat, members of Butler's third sex, the ooloi, are the active partners in the relationship. Rather than simply transmitting messages between men and women, ooloi initiate contact and determine the genetic content of the sexual message, designing offspring from among the hereditary possibilities carried by its partners.

Whereas gynandrous beings like Pat lack visible signs of gender, the ooloi are over-endowed. They have two hearts, four arms, seven fingers on each hand, an internal reproductive organ called the "yashi," and wriggling sensory tentacles in various places. They do not have genitals but their sexual equipment includes both the womb-like yashi and the phallic sensory arms. They are attractive to members of both other sexes and can temporarily develop breasts and other secondary characteristics of either human sex.

Not products of mutation or surgical mutilation, the ooloi originate among an alien race, the Oankali, who are essentially genetic traders. They travel from world to world mating with the peoples they find, transforming those other races and being transformed by them. The ability to bring diverse species together both sexually and genetically rests among the ooloi, whose name is variously translated as " 'Treasured stranger.' 'Bridge.' 'Life trader.' 'Weaver.' 'Magnet' " (*Imago* 513). Each of these translations is a description of gender, variously naming the ooloi's features, functions, and desirability. There are male and female Oankali as well as ooloi; a full mating complement includes one of each of those three groups plus female and male humans (or whatever race the Oankali are currently courting). By the last volume of the series, the first human/Oankali hybrid ooloi have appeared, a development that marks a new level of maturity for humanity.

One effect of adding ooloi to the human sexual equation is to make females and males appear more alike than different, because both are treated the same way by the ooloi. The ooloi uses its sensory arms to enter both the male and female bodies. It receives from each the gametes out of which it constructs a new individual. It differs from men and women in being immensely powerful, able to kill with a touch but also to heal, and capable of stimulating (and receiving) unearthly pleasure. The partly human ooloi Jodahs describes its first adult sexual experience:

> I lay down and moved close against Tomàs so that all the sensory tentacles on his side of my body could reach him. Linking into him was such a sharp, sweet shock that for a moment, I could not see. When the shock had traveled through me, I became aware of Jesusa watching. I reached up and pulled her down with us. She gasped as the contact was completed. Then she groaned and twisted her body so that she could bring more of it into contact with me. Tomàs, not really awake yet, did the same, and we lay utterly submerged in one another. (620)

Like Bradley's *chieri,* the ooloi confer the gift of psychic as well as physical closeness to their sexual partners. The merging that takes place when an ooloi mates is not telepathic, but chemical—it reads the chemical traces of its mates' responses and speaks to them in the same language—but the effect is the same. The sexual partners also become soulmates.

Not everyone is eager to merge with the ooloi. Butler's male characters express considerable apprehension at the prospect of such physical and psychic closeness. One prospective male mate says to Jodahs, the ooloi, "I know what you do—your kind. You take men as though they were women!" (581). His take on the third sex expresses the gynandrous viewpoint, whereas the rest of the narrative emphasizes the androgynous. He sees the ooloi in terms of invasion, violence, loss of prestige, loss of integrity. The action of the story represents them in terms of plenitude, power, psychic merging, sexual satisfaction, evolutionary advancement. Though both signs, or both viewpoints on the shifting sign, are present, the author's identity as well as the story's resolution give more weight to androgyny than to gynandry. Still, novels are, as Mikhael Bakhtin pointed out, multiple-voiced texts. Different readers may perceive the interacting voices differently, some hearing the gynandrous message more clearly than the androgynous.

And what about the voice of androgynes themselves? Jodahs narrates the third volume of Butler's trilogy. Genly Ai and Ong Tot Oppong are not the only commentators in *The Left Hand of Darkness:* Estraven narrates some key scenes. In the latter case, a good Bakhtinian hears at least three voices at once. The framework of the book indicates that it is Genly who has chosen to present Estraven's narratives and is thus speaking through them, inhabiting them temporarily. And Genly is given voice only by being invented by the author herself. Which version of the shifter is present when a women speaks through a man speaking through an ambisexual Gethenian? Part of the power of the sign is its ability to make us ask that question.

If we could take the androgynous voice as something other than a stand-in for a man or a woman—as a genuine alternative social position and perspective—then that voice could offer a more significant challenge to the dualities that pervade cultures. But how can myth speak?

Recent stories have brought the shiftiness of the androgyne to the foreground as a way of investigating the nature of all such gender signifiers. In Kelley Eskridge's "And Salome Danced" (1994), the meaning hinges partly on our inability to pin down the gender of the speaker and thence the identity of characters as either androgynous or gynandrous.

Eskridge's story invokes many different ways of signifying sexual ambiguity, including those exploited by Oscar Wilde in the play that Eskridge's characters are performing and those envisioned by Aubrey Beardsley for his illustrations to Wilde's play. Eskridge introduces a character, Joe Sand, who first comes to audition to play John the Baptist. But Joe is a shifting Sand; he returns to the auditions the next day as Jo, to read for and win the part of

Salome. Like a Beardsley figure, Sand looks male one moment, female the next, and sinister in either guise.

The narrative does not equivocate about Sand's sexual chameleonism. Joe is clearly male; Jo just as definitely female; both are indubitably the same individual. But it is not clear whether this double gender is promise or threat, whether it stands for androgyny or gynandry, for the narrator who describes Joe/Jo to us is never clearly identified as man or woman. The director, Mars, is more attracted to Jo than to Joe; the reader can decide whether Mars is a heterosexual man or a lesbian. We also know that Mars is primarily attracted to neither of Sand's bodily shapes but to his or her ability to perform gender. It is Jo the actor, not Joe the potential sexual partner who intrigues and disturbs Mars. Jo is a director's dream, someone who can reach into Mars's mind, find the images there, and impersonate them on the stage. Jo exemplifies Judith Butler's description of gender as something enacted *upon* the body. For Butler, gender is not an identity but a performed sign; it is called into existence by the very acts that purport to express something already there (136). Jo's virtuosic performance of gender seems to Mars to be both consummation and consumption: how long, Mars wonders, will it take Jo "to eat me, bit by bit?" (161).

Jo/Joe's androgyny complements that of Mars, though Mars is not portrayed as anything but an ordinary human. Kelley Eskridge says of the story that

> I think that most readers will simply make assumptions about Mars' gender: I think it's what we do. But when I wrote the story, Mars became genderless for me in a way that was exhilarating: I wore Mars like a mask, and did not stop to look at my own reflection. Mars was free to behave in one of the ways that a human being might respond in such a situation, without consideration of biology or social behavior. Mars' identity, and all our identities, are much more about what we desire to become and what we fear ourselves to be, than about whether we behave like Tab A or Slot B. ("Identity" 182)

So which is Jo/Joe Sand: androgyne or gynander? Is Sand the fulfillment of desire or the threat of dissolution? Either or both, depending on how the reader chooses to inhabit the narrative voice of Mars.

Even two names are not enough to describe this shifting signifier. As Susan Suleiman says in the introduction to *The Female Body in Western Culture,* "Androgyny in a new key? Why not? Or better still, androgynandry, gynandrogyny" (quoted in Weil 144). This multiplicity is even more explicitly addressed in Raphael Carter's Tiptree-Award-winning story, "Congenital Agenesis of Gender Ideation, by K. N. Sirsi and Sandra Botkin" (1998).

Carter's story is disguised as a scientific paper. Its collaborative authorship already challenges the notion of a gendered speaker, for Botkin is female and Sirsi male. They speak as one, but refer to individual experiences that are shaped by gender, such as Sirsi's difficulties in dealing with the parents of the children he is investigating or Botkin's negotiating the social environment of the hospital where she works. Sirsi is a neurologist, a research scientist (albeit in a non-tenure-track position); Botkin is an occupational therapist, someone with considerably less clout in the world of medical research. Which position represents the degree of authority of the collective author of the piece?

What Botkin and Sirsi are investigating is a genetic quirk among certain families that results in individuals' inability to distinguish males from females. They try showing their subjects photographs of movie stars, with or without linguistic clues as to whether the picture shows an actor or actress: "On questions that provided no clue to the actor's gender, at least forty percent of the time they referred to Arnold Schwarzenegger as 'she' and Meryl Streep as 'he.' A control group achieved one hundred percent accuracy in this task." (98).

But further investigation reveals that the subjects are not gender-blind so much as overwhelmed by too many possibilities. A pair of twins with the condition turn out to be able to identify not two but twenty-two categories of people, representing several seemingly incommensurable features:

> Botkin numbered these categories and began to investigate what they might mean. Categories 9 and 21 proved to identify women born with clitoromegaly and men born with hypospadias, respectively, even though these are minor cosmetic conditions of the genitals with no known effect on clothed appearance. Category 6 comprised people with high scores on the Bem test of psychological androgyny. Again, it is not clear how this could be distinguished from a photograph, but the twins' identifications have proved to be repeatable. Number 18, whose exact biological meaning is unclear, includes a disproportionate number of people with a family history of osteoporosis; two women and one man in the category have since been diagnosed with bone loss themselves. Perhaps most strikingly, categories 4 and 9 identified men and women who took artificial sex hormones rather than producing them naturally, even when this was the result of hysterectomy or accidental castration rather than of genetic difference. (103)

This hodgepodge of features corresponds, Carter is saying, to what we already do with the category of gender. Sometimes gender corresponds to body type, sometimes to sexual behavior, sometimes to self-definition, sometimes to social role. Yet we group all these together as if they were the same thing. Sirsi and Botkin ponder whether their findings tell them something about the real world or about perception, or whether there is any way to tell the difference. "Our knowledge of the world," they suggest, "is filtered through an unreliable narrator whose biases deny us direct access to the truth" (106).

Yet they, unreliable narrators themselves, do suggest the possibility of glimpsing truth slantwise, by trying on different points of view and borrowing others' metaphors. Botkin confesses at the end of the story that she is beginning to be able to see what the twins see—and forgetting how to see what they do not:

> Most days I don't even think about the implications of what we've found. And then I'll meet someone, and I'll start thinking, "He's a twelve. I know he's a twelve. How do I know he's a man?" (106)

The story not only posits a broad range of gender possibilities, including several that traditionally fall under the heading of androgyny, but also questions the stability of the categories we use as standpoints from which to view gender. It is not just the putative authors of the scientific paper, but the story's author as well who is well positioned to issue such a challenge to "gender ideation." Raphael Carter's self-identified gender is neither feminine nor masculine. Carter's home page on the World Wide Web offers several witty commentaries on gender ambiguity, including "M. Manners' Guide to Excruciatingly Correct Behavior toward (and by) Androgynes: Or, Brother-sister Raphael Explains it All to You." Among other topics, this document takes up the question of what one calls a person of other than conventional gender (a question with which I have been wrestling throughout this chapter). Carter's suggestions: for pronouns, *zie* and *zir;* for nouns, *androgyne, epicene, gender outlaw, hermaphrodite, gender refusenik,* the extremely obscure *arenotelicon, transgendered person, intersexual,* and the only traditional term of Old English origin, *scrat* ("Angel's" 1–5). As in most cases of questionable terminology, M. Manners suggests simply asking what the person would like to be called: "M. Manners' own preference, incidentally, is 'whatever makes you feel comfortable.' Some friends refer to zir as 'he,' some as 'she,' and that's perfectly fine by zir."

So we might refer to Carter's version of the signifier—both in the story and in the group of texts on the home page—neither as *androgyny* nor as *gynandry* but as any other we choose from the list. I like the impudent and completely non-medical sound of *scrat* myself, so I will say that Carter's self-representation constitutes *scratdom.* Or would it be *scrathood? Scratdom* is the androgyne's view of zirself. Although I said above that androgyny is not a condition but a signifier, that statement itself might mean two different things, depending on the meaning of *signifier.* A *scrat* can be either that which stands for a signified or the one who constructs significance: the speaker, meaning-maker, performer of gender.

Carter describes zirself as inhabiting the space we have taken for imaginary in earlier texts. Zie speaks in a voice that shares registers with Butler's Jodahs and Sturgeon's Ledom and Le Guin's Estraven. Zie can talk about the androgyne as the norm, as simply "what I am." And one doesn't ordinarily see oneself as either dangerous or complementary, though Carter's rendering of gender issues is both a complement to earlier treatments and a threat to any sort of complacency.

A third alternative to any binary system disrupts its logic. "Either this or that" becomes "maybe or maybe not." In ordinary language, binary pairs easily slip into a relationship of positive and negative: one turns into the negative of the other. To be feminine is to lack whatever makes one masculine. But when more signs are added to the category, this on/off switching can no longer take place automatically. What does a male have that an androgyne does not? What if the binary choice is between single-sexed or double? Which is the plus, which the minus?

Texts that perform *scratdom* also transform earlier treatments of androgyny and gynandry. When the voice of the scrat is heard in the land, it becomes difficult to read *The Left Hand of Darkness* as a denial of difference, and easier to read it as Le Guin says she intended it to be read: as a thought experiment eliminating gender "to find out what was left. Whatever was left would be, presumably, simply human. It would define the area that is shared by men and women alike" ("Is Gender" 10). However, the sign of the androgyne says that humanity is an area shared by men and women, not alike, but differently.

The choice of words is less important than the sense that some word is needed. Stories like these suggest that we need more words for gender in order to understand even the genders we already have words for. Carter cites a study (an actual one) in which a chimpanzee was offered a choice of two unequal piles of candy and then given whichever he did *not* select. Though the chimp seemed to understand the game, he could not stop himself from selecting, and thereby forfeiting, the larger stack.

> When the experimenters taught the chimpanzee Arabic numerals, however, he could readily chose the smaller number to get the larger treat. Using numbers rather than real candy seemed to help the chimp overcome an instinctive response and use general cognition instead. Sirsi suggests that humans may prove "as smart as chimps"—we, too, may be able to use general cognition to overcome our innate ideas, if we cling fast to symbolic manipulation and quantification and try to ignore common sense. ("Congenital" 105)

Ignoring common sense is how most science progresses. The thought experiments of SF have given us new symbols to manipulate and new ways of manipulating them. It may not be possible, outside the realm of fiction, to overcome innate and cultural patterns that result in some of us getting the short stack, but it certainly seems worth trying.

The different forms of androgyny worked out by writers from Sturgeon to Carter are available for subsequent writers, who need not be bound even by the social and psychological dynamics that divide androgyny from gynandry. A male writer like John Varley, in his tales of a gender-switching future, can invoke the sign that implies wholeness and interpenetration along with that of loss and fear. Varley's "Options" (1979) describes a woman who chooses to become male for a time. She finds that experience turns her into "one whole person"—though her husband resents her experience and refuses to make a change himself (180). In *Steel Beach* (1992), the central character is a depressed loner, a tough guy modeled, as a number of allusions make clear, after the heroes of Robert A. Heinlein. Yet this tough guy was born Maria Cabrini (494), and the solution to his depression necessitates taking another try at femaleness and performing an exaggerated version of femininity peculiar to the revived nineteenth-century culture of an ersatz Texas "Disneyland."

Likewise, a female writer can contemplate the danger and absence that accompany the sign of the gynander even while invoking the sign of the androgyne, as Gwyneth Jones does in her story "Balinese Dancer" (1997). Jones's male viewpoint character Spence, a writer, observes the social breakdowns that follow discovery of a genetic shift away from sexual differentiation. His biologist wife Anna sees the same changes more positively, in terms of evolutionary development. The poignant tone of the "Spence" sections may reflect not only the character's fear of losing masculine prerogatives but also the high valuation of her own gender on the part of a contemporary women writer like Jones. Movement away from a feminine identity can now be seen as sacrificing distinctiveness, rather than as simply gaining power.

Like chromosome sequences on the genes that Jones writes about, signs like androgyny may occasionally jump locations, thereby generating new expressions of identity, new ways of seeing ourselves. And, as Anna protests, "this isn't like global warming or holes in the ozone layer. It's not a punishment, it's not an awful threat. Something is happening, that's all. It's just evolution" (297). The sign of androgyny is evolving, and with it, perhaps, something of human consciousness.

CHAPTER

"BUT AREN'T THOSE JUST . . . YOU KNOW, METAPHORS?"

The two-mile-long corpse of God is found floating in the Atlantic Ocean. Alien scam artists invade earth. These are the premises— Hollywood would call them high concepts—that launch two major fictional projects of the 1990s: James Morrow's Godhead Trilogy and Gwyneth Jones's Aleutian Trilogy. In each instance, the wildly inventive concept is only the entry into a series of encounters that dramatize issues central to both SF and postmodernism.

Both SF and postmodernism concern themselves with ways of knowing. SF has generally upheld the notion of a fully comprehensible universe, while postmodernism seems to deny the possibility of objective truth. The challenge for both scientists and SF writers is to find a way to incorporate the skepticism about scientific paradigms that followed Thomas Kuhn's *The Structure of Scientific Revolutions* (1962) without letting go of the search for scientific validity. Jones and Morrow might seem to be more closely allied with the postmodern school. Their characters strive and suffer, as if mustered into the armies of Jean Baudrillard, Jacques Lacan, and Michel Foucault, on behalf of sign systems, textualized identities, and the master narratives through which we interpret the world. Although both series call such epistemological habits into question, they retain SF's traditional respect for scientific methods and

Figure 6. The Word Made Flesh. Simon Ng's cover illustration for James Morrow's *Towing Jehovah.*

goals. One way they manage to hold this middle ground is by directing attention to the gender-marked body as a basis for knowledge and judgment.

Many commentators have noted the close relationship between SF and postmodern literature. The works of Thomas Pynchon, William Burroughs, and Russell Hoban are informed by SF tropes while writers like William Gibson, J. G. Ballard, and Philip K. Dick have emerged from the SF community to be embraced by critical fashion. The very theories that attempt to account for postmodern sensibility are couched in science fictional terms: Fredric Jameson's architectural *hyperspaces* (43–44), Brian McHale's narrative *zones* (45), Jean Baudrillard's *simulacra* (309), and Donna Haraway's *cyborgs* (149).

All these terms designate constructed or virtual realities; all imply that reality itself is an artifact of the ways we represent it. The great insight of cultural critics such as Jean-François Lyotard is that we acquire much of our understanding of the world in the form of stories passed on by culture. Such master narratives authorize society's institutions without having to be justified by experience (Bukatman 106–07). Some of these master narratives may be, in essence, fictions about science disguised as universal truths. Hence SF itself, as a mechanism for generating signs for things that do not exist, is a useful metaphor for the postmodern critic who wishes to prove such a-referentiality to be the condition of all signs. We can't know; there is nothing to know; our illusion of knowing is all there is—this is the position of the most extreme postmodern theorists.

With their reality slippages and affectless apocalypses, William S. Burroughs, J. G. Ballard, and Philip K. Dick might almost have written expressly to illustrate the theory—had they not preceded it. It is no wonder that these are among the "usual suspects" of postmodern SF criticism (at least its masculine division), discussed at length by Baudrillard, Jameson, Scott Bukatman, and contributors to the special issue of *Science-Fiction Studies* devoted to "Science Fiction and Postmodernism." Many of those contributors followed Baudrillard in using Ballard's novel *Crash* as a test case.

However, the interrogation of master narratives, including the scientific megatext, can lead to other places than Ballardian crash sites. Among many postmodernisms, some varieties attempt to mediate between blind faith in traditional epistemologies and absolute rejection of objectivity. This middle way usually involves acknowledging the shaping power of the spectator's perspective while still looking for ways to test observations and theories against an external reality. Writers working along these lines treat our lenses on the world—perception, language, and scientific methodology—as neither transparent nor opaque. They see the observer's cultural biases and physical limitations not as bars to knowledge but as determiners of its form. Hence they come closer to the spirit of contemporary science than do novelists who use *chaos* or *uncertainty* as if they meant emptiness and unknowability.

Both Gwyneth Jones and James Morrow dramatize the importance of perspective in their SF. In her Aleutian novels, for instance, Jones invokes the scientific spirit with a thought experiment about aliens whose physical similarity to human beings leads to chaotic mutual misunderstanding and thence to new discoveries. In his Godhead trilogy, Morrow writes about scientific spirituality: the physicist's quest for a grand unifying theory converges with the metaphysician's quest for a glimpse into the (implicitly embodied) mind of God. Both writers investigate the way understanding and communication are grounded in physical being—we learn the universe by mapping it onto our own bodies. The very language in which we communicate our discoveries is colored, as Evelyn Fox Keller and other have pointed out, by social relations such as gender difference. Hence, the universe we perceive and describe depends on who *we* are and what shapes our bodies may take.

In Morrow's *Towing Jehovah* (1994) and its sequels, the body in question is human, male, alarmingly solid, embarrassingly equipped. This particular body is divine: it is that which, in Western religious narrative, made not only humans but the universe in its own image. It is also dead. The death of the prototype leaves human beings and all of physical reality in the condition of Baudrillardian simulacra—imitations of nothing. Hence, characters throughout the three volumes are in search of some new source of measure and meaning to replace the one provided, in the Christian master narrative, by the bodily image of a divine father.

The divine corpse does not appear on stage at the beginning of the book. Instead, the archangel Raphael manifests himself to Captain Anthony Van Horne in an inverted annunciation. Raphael, like the other angels, is dying, his feathers falling out and his halo fading. "Our mutual Creator has passed away," says the angel to Van Horne, who is to usher the body out of the world. Van Horne is returned to command of the supertanker *Carpco Valparaíso* and commissioned by the Vatican to haul the body to a secret ice cavern in the Arctic.

Van Horne is a reasonable choice for the task, because he is already towing a supertanker-sized load of guilt. Under his watch, the *Valparaíso* was involved in an incident that resulted in a devastating oil spill. Though Van Horne did not cause the accident, and indeed could not have prevented it, he blames himself, and his guilty conscience is inflamed by his father. A famous sailor himself—"the handsome, dashing master of the *Amoco Caracas,* the *Exxon Fairbanks,* and a dozen other classic ships" (6)—the senior Van Horne is also an arrogant, womanizing, fiercely competitive father, impossible to please or to live up to. If Anthony has been able to bear up under that load of paternity, then he is up to the task of hauling another father-figure to His icy tomb.

An Ahab in search of redemption rather than revenge, Captain Van Horne regains his ship and acquires a crew that is a Melvillean microcosm of American society. Among the diverse crew members, two become major viewpoint characters sharing the narrative with Van Horn: the Vatican's representative Father Thomas Ockham and the rescued castaway Cassie Fowler.

Both are scientists. Fowler is a biologist who had been retracing her hero Charles Darwin's voyage when the *Beagle II* was shipwrecked (perhaps in a spiteful last Act of God). Rescued by the *Valparaíso,* she is appalled when she discovers what sort of voyage she has shipped onto: "this damn body is *exactly* what the patriarchy has been waiting for—evidence that the world was created by the male chauvinist bully of the Old Testament" (100). The existence of the divine corpse undercuts not only her secular viewpoint but also her feminism.

Ockham's beliefs are less disturbed by the discovery, though one would think the death of God would throw some kinks into the faith even of a proverbial Jesuit. Ockham is a physicist as well as a priest affiliated with the Society of Jesus and has made a successful career out of combining both pursuits. He is the author of such books as *Superstrings and Salvation* and *The Mechanics of Grace,* "his revolutionary reconciliation of post-Newtonian physics with the Eucharist" (22).

For Ockham, the *corpus dei* represents the ultimate truth he has been seeking, the answer to the questions of both science and faith. On getting his first glimpse, from footward, of the supine body of God, he comments that "it's rather poetic, seeing the toes first. The word has special meaning in my field. T-O-E: Theory of Everything" (80). Those toes, "a series of tall, rounded forms, all aspiring to heaven" (79), hold the secrets of the universe. Like Moses getting a peek at God's nether parts, Ockham looks to the toes for insights hitherto withheld. His desire for scientific knowledge is bound together with his need to comprehend God in human terms:

> "At the moment, we've got TOE equations that work on the submicroscopic level, but nothing that"—voice splintered—"handles gravity too. It's so horrible."
> "Not having a TOE?"
> "Not having a heavenly father" (80)

As a priest of science, Ockham is accustomed to mediating between divine mystery and the ordinary communicant—whom both the church and the scientific establishment refer to as a *layman*. His double calling places certain demands upon him, requiring, for instance, a denial of his own bodily desires in order better to serve "the Mystical Body of Christ" that is the church (21). This phrasing suggests a deferring, rather than a canceling, of desire, locating fulfillment beyond the end of life. How much greater the satisfactions of a mystical, universal body must be than those of a merely contingent and personal one.

However, this deferring of desire may also be analyzed as a way of seeming to deny the body while actually ensconcing it at the very center of faith. Christ's mystical body can be known only by reference to its humbler earthly type, the priest's own male form—which is why priests must traditionally be male. In Ockham's other calling, cosmology, the observer's material self is likewise displaced into symbolism. While physics does not talk about the Body of Christ, it does make use of a similar set of metaphors to transform the observer's material self and desires into a "body of knowledge" to which each researcher hopes to contribute.

Science is, in theory, less wedded to its symbol system than is the priesthood. Still, traditional ways of describing the universe and the observer's relation to it embed images of male sexuality. As noted in earlier chapters, this habit carries over from science to science fiction, where descriptions of the penetration of space and the seeding of worlds can become positively torrid. The more invisible the male body becomes within physics and religion, the more omnipresently it manifests itself in the language and culture of both endeavors.

Towing Jehovah's elaborate metaphoric system brings together the divine corpse, the paternal body that lurks in language, and the repressed desires of the male priest and theorist. In doing so, the novel only reinforces longstanding linkages within the cultures of both professions. Physics has always been a quasi-priestly calling, argues Margaret Wertheim in her book *Pythagoras's Trousers,* dealing as it does with "our conception of the universe, and of how we humans might function within it" (6). For this very reason, the field of physics has been, of all scientific endeavors, most resistant to incursion by women. It is, says Wertheim, "the Catholic Church of science" (9). Its inner circle consists of those who fit the priestly image—male but pure, that is, sexually noncompetitive and free of womanly taint. The pocket protector is the scientific equivalent of the clerical collar.

Ockham is authorized to seek out God's TOE by the fact that his own body corresponds feature by feature with the body of the deity. The angel Raphael explains to Van Horne:

> "Religion's become too abstract of late. God as spirit, light, love—forget
> that neo-Platonic twaddle. God's a Person, Anthony. He made you in
> His own image, Genesis 1:26. He has a nose, Genesis 8:20. Buttocks,
> Exodus 33:23. He gets excrement on His feet, Deuteronomy 23:14."
>
> Van Horne objects:
> "But aren't those just . . . ?"
> "What?"
> "You know. Metaphors."
> Raphel answers,
> "Everything's a metaphor." (12)

Everything, though, is not just any kind of metaphor. These are metaphors that impose the human body upon the universe. Like the demolished giant Ymir of Norse myth—whose skull becomes the sky, his blood the seas, his bones the rocks, and so on—the apotheosized male body is figuratively strewn across the cosmos.

It is easy to see how mythological narratives, whether Norse or Christian, might involve various sorts of figurative linkages between, say, one's own parents and the forces of creation, or the mystical center of the universe and one's navel. Less obviously, though, the language of science is likewise irreducibly metaphoric. In a series of individual studies and collaborations, linguist George Lakoff and philosopher Mark Johnson have made a compelling case for metaphor as the basis for all thought and communication, including scientific discourse—though metaphor, in their analysis, does not imply the arbitrariness that Lyotard ascribes to master narratives.

Johnson's *The Body in the Mind* offers, as an example, the many kinds of bodily experience implicated in an apparently abstract scientific term like *equilibrium*. This concept grows from humble beginnings, such as a toddler's first lurching steps. This initial balancing act is reinforced by other physical sensations: "There is too much acid in the stomach, the hands are too cold, the head is too hot, the bladder is distended, the sinuses are swollen, the mouth is dry." (75). Feeling ourselves to be "out of balance," we respond by adding warmth, emptying or replenishing fluids, and so on until equilibrium is restored. Such bodily experiences form the ground, the schema, upon which we build our understanding of other sorts of balance: visual symmetry, the principle of the fulcrum, ecological systems, psychological stability, mathematical equations, and the scales of justice (82–90). Somewhere inside the scientist who senses the existence of pattern with each of these systems is the memory of a baby struggling to stay upright.

Other linkages similarly emerge from experience to provide the "source domain" for whole families of metaphor, including the notions of force, flow, and even category—the idea of something fitting into a category is figuratively extended from images of containers and their contents (Johnson 39). Picking one of these schemata to describe a given phenomenon, a choice often governed more by cultural habit than logic, can affect the scientist's ability to make discoveries.

In the nineteenth century, for instance, the term *entropy* invoked a whole set of cultural attitudes regarding the maintenance of order within the British Empire. "To Kelvin and his fellow thermodynamicists," says N. Katherine Hayles, "entropy represented the tendency of the universe to run down, despite the best efforts of British rectitude to prevent it from doing so." (40). The loss of energy from a higher to a lower state suggested a similar leakage of dynamism within the British state as it poured itself into the more chaotic systems of the colonies. Only after the borders of Empire were breached did new metaphors suggest themselves, including the understanding of entropy as increase, rather than loss, of information.

Morrow's novels can be read as reenacting precisely this metaphoric shift. In *Towing Jehovah,* the death of God reverberates through society and the cosmos as both threaten to run down. Entropy as both physical fact and social symbol is figured forth in the bodies of God's emissaries, the angels, who seem to be falling to bits throughout the story. Having lost their progenitor and prototype, they drop feathers, fade, and finally fall into disorder and death: "the archangel's eyes liquefied, his hands melted, and his torso disintegrated like the Tower of Babel crumbling beneath God's withering breath." (360). Like the phallic tower of the Babylonian empire, the universe itself threatens to collapse without its masculine principles of order and uprightness. Only in Morrow's sequels, as characters begin to learn to live with uncertainty and social chaos, do pockets of organization begin to form around new, less rigid understandings of self and universe.

The metaphoric linkage described above, between universe and empire, suggests that both are being metaphorically mapped onto the individual body—a male body. Loss of energy, loss of heat, loss of firmness are the consequences of contact with women, according to the belief systems held by many men. Entropy not only threatens civil order but also the integrity of the male body. To overturn this view of entropy required not only a different choice of metaphor but also a reconfiguring of gender. Entropy's threat to masculine order and integrity might not seem so dangerous to a society figured as feminine.

Generally, we can ignore differences in the metaphorized bodies that pervade language. We can speak, especially in scientific contexts, as if these represented "the body" rather than individual bodies. Just because I am, say, six-foot-three and you are a hair under five feet does not mean our experiences of verticality are not translatable. You speak of the temperature rising; I comment that the stock market is up; we each translate the other's comment into our own frame of reference and are satisfied that we understand one another. Your experience of looking into other people's midsections and my familiarity with the tops of their heads may enter into our images of up and down, but we can treat the difference as nonsignificant.

However, one difference that is rarely insignificant is the difference between male and female, especially as that difference is caught up in various cultural systems. For example, male bodies have traditionally been equated with strength, integrity, and the spark of the divine, and female bodies with animal nature and original sin. It is not any old "the body" that feels threatened by femininity, any more than it is "the body" that emerges from pain with a newborn baby in its arms.

Though Lakoff and Johnson generally do speak as if the gender of the metaphorized body were irrelevant, Johnson, in his discussion of the concept of force, chooses a particularly gender-charged example. In a series of prison interviews, one man's testimony includes a number of comparisons all growing out of the metaphoric schema that Johnson calls "PHYSICAL APPEARANCE IS A PHYSICAL FORCE":

> . . . she's *giving off* very feminine, sexy *vibes.*
> . . . I'm supposed to stand there and *take it.*
> . . . the woman has *forced me* to turn off my feelings and *react* . . .
> . . . they have *power over* me just by their presence.
> Just the fact that they can come up to me, and just *melt me* . . . (7)

The metaphoric system serves as the basis for a sequence of inferences, leading ultimately, in this case, to a rationalization for rape. The rapist sees himself as simply restoring the balance of justice (8–9).

Thus, both *balance* and *force* can be invoked metaphorically to justify male violence against women. Can the use of either term, then, be completely gender-neutral, even in a discussion of the amount of rocket fuel needed to balance the force of gravity? Or is the pull of the earth likely to stir memories of maternal constraint or unrelieved desire, while the rocket becomes the escaping or ejaculating male?

All this load of uneasy, aggressive, overweening masculinity, which is usually allowed to imprint itself invisibly on language and thought, is given form and substance in Morrow's God. The floating corpse, accordingly, is the figure of a figure. It stands for metaphoric schemata that preside over physics as well as philosophy. The exploration of the corpse's nooks and crannies—the peaks of its nose and chin, the broad plain of its chest, the intricacies of its inner ear—these are investigations into the ur-form of both man and universe. In exploring God's body, Ockham and the others metaphorically venture out into the cosmos. Everything they find, though, is at the same time already familiar, for it is themselves figured large.

The metaphor does not, however, figure forth their feminine selves. The body projected across nature, culture, and psyche is, as Cassie Fowler bemoans, "the gender the universe fully endorsed. Womankind was a mere shadow of the prototype" (90). This lesson is hammered home with the first "truly unnerving sight" of God's genitals (115).

> Why would a mateless God need genitals, wonders Ockham, and answers his own question:
> Technically, of course His gonads made no sense; they might even be marshaled to dispute the corpse's authenticity. But such an objection, Thomas felt, smacked of hubris. If their Creator had once wanted (for whatever reasons) to reshape Himself in the image of His products, He'd have gone ahead and done so. "Let there be a penis," and there would be a penis. Indeed, the more Thomas thought about it, the more inevitable the appendage became. A God without a penis would be a *limited* God, a God to whom some possibility had been closed, hence not God at all. In a way it was rather noble of Him to have endorsed this most controversial of organs. Inevitably, Thomas thought of Paul's beautiful First Letter to the Corinthians: "And those members of the body which we think to be less honorable, upon these we bestow more abundant honor. . . ." (116)

The quotation from *Corinthians* is yet another metaphor turned back on itself, reliteralized, by Morrow. There is no name for this rhetorical figure, the metaphor driven relentlessly back toward concrete literality, but its effect is not so much to erase the figuration as to compound it: metaphor squared. As its use here indicates, the taboo is simply the other face (or some other part) of the sacred. We perceive the holy as well as the forbidden through reference to corporeal experiences, even—or especially—erotic experiences. Both aspects of the divine are given shape through metaphor: man-shape.

In the course of the novel, it becomes clear that there is no way to evade God's body, nor even to destroy it. Van Horne, Ockham, and even Fowler become reconciled to the idea that the only way to cope with the body is to take charge of it. They complete their quest in the face of a fully staged (in the theatrical as well as the military sense) air and sea attack. Furthermore, Ockham decides it is not enough to put God in cold storage, hiding the fact of his demise. The world should be informed, the body put on view, in order that humanity be forced out of its childhood, as Ockham believes God has intended all along.

This decision corresponds with Morrow's storytelling technique: forcing that which is implicit into plain sight, taking metaphor more literally even than Biblical literalists do. There is no way to get outside the metaphor, implies Morrow; one can only work one's way through it to some sense of a reality beyond. It is this literalizing technique that differentiates Morrow's novel from metafictional fables like Donald Barthelme's *The Dead Father,* J. G. Ballard's "The Drowned Giant," and Gabriel García Márquez's "The Handsomest Drowned Man in the World," all of which echo Morrow's central image (though Morrow mentions that he was not aware of any of them when he began writing the novel; Delany 138–39). As F. Brett Cox points out, it is Morrow's consistent working out of the material implications of the metaphor—his insistence on "the brute facticity of the corpse," to quote Cox quoting Morrow—that makes his work readable as science fiction as well as postmodern parable (Cox 20).

The next two novels of the trilogy project the results of making the world aware of God's death further into the future. In *Blameless in Abaddon* (1996), the body, now hooked up to life support and serving as central attraction in a fundamentalist Christian theme park, becomes the object of a courtroom battle that combines an exploration of the problem of evil with a debate over medical intervention in a case of probable brain-death. By the third volume, *The Eternal Footman* (1999), the body has disintegrated, but God's skull orbits the earth, a gigantic *memento mori* in the sky. In these two books, as the humor grows more mordant and the irony more wrenching, the emphasis shifts from epistemology to ethics and the relationship between art and faith.

The later novels, however, continue to explore the role of metaphor in thought and belief. They demonstrate how substantial an image can be, even while solid matter is revealed to be something less than real. As the archangel explains right at the beginning:

> "Bodies *are* immaterial, essentially. Any physicist will tell you as much."
> Groaning softly, Raphael aimed his left wing toward the Late Gothic Hall and took off, flying in the halting, stumbling manner of a damaged moth. As Anthony followed, he noticed that the angel was disintegrating. Feathers drifted through the air like the residue of a pillow fight.
> "Insubstantial stuff, matter," Raphael continued, hovering. "Quirky. Quarky. It's barely there. Ask Father Ockham." (*Towing Jehovah* 12)

Towing Jehovah suggests that the best way to comprehend the power of metaphor is to look directly at the male body writ large across the cosmos, to see how we use it to maintain the illusion that science's quirks and quarks constitute a substantial common-sense reality. We are stuck with God the Father's body, one way or another. Though we can transform its image through art, through reason, and through compassion, we cannot transcend it.

Rather than trying to transcend gendered perceptions, Gwyneth Jones, in *White Queen* (1991) and its sequels, proposes another tactic: to try looking through an alternative set of metaphoric lenses. Repositioning one's viewpoint even slightly might lead to new formulations of fundamental principles. Like Morrow, she investigates what Mark Johnson calls "the body in the mind." Unlike him, she explores the possibility that there might be other sorts of minds incorporating other shapes of bodies.

The two rival metaphoric schemata in Jones's novels might be expressed, in Lakoff and Johnson's notation, as "THE WORLD IS AN EXTENSION OF MYSELF" versus "DIFFERENT IS ALIEN." The former metaphoric system corresponds roughly to the one Morrow has investigated: we make sense of the universe by mapping it onto our own bodies. In the latter system, gender is the primary difference that serves as source domain. Taking off from bodily differences and the social distinctions that arise from them, Jones generates alternative ways of seeing self, other, communication, and universe. The Aleutians (as her aliens choose to call themselves) inhabit a different universe from ours because theirs is figured forth not only in terms of a different body shape but a different set of differences. There are masculine Aleutians and feminine ones, for instance, yet the distinction has nothing to do with reproduction or divergence from a divine prototype and everything to do with desire and the presentation of self. Whose body, then, is enthroned in Aleutian scientific paradigms?

Ironically, it is the Aleutians who see the universe in terms of sameness, while the "DIFFERENT IS ALIEN" paradigm governs the reactions of most of earth's natives. Humans see only the Aleutians' difference from themselves, while the aliens find nothing alien about us. Both perspectives lead to major misunderstandings and social disasters, but both are, at some level, truths about the nature of reality.

The landing of the Aleutians unsettles every aspect of human culture. Like an invasion of French theorists landing on the American shore, they call into question the most commonsense assumptions about both social relations and physical being. What is a parent and what is a child? Where does self end and other begin? What is desire? How do we distinguish between humans and their technological products? Conventional answers to these questions are thrown into doubt by the existence of the aliens.

Jones's novels evoke three aspects of postmodernism: first, the investigation of authority and meaning within the humanities; second, the paradigm shift within physics and mathematics; and, third, possible linkages between the first two. In the new physics, chaos is both deeply ordered and creative, and entropy can be viewed not as loss of integrity but as the accumulation of information (Hayles 10, 45). These shifts in perspective could not have occurred without prior cultural changes allowing new metaphor systems to come to prominence. The shift to nonlinear mathematics or chaos theory, Katherine Hayles suggests, is as fundamental as that which replaced angels with angles of force (170). It could not have taken place without a major reshuffling of basic concepts such as closure, predictability, and otherness.

Each of these concepts is metaphorically bound up with gender. Hayles offers, almost as an aside, an analysis of the biographical vignettes that James Gleick scatters throughout his book on chaos theory, pointing out that in all this richly textured detail, women never appear. The impression is that none of these men has a relationship with a woman which is important in his intellectual life; none works with a female collaborator who is an important contributor; and none spends much time with women. (173)

Despite the disappearance of women from Gleick's narrative, however, the feminine is not absent. Rather "[c]haotic unpredictability and nonlinear thinking . . . are just the aspects of life that have tended to be culturally encoded as feminine" (173).

Just as nineteenth-century scientists identified themselves with their subject matter, researchers in the new physics must imaginatively identify themselves with chaos in order to understand it. However, because chaos in Western thought has always "played the role of the other—the unrepresented, the unarticulated, the unformed, the unthought," identifying with it aligns the researcher with the feminine Other (Hayles 173). If chaos is feminine, then those who study it become feminized. To avert cultural sanctions against such symbolic cross-dressing, Gleick and the others incorporate the feminine as a set of abstractions while eliminating any actual female presence from their texts, leaving science "as monolithically masculine as ever" (174).

Reversing such a deeply ingrained cultural pattern as the association of chaos with the feminine requires more than simply reinserting women into narratives. One way to reshuffle the cards is to postulate a different set of gender differences, setting up contrasting identities that seem to correspond to, but are ultimately not congruent with, the ones we take for granted. Gwyneth Jones performs just such a transformation of gender symbolism, with the ultimate effect of displacing the masculine from its privileged position in epistemology.

Let's pretend, says the first of her Aleutian novels, that there are people who do not know sexual difference. Without sexual reproduction, they must have some other mechanism for reshuffling genes, so let's suppose that each one carries a multiplicity of genotypes, only one of which is expressed in the individual. It is as if all the recessive genes each of us carries made up a separate potential person to which one might give birth—only multiplied millions of times over. Each Aleutian individual resides, *in potentio,* within the genetic memory of every other, and might be reborn at any time, to any parent. So there are not only no males and females among the Aleutians, there are no family lines either, no patriarchal lines of kinship and inheritance. All are family. No one is Other. All are Self.

Jones goes even further to blur the boundaries between individual Aleutians. Using as a model the air-borne chemical signals called pheromones, she imagines an even broader channel of chemical communication. The Aleutians give off insect-sized lumps of themselves, capable of carrying information about complex emotional states and even specific memories. These "wanderers" fill the air and crawl over the skin; they can be emitted deliberately as a record of important events; they can be ingested and "read" by others; and they can even make their way back into the common gene pool to make permanent alterations in the blueprint of oneself stored there.

Furthermore, the people of "Aleutia" share this genetic link with the other life forms on their world. Indeed, many or all of these other organisms were made to order, generated from their own bodies to serve as food sources or tools. It is a world of commensals, an ecosystem that is truly, as etymology indicates, an *oikos,* a single big household.

All this is very strange, very alien, very Other. Yet everything the Aleutians do is familiar. They eat, sleep, defecate, make love, make war, make jokes, make discoveries, bargain, commit fraud, argue, and write poems. They even divide themselves into genders, according to temperamental patterns:

> Feminine people, according to the lore of Atha's kind, are the people who'd rather work through the night in the dark than call someone who can fix the light. The kind of people who chatter when they're exhausted and go to sleep when they're happy. The kind of people who can't live without being needed but refuse to need anything from anyone. Masculine people, on the other hand, can never leave well enough alone, break things by way of improving them, will do absolutely anything for a kiss and a kind word. . . . (123; ellipses in original)

For the Aleutians, gender is something between a parlor game and a cult, like astrology. What sign are you: feminine or masculine? One fascinating trace to follow throughout the three books is the use of personal pronouns among the aliens: *he*'s can unexpectedly morph into *she*'s, and Aleutians will, with arrogant assurance, assign gender to humans without regard to biological sex.

When Aleutians meet earthlings, they are constitutionally and culturally predisposed to see sameness. It is all they know: extensions of self. In contrast, people of earth are predisposed to see difference, because they have always seen themselves as either/or. "People will tell you duality was invented by a chap called René Descartes," comments one human character in *White Queen,* and continues:

> It's nonsense, we were always like it. We have our persistent fantasies that everything is one, man. But our experience has never borne that out, never. I look at you, you look at me. Something passes from my eyes to yours: Well, that can't happen, because the space between is 'empty.' No action at a distance. That's our predicament We are alone. Even when we speak or touch each other separation remains what we believe in, it's our default state. (181)

And so the people of earth expect alien visitors to be absolutely alien: mysterious, inexplicable, anything but folks like us. Ecological disasters and wars having set up conditions for a worldwide Cargo Cult, when strange beings from space announce themselves, most humans are ready to roll over and play dead for them. Because we habitually turn alternatives into hierarchies, the aliens must be either inferior or superior to ourselves, and the fact that they, and not we, have initiated contact indicates that they must be top dogs. They are the Conquistadors, we the Incas; they are the masculine to our feminine.

For the Aleutians, though, landing on earth is business as usual. They are not saviors or conquerors, or even really explorers—though they are perfectly willing to play whatever part they are assigned, so long as it gives them bargaining power. If the people of earth want to believe they are superbeings with a faster-than-light ship, they will concoct stories about such a ship, though they, like human scientists, know it to be an impossibility.

In reality, the Aleutians are a trading expedition that has gotten a little lost. They assume that the people of earth are basically funny-looking Aleutians, and they view the earth itself as an untidy version of the homeworld. One of the Aleutians notes this familiarity as he studies an earthly leaf:

> He laid his own hand next to the hand of a fallen leaf. Even to the stubby fifth leaflet the shape was an echo, an echo of home; an echo of self. To give and to receive the Self makes open palms. He shook hands with the fallen leaf, wondering what tiny faraway contact the local people felt. (19–20)

What a disappointment, he thinks (being a poet—none of the others are much bothered):

> I came to find the new, but there is nothing new. There is only the World-Self, perceiving itself. Any shelter out of which I look is that of my own body. Any leaf is my hand. I cannot escape; I can never leave home. (20)

A leaf is a hand; the self is the world—so metaphor allows the Aleutians to construct the universe in their own image. In this they are not so different from humans after all. They are enough like us to project an idealized version of the self on another individual, turning that one into the Beloved. This particular application of metaphor—the lover as twin, as soulmate, as second self—turns the meeting of Aleutian and human into tragicomedy when the poet falls in love with Johnny Guglioli, with repercussions that cascade through two cultures and three books.

For Johnny, a disgraced journalist, the aliens represent a great story, a scoop, a chance to redeem himself. His meeting with the poet is the first real contact between the races, and, like all subsequent interactions, is a mixture of misperceptions and surprisingly easy connections. Johnny sees the Aleutian poet Agnès sometimes as "the creature" and sometimes as "the alien girl" (56). The variation indicates his complex response to "her": fear, eagerness, disorientation, desire, alarm at his own apparent ability to speak telepathically with Agnès.

"How do you make me understand you?" he asks. "Have you learned my language or am I—uh—doing my own translation somehow?" Agnès is puzzled by his puzzlement: "This is my language. Surely Common Tongue is the same everywhere?" (58).

Each is writing the script of their conversations as he goes along, revising to fit unexpected responses, seeking familiar scenarios within which to place the encounter. For Johnny it is by turns the science fictional First Contact, the Exclusive Interview, the Mental Invasion by a Super Being. For the alien it is Initiating a Bargain, Trading Half-Truths, and ultimately, the Aleutian romantic ideal of Truechild Finding Trueparent, the meeting of two incarnations of the same person. Even though their scenarios fail to match up, there is no way to approach the other without a script. No unmediated perception can occur when perception itself is the medium that divides. As Agnès muses,

> The eye attached to the word-filled mind finds it extremely difficult to come to any image 'empty': simply to see. The farther a human artist strays from representation, the more literary a picture becomes, not less. Agnès did not struggle with the paradox. She called this a poem. (59)

Agnès, now calling himself Clavel, fills his own mind with love poems and sees those instead of the "real" Johnny. In Aleutian cultural terms, this is a perfectly appropriate way to carry on a relationship. If Johnny were an Aleutian, the "Johnny" imagined by Agnès/Clavel would grow out of shared genetic memories and would be continually corrected by chemical communion. If the individual departed greatly from the mental image, it would be as much Johnny's duty to shape himself to the image as Clavel's to readjust it.

The Aleutians believe themselves to be telepathic because of a combination of shared genes, chemical signals, close attention to body language, and lifetimes of common experience recorded and studied as part of Aleutian religion. These together constitute the Common Tongue mentioned by Clavel, a form of communication so effective that the majority of Aleutians do not speak in any other way. In Common Tongue, the body functions not as metaphor but as a continual presence. Only "signifiers"—poets like Clavel—bother with the disembodied "formal language."

Perhaps it is Clavel's "word-filled mind" that leads him astray in dealing with Johnny. The Johnny he is in love with is sign, not referent, not the complex and conflicted human being. The gap between referent and sign turns Clavel's lovemaking into an act of rape. Afterward, he is baffled by Johnny's rage and revulsion, which are tied into Johnny's sense of his own signification as *Johnny*, as *human being*, and especially as *man*. He asks Johnny's human lover Braemar Wilson, "Are you a woman? I thought I knew what that meant, so far as it matters. But the worst thing was I tried to *treat him like a woman*. What does that mean?" (211).

For Johnny and for Clavel, their soured Romeo-and-Juliet affair defines the entire contact between Aleutians and humans. The romance-conditioned reader, too, tends to focus on that part of the plot. But Jones draws back occasionally to show that contact between any pair of individuals is only part of a larger, more convoluted line of contact. As one of the characters observes, human society and Aleutian form "two almost identical surfaces, at first glance seamlessly meeting: at a closer look hopelessly just out of sync, in every tiny cog of detail" (313). Johnny and Clavel's meeting is just one such cog, one promontory on a coastline. All along that coastline, similar but different sorts of interactions are taking place.

This image of a coastline seen close up and from a distance is one of the important teaching tools of chaos theorists. From high in the air, a particular stretch of coast looks smooth, easy to measure. Nearby, it reveals a more elaborate design, which in turn is made up, on close inspection, of even more convoluted forms. The length of such a coastline approaches infinity. To measure it, one must choose a scale and gauge only what is apparent at that scale, ignoring finer divergences from the broad pattern. The result depends on the scale one selects. Though the obvious source domain for this metaphor is geography, a coastline is also a figure for the bounded Self, continually in danger of being invaded by an oceanic Other. Our skins are fractal.

Applying the analogy to Jones's storytelling, the tiny perturbations that mark Clavel's relationship with Johnny hardly appear on the map of general Aleutian/human interaction. Most people don't know who Johnny is. Clavel is not the Aleutian leader, the "poet-princess" that the humans take him for. Their misadventure makes scarcely a ripple in the larger story of Aleutian conquest. However, there is one more peculiar feature of chaotic systems with regard to scale: A tiny alteration can, under the right conditions, create completely disproportionate effects. This is the famous Butterfly Effect: within the system of chaotic interactions that produce weather, the flap of a butterfly's wings in one part of the globe might trigger a hurricane far away.

Just so, Johnny and Clavel's failed mating dance continues to ripple through both worlds, a tiny spot of turbulence that redefines the whole system. They are its strange attractors: the apparently insignificant points around which the whole figure revolves. There is no obvious reason why Johnny should find himself involved in the anti-Aleutian conspiracy called White Queen, why he and Braemar Wilson should be the ones to get the secret of instantaneous travel from an eccentric scientist named Peenemünd Buonarotti, why this act should thereby get Johnny killed in an attempt to destroy the Aleutian shipworld. How does Clavel's attempt to assuage his guilt by cloning Johnny in an Aleutian body lead, in *North Wind* (1994), to the rediscovery of that same Buonarotti device? When Clavel remakes himself into a human woman in *Phoenix Café* (1997), who would expect that Clavel/Catherine should be instrumental in making Buonarotti's invention accessible to humans as well as Aleutians. Why Johnny? Why Clavel? Why this butterfly and not that?

But perhaps their little flap is unique, after all. Other humans learn to control their use of Common Tongue, but only Johnny experiences it as the

Aleutians do, as a direct meeting of minds. Something passes between the two of them, however imperfectly, and each is transformed by the exchange. This transformation is the "fixed point" of symmetry that "allows coupling to take place between different levels" in a chaotic system (Hayles 156). It is the tiny ripple that pulls the whole system into a new state of equilibrium. Braemar Wilson notes,

> Everything that we are not they are, everything that we can't do they can. But the join is not completely sealed, a tiny trickle breathes through. Aleutia lives on the edge of our possibilities. (290)

Johnny and Clavel are not the same individual, as Clavel thinks. But there is symmetry between them, which Clavel's act of signification transforms into similarity. His metaphor remakes two worlds.

The Aleutian novels not only incorporate imagery from the science of chaos, but they also enact the sort of cultural reorganization that made possible the paradigm shifts of chaos theory. These books are informed throughout by postmodern notions about language, psychology, and history. Jones confesses that in her invention of the Aleutians' chemical communication, a "soup of shared presence," she was reinventing "the unconscious in the version proposed by Lacan, the unspoken plenum of experience that is implicit in all human discourse" ("Aliens in the Fourth Dimension," *Deconstructing* 118). Lacan and Derrida even make cameo appearances in *Phoenix Café* as two of "those structuralists, post-structuralists, semioticists of the pre-contact so forgotten now" but whose "influence on Buonarotti has never been properly realized" (196).

Science fiction, a form that relies on both human interest and scientific curiosity, is uniquely suited to helping us realize the influence of Lacan on Buonarotti, or more precisely, of culture and the imagined self (as represented by a major psychoanalytic structuralist) on scientific paradigms (as represented by the fictional physicist). Science fiction exists, as Jones says, on "the boundary area between our knowledge of the world out there, our science and its technologies, and the reports we have from the inner world of subjective experience: ideology, interpretation, metaphor, myth" ("Fools: The Neuroscience of Cyberspace," *Deconstructing* 76).

The genre does not always live up to its potential, though. Not all contemporary SF writers take advantage, as do Jones and Morrow, of postmodern methods of critique. All too often writers take a current paradigm for granted, using it as a backdrop to hang behind the conventionalized actions of their scientist heroes.

Taking a scientific model for granted is possible, though, only if one already has a place within the paradigm. Just as the scientist tends to identify with the object of study, the typical science fiction writer identifies with the scientists he is writing about, the clerics of the Church of Physics described by Margaret Wertheim. But Gwyneth Jones does not resemble those priestly scientists. It is a church that by tradition excludes her and those like her. In return, she feels free to cast a skeptical eye on the paradigm—to deconstruct the starships, as she says in the title of her collection of critical essays.

Finding herself omitted on account of her sex from the master narrative of science, Jones has looked for other silenced, excluded, Othered categories, including the native peoples of all the continents except Europe. Her Aleutians are composites of many such groups:

> I planned to give my alien conquerors the characteristics, all the supposed deficiencies, that Europeans came to see in their subject races in darkest Africa and the mystic East—'animal' nature, irrationality, intuition; mechanical incompetence, indifference to time, helpless aversion to theory and measurement: and I planned to have them win the territorial battle this time. ("Aliens" 110)

These are also, she points out, precisely the characteristics men ascribe to women. Accordingly,

> I often awarded my Aleutians quirks of taste and opinion belonging to one uniquely different middle-aged, middle-class, leftish Englishwoman. And I was entertained to find them hailed by US critics as 'the most convincingly *alien* beings to grace science fiction in years'. (111)

The strangeness of the Aleutians, then, is strange only by Western male standards. Their interconnectedness, their silence, their willingness to pretend to be what they are taken for—all these are part of what Jones sees as the condition of subjugated peoples of all sorts, including women. Even the peculiar physiology of the Aleutians can be seen as a metaphor for femaleness in a male-defined culture. I mentioned above, as an instance of the similarity between Aleutians and humans, the fact that they defecate. In fact, the Aleutians like to imagine that they don't—they have adjusted their diet to produce a minimal amount of insubstantial waste, which they then cope with by wearing disposable pads. "I made this up," says Jones, "because I liked the image of the alien arriving and saying *Quickly, take me somewhere I can buy some sanitary pads . . .* " (114).

A male writer (Morrow, perhaps) might be able to invent such an image. But it is highly unlikely, as unlikely as the prospect of a male writer describing a form of selfhood that is not contained within one's skin. Such a self cannot possibly be violated by penetration of the body the way Johnny Guglioli feels he has been violated. It is this sense of the boundaried and therefore violable self that must be overcome, within the story, before humans can use the Buonarotti device and travel freely through the cosmos. The imagined world must change before science can follow. Nothing new can be uttered until there is a language to say it in and a self capable of speaking it.

Like Morrow, Jones stops short of turning science into a language game. The Aleutians may describe the universe and the self in terms wildly unlike ours. They may assume that telepathy is possible, gender a joke, and permanent death merely a curious local legend. However, they subject their scientific accounts to the same verification we do. They have discovered the same universal speed limit that Einstein described (the Buonarotti device enables consciousness, not matter, to cross the cosmos faster than light).

Just because "everything is a metaphor" doesn't mean that one can choose any old metaphor one wishes. According to Jones, the "science" part of *science fiction* means

> that whatever phenomenon or speculation is treated in the fiction, there is a claim that it is going to be studied to some extent scientifically—that is objectively, rigorously; in a controlled environment. ("Introduction," *Deconstructing* 4)

Still, within those limitations, the science fiction writer can conduct any sort of thought experiment her borrowed, adapted, figurative, reliteralized language allows her to imagine. Morrow, in the third volume of his trilogy, has characters meeting their death-bringing doppelgangers. Only after his protagonists begin to adopt the perspective of the demonic Others, seeing the world from outside their own bodies, can they join in constructing a new, rationally spiritual (or spiritually rational) post-Jehovan world. Jones's experiment involves aliens who are not women but whose differentness—and sameness—can stand metaphorically for the differences between the genders. She imagines a meeting between aliens and humans that results in chaos, and then shows how that chaos transforms information into new patterns of meaning, including the liberating Buonarotti device.

Both Jones and Morrow play postmodern skepticism and gender-bound scientific paradigms against one another to generate fables about the emergence of new, self-critical, and self-revealing forms of knowledge. As those forms of knowledge emerge, according to both writers, they will result in futures—or at least fictions about the future—that are funny, disturbing, dangerous, fractally complex, and enriched by all the sorts of alienness that human beings can generate.

CHAPTER

WHO FARMS THE FUTURE?

Not everyone would agree that the examples studied in the previous chapter are at the forefront of contemporary science fiction. Some would argue about their importance or centrality; others might object that Gwyneth Jones's work is too oblique and too feminist, or take issue with the claim that James Morrow's work is SF at all. And neither series caters to the traditional audience of young male technophiles—there isn't a Very Large Hard Object in any of the six volumes.

There have always been debates among fans about generic boundaries and touchstones. Those debates grow more urgent as SF emerges from its subcultural ghetto to permeate popular culture, the academy, and everyday language. SF is taking over the world, but there is little consensus on which version of SF that might be. There are so many options: hard and soft, eco-feminist and libertarian-militaristic, North American and Everywhere Elsian, SF on the page and SF on screen. Some outgrowths of the genre have so little in common that they hardly seem to constitute a single category. Yet if they share few features, all the myriad manifestations of SF may still be analyzed as products of a single process. All result from negotiated exchanges between different segments of culture. And in all cases, the negotiation aims at establishing one particular version of the future as the most probable or desirable. Furthermore, in the instances where this process of negotiation is most visible, the primary factions are defined by gender.

Archer's Goon, a witty and intricate fantasy by Diana Wynne Jones, can be read as a parable about the contemporary condition of science fiction. It explains why members of the SF community feel they must compete for the right to be represented in SF and strive for the privilege of choosing fictional formulas for representing scientific and social change. The competition grows fiercer as SF's images and ideas begin to emerge in contexts ranging from ads on television to texts studied in a college classroom.

In Jones's book, the main character, a boy named Howard, discovers that his world is under the management of a shadowy set of superbeings. A modern-day pantheon, they have carved off territories to govern, but instead of sea and sky, war and wisdom, these seven siblings have assigned themselves such fiefdoms as crime, the arts, the power grid, and even the sewer system. Each is said to "farm" that aspect of society, directing activities and skimming off the profits. One of the more unlikely domains is the future, farmed by the youngest brother, Venturus.

What does it mean to farm the future? How can one control what has not yet happened? Where is the profit in future events? As Jones describes his operations, Venturus's territory includes the construction industry (reaping profits on buildings that do not yet exist), schools (manufacturing citizens of the future) and, dearest to Venturus's heart, space exploration. Venturus's headquarters, located in an as-yet-unfinished monument, house an army of robots constructing a gleaming ship to extend Venturus's realm to infinity.

Who farms our future? Jones's parable invites us to look for forces at work today to shape and to profit from things that have not yet come about. Who are our futures traders, and what kind of commodities do they deal in?

The easiest place to see the future being bought and sold is Hollywood. Movies about alien invasions, time travellers, and space fleets form a significant and profitable part of the film industry, especially with the advent of computer-generated imagery to replace clunkier and more expensive special effects. On television, the newer networks are particularly amenable to science fictional concepts, though they do not always know how to develop or market those concepts. And older series never die; they just go into syndication or end up on cable's Sci-Fi Channel. These futuristic film and television productions spin off other commodities: video games, action figures, comic books, novelizations, costumes, board games, and even movies *about* SF culture—metamedia—such as *Trekkies* (1997), *Free Enterprise* (1998), and *Galaxy Quest* (1999). The future is already for sale, and the potential profits are enormous.

But longtime fans of written SF are not eager to pay allegiance to the Venturus who governs video games. It is useful to be able to distinguish the popularized and mediated version of the future from the more complex, ambitious, and ambiguous visions of writers like Joe Haldeman or Ursula K.

Le Guin, and rival acronyms adopted by fans and the media provide just such a distinction. Written science fiction is SF, a coinage that has been used to stand not only for science fiction but also for speculative fiction and even structural fabulation (Wolfe 117). Sci-fi, which SF fans often pronounce "skiffy," is what comes out of Hollywood: both the popular entertainments and the non-SF-reading public's impression of what the field is all about (Wolfe 114–15).

Most people think not of SF but of sci-fi when they describe aspects of contemporary life as science fictional: cloning, the internet, gene therapy, surveillance technology, weapons like "smart" bombs, designer drugs, and ecological shifts such as global warming. Movies and books disagree on what sort of *story* this futuristic hardware throws us into: are we evolving toward utopia, falling into a Cold War-era cataclysm, savoring the self-reflexive ironies of a postmodernist fable, or acting out one of Hollywood's high-tech shoot-em-ups? If the future is already here, the selection of a scenario becomes more than a choice among amusements. As people become accustomed to seeing themselves as living in the future, more and more products are pitched in terms of futurity. Politicians must present their policies as representing, not current needs, but coming trends. To be merely up to date is to be outdated.

Most of the futuristic images and metaphors that circulate through popular media were originally developed by writers of SF novels and short stories, rather than by Hollywood screenwriters or hucksters. The relationship between printed SF and the sci-fi of film or television or political rhetoric is a complex negotiation whereby certain images are rejected while others are simplified, intensified, and redirected. The information about orbits, antibodies, or relativistic effects that is an important feature of much SF devolves in sci-fi into mere technobabble. The scientific explorer hero of SF is turned into a foil for the cinematic action hero. He is the guy in glasses who says, "Don't shoot; this is a unique scientific opportunity," just before the alien eats him.

These are problematic trade-offs for the SF fan, especially the redefinition of the masculine image, but they are part of the contract by which producers and directors agree to put on screen a few plot components and some measure of SF atmosphere. SF gives up control over its inventions; in return it gets to see them circulated beyond the confines of the relatively tiny community of serious readers.

The process is similar to the kinds of exchanges within Elizabethan society analyzed by Stephen Greenblatt. Greenblatt identifies the Elizabethan stage as an arena in which society's central issues found expression. Not only was the theater the chief form of public entertainment for Londoners, where social classes mingled and contemporary fashions were paraded, but playwrights and actors also had the power to invoke England's most intense political, religious, and sexual conflicts and thereby transfer some of that intensity and "social energy" to their staged entertainments (Greenblatt 6). Theatrical companies could do so partly because each area of conflict was already being enacted dramatically. Elizabeth, for instance, conducted her royal court as a traveling pageant or masque (136). The rivalry between Protestant and Catholic was played out through ritualized dramas such as exorcism, condemned by Protestant clergyman Samuel Harsnett as a dialogue between devils (98). The privileges of manhood and the obligations of women were tested by cases of sexual masquerade (92–93). Shakespeare was able to transfer these actions to the stage, then, because what he appropriated was already a form of drama. "When Shakespeare borrows from Harsnett, who knows if Harsnett has not already, in a deep sense, borrowed from Shakespeare's theater what Shakespeare borrows back?" (95).

Similarly, when movies, television, advertising, and political rhetoric borrow SF's images and ideas about the future, they are borrowing what has already been conceived of in terms of sci-fi. The future that makes its way into the movies is, with few exceptions, the future we have already seen in the movies.

Yet the same is true of SF, for scientific ideas are transformed into narrative components through a similar process of negotiation. SF too is most willing to "buy" what it already owns: those concepts that have already established themselves as reliable motivators of character, setting, and plot. In the 1940s, story after story retraced a sequence of atomic devastation followed by mutation of human beings into monsters and supermen. Before Henry Kuttner and A. E. Van Vogt led the way, however, the prospect of nuclear holocaust was not a particularly appealing plotline. Only when it became part of a story of rebirth, transformation, and masculine triumph could the threat of atomic war be assimilated within SF's adventure-romance mode. The story line tamed the idea just enough to harness its energy.

Forty years later, the most popular match-up of idea with narrative structure involved immersion into a computer-simulated environment. The cyberpunk movement could happen, however, only after Vernor Vinge, in *True Names* (1981), and William Gibson, in "Johnny Mnemonic" (1981), demonstrated that a dull gray box full tiny switches could be transformed into a kaleidoscopic backdrop for adventure. Furthermore, the cybernetic universe is depicted as a feminine "matrix," lending a strongly sexual charge to the act of "jacking in" (Nixon 226–27). No wonder not only writers and film makers but also engineers and software designers continue to draw on the social energy generated in Gibson's stories.

Not every scientific idea captures the imagination of SF readers and writers. Some branches of science generate whole subgenres, while others are represented spottily if at all. The humanoid robot, an invention for which the engineering and the necessity may never arrive, has been an SF staple for decades, whereas the genuinely weird adaptive mechanisms of plants show up in a bare handful of stories. Pseudosciences like psionics produce far more fiction than authentic enterprises such as plate tectonics. The scientific ideas most likely to cross over into SF are those that offer connections to issues that matter to people: issues of identity, power, desire, and social change. Anyone wishing to guide the future must offer power and fulfillment in exchange— or seem to.

In the most effective SF, the disorienting element that Darko Suvin calls a novum, which can be anything from a new invention to an alien invasion, corresponds to something already inherent in the characters: a buried fear, an unforeseen capability, a potential reshuffling of basic beliefs. In confronting the novum, characters are forced to rewrite their own stories, not only their individual life histories but also the historical, religious, and scientific trajectories— the masterplots—within which they make sense of their lives. The SF writer, then, is not simply a popularizer of scientific ideas, but someone who links those ideas to cultural narratives.

In the bargain between science and SF, the stock-in-trade on one side is new discoveries, new theories, new systems of thought. The other side offers a place for those ideas within stories of heroic exploration, tragic overreaching, social evolution, moral regeneration, or erotic fulfillment. Both sides gain when the resulting narrative catches hold of the reader's imagination. The social energy Greenblatt talks about is generated not by ideas alone or by the story lines but by their fusion. Embodied within a story, a concept such as virtual reality takes on emotional weight, social status, and intentionality— we learn not only what it is, but where it is going, pulling ourselves along with it. It becomes part of our story, and we become part of its. As Pat Cadigan suggests in her cyberpunk classic *Synners,* we have been conditioned by SF to believe that we must either "change for the machines" or get left out of the future (97).

What SF fans worry is that as the future is traded away to Hollywood, they and their concerns will be ignored or changed beyond recognition. Having long thought of themselves as Venturus's acolytes and initiates, they are disturbed to find themselves standing outside the temple. The SF community has lamented for decades Hollywood's inability to produce real science fiction, with legitimate science, consistent plots, intelligent characters, and serious themes. When scientists become monster-fodder, where does the serious reader find herself on screen? Hollywood's version of Venturus, ruler of the future, tends to look like Arnold Schwarzenegger. Anyone who is not so white, male, straight, and muscular gets pushed to the side, or off screen entirely.

That absence would not matter if sci-fi weren't so persuasive. At their best, movies create moments of breathtaking vision, like the opening panorama of *Blade Runner* (1982); gestures of emotional intensity and moral weight, such as the dismantling of the intelligent computer Hal in *2001: A Space Odyssey* (1968); vista-opening technological images from the goofy robot of *Forbidden Planet* (1956) to the wall-walking of *The Matrix* (1999); and heroes of integrity and strength, such as Sigourney Weaver's Ripley in *Aliens* (1986). These are the things movie-makers are proficient at; these are the goods that Hollywood is willing to buy back from writers. Occasionally, as part of the package, an idea or two slips in and, if it finds compelling visual analogues, becomes currency for later exchanges.

Because of its dependence on recycling its own products, Hollywood's future is often retro, sometimes self-consciously so, as in the *Star Wars* series. SF fans note that sci-fi in the movies is typically thirty years behind printed SF, which means that the movies should start discovering gender exploration any time now. But some fans, especially those whose gender or sexuality leaves them perennially at the edge of the movie screen, are not content to wait for the Hollywood mills to turn. They wish to enter into the negotiations themselves. One major sci-fi outlet, the Star Trek empire, consisting at last count of five live-action and one animated TV series plus several feature films and spin-offs in other media, has both raised and disappointed hopes that it will someday soon go where no sci-fi has gone before.

Star Trek fandom represents a highly visible effort on the part of sci-fi consumers to become Diana Wynne Jones's Venturus: to play a part in farming the future. The original *Star Trek* series (1966–69) encouraged broader fan involvement in several ways. For instance, its creator, Gene Roddenberry, chose to cast an African-American actress, Nichelle Nicholls, in the role of Uhura, the communications officer. Though Uhura played little part in most plots, still she was present on the bridge of the starship Enterprise as a black, female character of dignified intelligence and professional competence—a rare image in any medium in the mid-1960s.

Such casting was to become a regular feature of later series, with actors of various races moving into more substantial roles and women following slightly behind. By the time the studio spun off *Star Trek: Deep Space Nine* (1993–99), with its black commander, and *Star Trek: Voyager* (1995–2001), helmed by a female captain, the innovations were hardly noticeable, though neither of these characters could have been cast as leads in earlier versions of the Star Trek universe. A subtler breakthrough was achieved when black, Asian, and Latino actors began to play aliens. It is one thing to make the crew of an earth vessel multi-ethnic, but it takes a more profound rethinking of race to give other worlds racial differences and especially to imply that earthly hierarchies are irrelevant to those alien civilizations. The presence of strong female and non-white characters brought to Star Trek a female following that had not previously paid much attention to SF (Bainbridge 177).

Roddenberry made another important decision in his first *Star Trek* series: to commission scripts from established SF writers like Harlan Ellison and Theodore Sturgeon and, even more daringly, to produce scripts sent in by unknown fans David Gerrold (who went on to write successful SF) and Jeri Taylor (who eventually became one of Star Trek's producers). The resulting episodes were among the most successful (and least predictable) of the series, and the invitation had thereby been offered to fans to take control of their own futures.

That invitation was taken up in ways undreamed by Roddenberry or Paramount Studios. An entire subculture of fans formed around the idea of writing fiction within the framework of the series. In the early days, the fiction was mimeographed and distributed by mail and at fan gatherings. Later, the Internet provided a venue both for publishing and for critiquing the efforts of non-professional writers. Though the series stopped using unsolicited screenplays, some of the fan fiction found its way into the series of novels published as an adjunct to the show (Penley 144).

Perhaps the most original form of Star Trek fan fiction, and certainly the most notorious, is what was originally termed K/S, the initials joined by a slash signifying the idea of a romantic link between the two male characters Kirk and Spock. (Other slash phenomena, such as the S/H fiction written by fans of the action series *Starsky and Hutch,* seem to have followed the lead of the Star Trek slashers.) K/S fiction has been documented and analyzed by a number of scholars, including Henry Jenkins III, Constance Penley, and Camille Bacon-Smith, who see in slashing a counter-argument to theories of mass culture in which audiences are portrayed as Venturus's slaves: that is, as completely passive consumers of corporate ideology. These fans freely invent new races, bring back characters killed off on television, write and illustrate pornographic scenes between characters, and even produce video montages that reinterpret scenes from the series in terms of passionate longing. All of this textual poaching, as Jenkins calls it, must give the Paramount executives pause, but as it seems to increase the visibility of and profits from what is commonly called "the Franchise," they have not had their legal team clamp down on such fan activities.

But there is a difference between writing fantasy scenarios in which familiar TV characters are recast as gay lovers and actually seeing nonstandard sexuality acknowledged on the screen. The original slash community was made up largely of heterosexual women, who, according to Penley, found in the imaginary relationship between human and alien males a metaphoric portrayal of the kind of partnership between equals they would like to find in their own lives (156). Other groups, however, have since begun to emulate the example of these early slashers, including gay women and men. These fans are not necessarily looking to Star Trek to provide them with models for heterosexual marriage, but rather to validate their existence as a continuing component of humanity. They want to be told that gays won't go away, won't be legislated or engineered out of existence between now and the 24th century.

The demand for gay Star Trek characters has taken several forms, such as petitions, demonstrations at fan conventions, and "An Open Letter to the Producers of Voyager" that appeared on a "gay trek" website during the early run of that series. The letter refers to a promise said to have been made by Roddenberry to include gay characters in the next Star Trek series (Perkins 1). This promise would seem to be consistent with Roddenberry's liberal vision, best expressed in a religious slogan of his invented race, the Vulcans. They believe in "IDIC," or Infinite Diversity in Infinite Combination. After Roddenberry's death in 1991, however, Paramount and the producers evidently decided that some of those combinations were a little too diverse for television. No overtly gay characters appeared.

The writer of the "Open Letter" points out that this failure of nerve means something different from the inability of other television series to depict nonstereotypical homosexual characters. The absence of such characters in a futuristic drama gives ammunition to "the small-minded bigots we encounter on-line who say that the reason gays and lesbians aren't portrayed on Star Trek is that we have all died of AIDS or that science has found a 'cure' for our 'condition' and eliminated it" (Perkins 5). If those who farm the future decide that gay people aren't a viable crop, then that means they are already obsolete and therefore irrelevant.

So, in addition to writing letters, gay fans have attempted to remain part of the future's Infinite Diversity by inventing whole new series of their own. The resources of the World Wide Web allow for the development of fan sites for popular (and some not-so-popular) TV shows. One such fan site concerns a series called *Star Trek: Pioneers,* depicting the crew and mission of the *U.S.S. Mandela,* "a combined science vessel and university" (Gustavsson 2).

The *Mandela's* crew, like other ships of Star Trek's Federation of Planets, is a mix of humans and humanoid aliens with different sorts of expertise and various telegenic personality quirks. The fan site has mini-biographies of all the main characters, complete with photos in Star Fleet uniform. The ship's science officer, Deane Min Troie, is a man from Betazed, whose inhabitants, we know from earlier series, are empathic and rather open about sexual arrangements. Troie and the Terran chief engineer, Brian McDonald, are lovers.

This site is so convincingly similar to other fan sites, so circumstantial in its detailing of the show's characters, mission, and plots, that it is hard to remember that no such series exists. In some sense *Pioneers* is no less real than an authentic but obscure show like 1967's *Captain Scarlet and the Mysterons* (yes, it has its fan websites). The technology of the Web allows anyone with enough time and expertise to create a simulacrum of a TV series, and the difference between simulacrum and prototype grows more trivial as the technology advances. In this version of cultural negotiation, the fan offers up as already achieved something the studio has been reluctant to attempt.

Cultural critic Mark Dery has identified yet another tactic used by Star Trek fans to take charge of the future, and that is by laying claim to one of the series' resident species. A common story arc in various Star Trek incarnations is the introduction of hostile species who are gradually tamed and incorporated into the Federation. Last season's enemy is this season's troublesome crew member. The most striking new enemy to appear during the run of *Star Trek: The Next Generation* (1987–94) was the Borg, a race of cyborgs intent on assimilating the rest of the galaxy to their hive society. Borgs are alarming looking, with dead white skin, tight-fitting armor and mechanical appurtenances sprouting all over their bodies. They are immensely powerful, with technology far beyond that of the Federation. They are also, to judge from the numbers of Borg costumes at any Star Trek convention, really cool.

The appeal of the Borg has something to do with their coolness—that is, their indifference to emotional upheaval. It is also related to the promise of the cyborg: fusion with machines as a way of transforming humanity into something of vastly greater power, adaptability, and lifespan. But Dery points out how many of the Borgs' characteristics may also be read as markers of homosexuality, especially the homosexual bogeyman conjured up by conservatives of various convictions.

> Once "outed," the Borg appear to be so obviously and so variously wired into gay myth and metaphor that it seems almost unthinkable that the connections could have gone unnoticed. Like sailors, bikers, cops, and other stereotypical characters in homoerotic fantasy, the Borg are an all-male society living in close quarters. They are in constant physical communion with one another, literally bonded by electronic interconnection. . . .
>
> Anonymous and continuous, the exchange of fluid data among the Borg conjures the fleeting, faceless sex, in bars, bathrooms, and public parks of the gay sexual demimonde in the '70s and early '80s. The Borg's cadaverous pallor evokes urban nightcrawlers—sybarites who come out only after dark, like the androgynous vampires in Anne Rice's best-selling homoerotic novels. (2–3)

Pierced and leather-clad young men (female—lesbian?—Borgs appeared only later), an army of indistinguishable clones, these spectres threaten Federation (which is to say middle-American) stability and respectability. And the greatest threat of all is that of assimilation. The Borg can turn anyone into a Borg, including Captain Picard of the *Enterprise,* who in two memorable episodes was transformed into a more sinister (and sexier) alternative self called Locutus of Borg.

Slashing the entire species of Borg, reading them as gay, hardly takes any manipulation at all. Seeing them in positive terms, as Dery does, takes a little more effort. It may seem self-defeating, for a group seeking broader acceptance, voluntarily to assume an image that is everything their adversaries accuse them of being. However, as Dery indicates, assimilating the Borg may well be the most effective way for gay people to guarantee themselves a place in the sci-fi future. The rules of cultural negotiation say that Hollywood will accept back what it has already produced. If lesbians and gays, in the guise of the Borg, are already present in the Star Trek universe, then producers and writers can go on reusing and reimagining them.

No one familiar with the history of SF fandom should be surprised at the degree to which Star Trek's fans, including gay fans, resist being left out of the decision-making process that generates their entertainment. SF fans have always attempted to assert the right to farm their own future. They talk back in letters columns; publish their own magazines—with no clear boundary between the professional publication and the fanzine; write their own fiction, often becoming professional writers or editors along the way; offer sophisticated critiques of others' work; hold regional, national, and worldwide conventions; and reward their favorites with prizes like the Hugo Award.

Following these examples, feminist readers in the 1970s established their own convention, WisCon, where in the 1990s, at the instigation of writers Karen Joy Fowler and Pat Murphy, the James Tiptree, Jr., Award was created to honor SF that explores and expands ideas about gender. Gay fans, likewise, have held their own conventions and established the Lambda Award, for SF or fantasy dealing with homosexual themes. Both sorts of negotiations have paid off. Following the creation of the awards, publishers brought out anthologies of both feminist and gay SF. The Tiptree award has also stimulated more than one writer to write a "Tiptree story," meaning a novel or story that might be considered for the award. In addition, awards and anthologies are ways of reframing fiction as something more important and more lasting than popular entertainment: they invite us to read SF as literature.

Figure 7. Shelley's Heirs. Freddie Baer's artwork for the 1993 Tiptree Award T-shirt reinvents the female Gothic as a statement about new directions in gender coding.

The advantages of being classified as literature are obvious: major SF novels would get noticed by mainstream reviewers, classics would stay in print, SF's relationship to other fictional forms would be acknowledged. The disadvantages are not so evident, but they are closely related to a sense of cohesiveness within the SF community. This cohesiveness has been fostered by the same exclusions that prompt writers and fans to refer to the "science fiction ghetto." A ghetto can be a place of mutual support and strengthened resolve. It is not a place that welcomes challenges to its core identity.

The efforts of gay and feminist fans counter a widely-held assumption within the SF community that gender is a trivial issue. When older generations of fans met together to praise and publicize SF, when they wrote critiques of bad sci-fi movies and good SF novels, they were working to establish within the imaginary future a particular way of seeing the universe in rational and rapturous terms. They thought of themselves as promoting a philosophical, not a sexual, orientation. Though the SF of the 1930s through the '50s was never as upbeat as some fans remember it being, it did generally uphold a belief in reasoned solutions to human problems. Even when those solutions failed, the stories gave the characters credit for trying.

One story in particular has been cited again and again as an exemplar of the SF ethos. Tom Godwin's "The Cold Equations," with an ending possibly dictated by editor John W. Campbell, has been debated so hotly and so often within the SF community that I apologize for mentioning it again here, but it does encapsulate some central tenets of the SF faith. It is a tight little allegory about reason and sentiment, in which a space pilot on a mission of mercy must deal with a stowaway whose presence threatens his ability to save a colony. The pilot represents, not reason alone, but emotion tempered by rational considerations. The stowaway acts on emotional impulse—she wants to visit her brother on the colony world—without adequate information or understanding of the forces involved in space travel; she learns better, but not in time to save her life. After considering and rejecting various possible alternatives, the pilot has no choice (within the rules of the narrative) but to jettison her. Heroically, she accepts the need to sacrifice her own life to save others'.

The popularity of this story indicates that it is not really a story of failure, though the characters fail to solve the problem it *seems* to pose. It would be a different matter if the pilot fell short of completing his rescue operation, but he succeeds by virtue of his passenger's self-sacrifice and his own grasp of the "cold equations" that govern space travel. The real problem within the story is to weigh social conventions and emotional responses against the implacable demands of the physical universe. The pilot proves himself a hero by being able to make the decision that will give himself and his medical cargo a chance of arriving at their destination. It's nice that he feels bad about the girl, but she brought her own fate upon herself by venturing unprepared into the harsh reaches of space.

Readers who are fond of the story read it as a validation of their own scientific understanding and of science's willingness to test inherited values against empirical data. They view the equations that govern matter and movement as something like the Old Testament God: a stern and terrible judge that is also the source of all that is grand and transcendent. To offer oneself as sacrifice to such a god is not such a terrible fate; to be the priest who interprets the equations is even better.

And it is important to remember that the roles are not fixed. What distinguishes the pilot from the stowaway is not his identity but his knowledge. The decision about which stays inside the ship and which steps into the airlock is based entirely on the fact that she does not know enough to get the ship to its destination, while he does. It could easily have been the other way around: a naive young man and a veteran woman pilot. Couldn't it?

For some women readers, it could. They were able to make the mental switch that allowed identification with the technologically savvy male hero rather than with the foolish passenger. Marion Zimmer Bradley, a fan before she became a successful SF writer, says that "many women, myself among them, were fascinated by the stories of adventure and genuinely identified with the men in the stories—not the simpering scientist's cute daughter, but the tough adventurer" (27). For these readers, SF offered an escape from gender stereotyping, a chance to be "one of the boys, accepted as myself, in a milieu where no one knew *or cared* whether I was a girl" (Bradley 26).

Yet Bradley also mentions that one of her fellow fans, Lee Hoffman, "actually passed herself off as male, by carefully avoiding any mention of her gender in her letters" (26). Her experience indicates that being "one of the boys" was a more complicated matter even in the culture of SF than merely being accepted as oneself. It meant not only believing in such SF articles of faith as the inevitability of space exploration, the heroic scientist, the awe-inspiring mathematical order of the cosmos, and the benevolence of technocracy, but also representing oneself as ungendered, which is to say masculine (masculine being the unmarked case here, as in many aspects of culture). There was no place in SF's sleek vessel for such feminine stowaways as family ties, overt desire, domestic arrangements, and psychological complexity. The first qualification for being Venturus is to be an unattached male.

These excluded elements are associated not only with femininity but also with canonical fiction. The strand of SF represented by "The Cold Equations"—the tradition identified by its advocates as "hard science fiction"— has always prided itself on its distance from traditional high literature. As David Hartwell points out, fans of hard SF typically "harbor a deep suspicion of the self-consciously literary," (31), by which they mean both "consciously literary effects" (31) and too much attention to inner life and "the specific human condition of any individual today" (34), as opposed to broader pictures of humanity confronting the cosmos. Thus literariness itself is classed as one of the "soft" qualities that threaten to dilute the masculine intellectuality of the form.

The pilot of "The Cold Equations," like most heroes of hard SF, is generic—in more than one sense. His blankness, which traditional literary analysis might view as an aesthetic failing, can also be seen as a mechanism that allows for other sorts of resonance. His effacement allows the idea to serve as the story's real hero, in a manner distinctive to the genre. This sort of difference has prompted Samuel Delany to define SF as a form of "paraliterature," something that shares features with literature, but ultimately operates by its own rules. Yet even the SF hero has ties to characters in other fiction genres: the Western gunfighter, for instance, or the competent endurer of Hemingway's fishing stories. One can read SF looking for differences from traditional literature or for the many similarities. Individual works within the genre will respond better to one reading strategy or the other, literary or paraliterary. Delany himself, though, is a writer whose work can appeal to readers accustomed to either Proust or Heinlein—but most strongly to those familiar with both.

Literature is, along with Hollywood, a site of cultural brokerage where SF ideas might find wider circulation. Though the literary marketplace is neither as profitable nor as widely consumed as TV and movies, still, it has the sanction of institutions such as libraries and universities. This can mean, for a writer, long-term sales and status as author of a "classic." Getting into the canon can also mean greater freedom to engage in stylistic experimentation and thematic exploration, with assurance that readers will take the trouble to follow. The classroom, too, is a part of the future that can be farmed.

Like the movies, literary institutions demand certain payments for taking in the products of SF. One is the privilege of reading a text in ways other than that which upholds the hard-SF creed. "The Cold Equations" has been reprinted in anthologies used in literature classes, including James Gunn's *The Road to Science Fiction, Vol. 3* (1979), Robert Silverberg's *The Science Fiction Hall of Fame* (1970), and David Hartwell and Kathryn Cramer's *The Ascent of Wonder* (1994). A reprinted story becomes something other than the disposable entertainment implied by its first magazine appearance. Like a museum-style frame around a painting, the covers of a teaching anthology announce that the materials within should be studied carefully, with attention to nuance and implication. "The Cold Equations" becomes fair game for analysis of its form, language, and ideology.

And, sure enough, it has received such analysis from academically-trained readers like John Huntington, Darrell Schweitzer, and Andy Duncan. (The latter two are also SF writers.) They note all the details in Godwin's story that are not really needed for making its point about scientific knowledge and necessity. Why is the ship, for instance, so ridiculously underequipped for its emergency mission? Why does the story so insist on the stowaway's desirably, if impractically, feminine appearance—at various times mentioning her curly hair, perfume, pleated skirt, lipstick, and "little white gypsy sandals" (Godwin 249)—yet acknowledge no sexual response whatsoever from the pilot? Why does neither character notice the presence of articles mentioned in the story, such as the door of the closet she hides in, that might be ejected in her place to save the necessary fuel? If it is a story about *natural* law, why does the text first mention a *regulation* that "Any stowaway discovered in an EDS shall be jettisoned immediately following discovery" (247)? Questions like these raise the possibility of readings other than the one outlined above. Perhaps it is not a story about science at all, but about 1950s sexual politics or the way custom and authority ascribe to themselves the force of natural law.

James Gunn suggests that to read the story against its intentions is to misread both it and the genre of science fiction:

> If the reader doesn't understand it or appreciate what it is trying to say about humanity and its relationship to its environment, then that reader isn't likely to appreciate science fiction. If the reader keeps objecting that the ship should have posted a more specific warning, that the story indicts the coldbloodedness of the situation or the ruthlessness of the rules, that the pilot should have found a way to sacrifice himself in order to save the girl or died with her rather than letting her go out the airlock alone, then that reader isn't reading the story correctly. (235–46)

But the ideological readings proposed by Huntington or Duncan do not suggest rewriting the story's events, but rather reading them as literary constructs. It may be natural law that a ship's fuel can only transport a certain mass a certain distance, but it is not natural law that chooses to exploit this fact in a work of fiction, nor to surround it with signals of gender difference and unacknowledged desire.

The fear of many fans is that allowing SF to be taken up into the category of literature will subject it to the same sorts of distortions that accompany the transition to filmed sci-fi. Characters will be reevaluated; situations will become ambiguous or, worse, symbolic; exploration of ideas will get lost amid discussions of style and narrative technique. With an expanding readership untrained in generic codes, the newcomers will read SF wrong, and they will read the wrong SF. The genre will cease to be itself and become SF-Lit, which is to say SF-Lite—a simulacrum of true speculative fiction with all the trappings and none of the scientific rigor or the emotional payoffs.

Those fears have been triggered on a number of occasions: when English departments began offering courses in SF in the early 1960s; when a scholarly organization, the Science Fiction Research Association, was formed in 1970 to study the genre; when academic journals in the 1980s began using theories derived from Freud and Althusser and Foucault to talk about SF texts; and in the early 1990s when a press best-known for its massive teaching anthologies issued a volume devoted to SF. This last event, the publication of *The Norton Book of Science Fiction,* offers evidence of the anxiety and perhaps some justification for it as well.

The Norton Book of Science Fiction, NBSF for short, is not actually a fat and footnoted Norton Anthology of the sort many people remember from college survey courses. Textbook editors at Norton have been petitioned repeatedly to publish such an anthology and have not found the material sufficiently canonical.

It was a clever editor in the trade book division, Dan Conaway, who thought of evading the literature police by commissioning a volume devoted to SF within the "Norton Book of" series of thematic anthologies aimed at a general readership. In 1990, he invited a writer highly respected both inside and outside the SF community, Ursula K. Le Guin, to assemble the book. She invited two co-editors: one, Karen Joy Fowler, a writer with connections among the newer generation of SF writers and the other, myself, an academic who had taught and written about SF. Le Guin also suggested to the press that the book might just possibly have a second career as a textbook in some SF courses. Both suggestions were acceptable, though the press did not want three names on the book's spine and so Fowler became a "consultant" and was excused from a little of the drudge-work. To encourage classroom use, I was asked to write a teacher's guide to the anthology.

The three of us set to work happily, pestering acquaintances for suggestions, gathering lists of honored stories, and digging through piles of magazines, collections, and anthologies. We found the task daunting enough to set some arbitrary boundaries. We would limit ourselves to short fiction, rather than using excerpts; set beginning and ending cut-off dates of 1960 and 1990 to represent the contemporary state of the genre; and look only at untranslated work from North America, hoping that more knowledgeable readers from elsewhere in the world would supplement our work. We settled on a mix of familiar and unfamiliar stories that each of us, probably for different reasons, found compelling and representative of the various traditions of SF.

Reviews of the book fall into surprising patterns. Disappointingly few of the reviews have much to say about the stories themselves. More concern themselves with questioning the editors' motives. The typical review focuses, in descending order of importance, on the title page, on the editor's introduction by Le Guin, and on patterns the reviewer thinks he or she detects in the table of contents.

For the reviewers, the most important factors on the title page are two names: Norton and Le Guin. Le Guin represents, depending on one's outlook, any of three things: the highest level of SF achievement, or a writer who combines SF and literature in such a way that one can give her books to friends who don't see what you find so interesting in that stuff, or a spy from the literary world within the ranks of SF writers. Norton represents both literary respectability and a sort of embalming of texts, making them into fixed objects of study instead of parts of an ongoing discussion. A Norton Anthology (the distinction between "Book of" and "Anthology of" is hard to maintain outside the publishing house itself) is supposed to sum up years of critical thought on a particular category: it is not just the best but what is generally agreed upon as the best, and therefore what teachers will be teaching and critics will be writing about for years to come. In other words, it is itself a sort of farming of the future, at least the future of literary studies.

Of lesser concern are the other names on the title page: Fowler, for those who have already discovered her work, representing a postmodern take on SF that uses and at the same time questions its conventions; me representing not so much an individual as "an academic" (some reviews omit my name entirely, substituting that term). In other words, we are all suspiciously close to the world of literature. In addition, there is only one "Brian" to balance a "Karen" and an "Ursula." Is one male editor enough to guarantee selections of interest to the historically masculine readership of SF? The subtitle, *North American Science Fiction, 1960–1990,* also raises some issues, especially outside of North America.

All of this title-page information is read as an indication that SF might finally be getting some recognition from the literary community, but that those in charge of the project are not reliable selectors of the real thing. As Nortonizers of SF, we are expected to select from what is already, by consensus, the body of important stories; however, as representatives of various branches of non-SF literature, we are suspected of having divided loyalties that might interfere with our attention to that duty.

Le Guin's introduction did not allay fears. She defined SF not in terms of specific content but in terms of "techniques and imagery" (Le Guin 16), and, borrowing from me borrowing from Damien Broderick, Christine Brooke-Rose, and, ultimately, Philippe Hamon, of a "megatext" or body of thought against which any SF story asks to be read (Le Guin 23). She dismissed the idea that hard SF of the "Cold Equations" sort is the only or essential variety. She acknowledged our efforts to find voices from outside the dominant tradition. And she mentioned "complexity and human relevance" as desirable traits in "the fiction that uses the future as its metaphor" (18), thereby casting doubt on readings that emphasize direct, nonmetaphoric reference to technological developments and conceptual breakthroughs.

It remained only for some reviewers to count the numbers of men and women represented in the table of contents to respond with that familiar cry of anguish over loss of control: "Political Correctness." An anonymous reviewer on the Amazon.com website puts it bluntly:

> While there are some excellent stories in this volume, the editors excluded authors and stories because they didn't meet their politically correct feminist viewpoints. Accordingly, this book doesn't represent a true cross section of the SF field which greatly diminishes it's [sic] usefulness as a reference. ("Customer Reviews" 3)

Here, I suspect the reader is responding to Le Guin's statement in the introduction that she was not receptive to stories that were racist, homophobic, or misogynistic or that used "prolonged description of violence (against anybody) to provide the emotional whammy." (17). A careless reading of this acknowledgment fails to note Le Guin's further comment that "I cannot myself untangle ethical from aesthetic standards in these matters" (17). In other words, stories that substitute violent confrontation for real resolution of issues are probably not good stories, aesthetically as well as ethically. The big boom that short-circuits thematic complexity is a movie staple that some SF writers have borrowed, perhaps in hopes of selling it back to Hollywood. As someone who finds car chases and explosions the most boring parts of movies, I tend to agree with Le Guin, though neither of us would rule out violent scenes as legitimate components of film or fiction.

More to the point, the reader quoted above is making the assumption that the anthology is intended to be—or ought to be—a "cross-section of the SF field." Another reader on the same website agreed that "as an introduction to SF it is terrible," partly because of the word count: "Avowedly feminist—and female—authors put far more words into this volume than the male authors. This, in spite of the fact that most of the SF written today and yesterday is and was written by men" ("Customer Reviews" 1). Here again, the assumption is that the anthology should be a sort of representative democracy, with word count proportional to word issuance. This is not a constraint that the SF community has applied to anthologies which do not similarly imply SF's transition into the realm of literature (though, as mentioned earlier, some of these anthologies have been used in literature classrooms).

NBSF is only one of a number of substantial reprint volumes issued during the 1990s. Others include James Gunn's historical four-volume anthology *The Road to Science Fiction,* originally published in the 1970s but reissued twenty years later; David G. Hartwell and Kathryn Cramer's *The Ascent of Wonder* (1994); Tom Shippey's *The Oxford Book of Science Fiction Stories* (1992); Gardner Dozois's *Modern Classics of Science Fiction* (1991); and David Hartwell and Milton T. Wolf's *Visions of Wonder* (1996). Among them, these books make available hundreds of SF stories with surprisingly few overlaps. I find this breadth cause for celebration and evidence of both the strength and the unruliness of SF. Decades of winnowing have not created as much consensus as some SF fans like to think regarding which stories, writers, and themes form the core of the genre.

Having been put into a counting mood by the Amazon.com reviewers, I did my own survey of the anthologies. Including only the latter two volumes of Gunn's series, which focus on recent and contemporary work, I found that the overall proportion of male to female writers represented was 226 to 62, or, by percentages, 78.5% men to 21.5% women. This is a considerable improvement over the situation described decades ago by Joanna Russ, wherein the numbers of women represented in literary anthologies hover around 7% year in and year out. To keep this number constant, formerly prominent women writers like Willa Cather and Elizabeth Barrett Browning are periodically weeded out to make room for newer male counterparts (Russ 79). Interestingly, only one of the SF anthologies, *The Oxford Book of Science Fiction Stories,* matches the standard pre-feminist proportion, with two women to twenty-eight men, or 6.8%.

But numbers are not really to the point. The Oxford and Norton titles deviate about equally from the mean; in both cases, the editors were looking not for percentages but for stories they thought worthy of readers' attention. Although the phrase "politically correct" is a powerful piece of rhetoric, implying that one's opponents' taste and convictions are not only defective but not even genuinely their own, it does not provide much help in analyzing the patterns of choice that differentiate one anthology from another. Even the editors are not necessarily conscious of the criteria by which they choose this story over that one. For this reason, I find illuminating—of my own reading patterns and also of the interplay between literary and SF cultures—those reviews of *NBSF* that offer analytical, rather than rhetorical, characterizations of the book.

First, complaints most frequently address, not the important writers we left out, but some that we put in. Margaret Atwood's presence, for instance, raises a lot of hackles. Does a writer so acclaimed by the mainstream belong in a book that will be presented to students as a survey of SF?

One of the more sympathetic reviewers, John Clute, comments, in *TLS,* that the anthology includes "several women of moderate obscurity," a category from which he excludes Pat Cadigan, Carol Emshwiller, Lisa Goldstein, Nancy Kress, and Connie Willis (24). The obscurities, therefore, include two groups: writers not yet well established and writers whose reputations have dimmed. The former might include Eleanor Arnason, Molly Gloss, Candas Jane Dorsey, Pat Murphy, and perhaps even Octavia Butler and Karen Fowler, all of whom have made a considerably greater mark in the field since 1993, when we reprinted their stories. I am not sure who is included in the latter category: perhaps Katherine MacLean, Marion Zimmer Bradley, Sonya Dorman Hess, Zenna Henderson, Phyllis Gotlieb, and Suzette Haden Elgin. If these writers are obscure, it is through no failing of their own, but rather through the tendency Russ mentions for women writers to drop from sight more rapidly than men of equal (or sometimes lesser) achievement. They have not dropped out of sight, moreover, for feminist critics. Essays by Pamela Sargent, Jeanne Gomoll, Marleen Barr, Robin Roberts, Sarah Lefanu, Jane Donawerth, and Jenny Wolmark, have created an alternative canon of women's SF, within which someone like Suzette Haden Elgin is recognized an influential explorer of new issues.

The key is which issues are being explored. Elgin works primarily with ideas about language, political power, folk tradition, and gender. These are significant parts of human experience, but they are not easily codified into equations, cold or otherwise. They don't power spaceships. If one's notion of science is physics, astronomy, inorganic chemistry, a little math, and a lot of engineering, then Elgin's work is not science fiction at all.

Though some of the other women writers do pay more attention than Elgin to the "hard sciences," it is common for their fiction to portray scientific endeavors within the context of human societies and motivations. In place of the isolated and virtually anonymous pilot of Tom Godwin's story, Connie Willis, for instance, writes about the physicist Karl Schwarzschild, whose brilliant equations describing the capture of energy around a black hole did not save him from death on the Russian front in World War I ("Schwarzschild" 703). Willis is interested in exploring what it means to live with the equations: how they might play out in human actions and perceptions. She invites us to read physics both literally and metaphorically, whereas Godwin—at least as read by his hard science advocates—avoids making metaphoric applications of his story. Whatever possible earthly situation might be refracted in his scenario, whatever actual case might warrant jettisoning one part of humanity to rescue another, is left unexamined. This, to me, is a less significant use of fiction than Willis's redoubling of patterns and implications. Without ceasing to be SF, her story also functions in ways we associate with literary artists. In doing so, it fits into the tradition of writers such as Cordwainer Smith, Samuel R. Delany, Fritz Leiber, Katherine MacLean, Damon Knight, Theodore Sturgeon, Philip K. Dick, Zenna Henderson, and Frederik Pohl—some of my own particular touchstones of the genre.

The categories of literariness and feminism have often been conflated in discussions of *NBSF*. Clute might just as well have noted our inclusion of relatively obscure or forgotten male writers: David R. Bunch, for example. It is not Bunch's dense prose and dark irony, however, but the prominent presence of women writers that signals literary ambition even for a reader who applauds the editors' aspirations and deems the collection "almost as good as it could be" (Clute 24).

Like John Clute, Brian Stableford offers an analysis of *NBSF* that has helped me see some of the forces at work in our editorial choices. Contrasting many of the stories in the book with SF's traditional mission of cheerleading for science, Stableford points out how few of the stories have happy endings—twelve out of 67, by his count. Like him, I think the well-wrought happy ending is a rarity worth treasuring; my count, though, comes to 25. This is a considerable difference, and I suspect many of my happy endings fall under his "blackly comic through the satirically ironic to the perversely eccentric" (5). He might not have counted Carol Emshwiller's "The Start of the End of the World" as having a happy ending, for instance, although it concludes with the female narrator successfully sabotaging an alien invasion. Nor, I would guess, did his list include Eileen Gunn's "Stable Strategies for

Middle Management," in which an oppressed and bio-morphed worker literally bites her boss's head off.

"Happy" rather depends on whose point of view one takes. So does "funny": reviewers universally fail to comment on Gunn's or Emshwiller's brilliant humor, perhaps because it is largely at the expense of male ego. A majority of the stories in *NBSF* fit one or the other meaning of the word "comic"—either as a structure of reconciliation or as a source of amusement— but they do so in complicated ways. As Stableford points out, irony creeps in frequently. So do ambiguity, narrative unreliability, and irresolution, even with respect to the stories' scientific content. Few of the stories have us cheering for a new discovery or an ingenious new application of technology. "The Lake Is Full of Artificial Things," by Fowler, for instance, involves a new device for replaying brain waves in such a way as to generate therapeutic dreams, but it is unclear whether her protagonist achieves greater self-understanding thereby or falls into delusion.

Stableford is right that most of the stories in *NBSF* are ambivalent about scientific progress—more ambivalent, I suspect, than are the editors themselves. This ambivalence may have less to do with philosophy than with narrative technique. When fiction takes up an issue, it tends to chew on it, worry it about like a puppy with a rag, until the rag begins to unravel. Bits of hidden lining show up; bright blends of color become separate, darker. Out of playfulness comes complexity. At least, this is the case with literary fiction. Evidently the sort of SF that appealed to the editors of *NBSF* tends to function similarly. We favored stories in which the novum is presented playfully and complexly, partly because we were looking for stories that would function out of their original context, for readers who might not even remember when the ideas in them were new. The energy imparted by social anxiety remains when that provided by scientific novelty has dissipated. Writers whose relationship to the dominant culture is already complicated by their sex or their sexuality are more likely to bring such anxiety to the fore; perhaps that is why women's fiction tends toward the ironic and ambiguous in its approach to scientific breakthroughs.

Like cultural negotiations on the Elizabethan stage, SF's distinctive forms of play exploit the tremendous social energy within troubling concepts. At present, these include manipulation of the human genome, alteration of ecosystems, the chemical and electrical origins of consciousness, the use of computers to simulate both consciousness and environments, and the mutability of social roles. Some of this energy will remain in the fiction even if the scientific paradigms that generate it fall by the wayside. Stories in which this happens will begin to function in ways that resemble literary art more than paraliterature.

For readers attuned both to paraliterary and literary sorts of readings, SF is uniquely positioned to mediate between the interests of the literary world and the investigations of science. Not every reader is or wishes to be so attuned. Hence it seems unlikely that SF will ever disappear into the category of literature. The debate over *NBSF* and other anthologies, for instance, has taken place almost entirely within SF's critical community, rather than the pages of *The New Yorker/Times/Review of Books. NBSF* has been adopted as a textbook in many college courses, but they are SF courses rather than, say, classes in contemporary literature or the art of the short story. Critics are beginning to discuss many of the selections (which is how touchstones are created), but they are SF scholars rather than mainstream academics. It seems less likely that SF will enter the literary canon than that SF will attract increasing numbers of literary readers among its contending factions.

To go back to my parable, the ending of *Archer's Goon* brings about two revelations about Venturus, the ruler of the future. One is that he has caused himself and everyone around him to reverse time and relive the span of his childhood—twice, in fact. The other is that the last go-round of growing up has made him into quite a different person from the Venturus he would have become. The original Venturus was solitary and self-centered, like most of his godlike siblings. All he was really interested in was his machinery, and that machinery was intended primarily to glorify himself. His spaceship, like the temple that housed it, was basically "Four towering statues of Venturus [that] held up a roof which was a head of Venturus, giant-size, looking heroic and noble and, to Howard's shamed eyes, utterly stupid" (230).

But Venturus has accidentally caused himself to grow up into someone else, into that very Howard who is so ashamed of Venturus's monument to Venturus. Why is Howard different from his earlier self? There are two factors: he has been raised by a human family, including a musician mother and a fiction-writing father; and he has been forced off center stage by acquiring a fierce-tempered younger sister—a female counterpart. Exposure to art, literature, and the feminine, one might say, has turned him into Howard, rather than Venturus.

Like Venturus, SF has had two histories, has grown up twice. In one history, SF develops from adventure stories like Edgar Rice Burroughs' Mars books into extrapolations of scientific concepts like Godwin's "The Cold Equations" and thence to elaborate virtual-reality playgrounds like those of cyberpunk. As the genre matures, it develops more sophisticated ways to represent scientific information and conceptual breakthroughs, but the narrative structure continues to revolve around masculine escape from physical limitations and social constraints.

The alternative history of SF involves writers exploring what happens to society, consciousness, emotion, and identity when those things are rethought by scientific investigation and remade through technology. This SF is complex, troubling, ironic, allusive, stylistically playful. Rather than being hostile to literature, it looks back to literary ancestors like Dante, Swift, and the

Shelleys, both Mary and her husband. From *Frankenstein* onward, this version of SF has been influenced by women writers and editors out of all proportion to their numbers.

Both of these histories are true; neither is complete. As in Diana Wynne Jones's story, they take place over exactly the same span of time but have very different outcomes. An important aspect of directing SF's future is asserting control over its past. The way SF represents itself and its tradition will affect what gets written and published in the future—and what ultimately makes its way into sci-fi and the popular imagination. Will science be reduced to a literary device, a trope? Can we continue to read "The Cold Equations" as a touchstone of the genre, and, if so, can we read it innocently or should we look for subtexts? Is gender an irrelevant distraction or a fundamental part of our mental equipment? Can SF become a broad enough category to include both Godwin and Atwood, or does appreciation for one preclude understanding the other?

College courses and historical surveys affect the answers to these questions. That is why anthologies are worth fighting about. Sci-fi matters too, but for different reasons. By using images of the future to describe the present, the popular media invite us to use futuristic scenarios as tests of viability. Any group that cannot negotiate a place for itself in the imagined future is already obsolete. The issue being debated in reviews and online discussions, in fan publications and websites, at conventions and awards ceremonies, in slash fiction and "respectable" anthologies is not only who gets to be Venturus, but also which version of Venturus it will be.

The anxiety felt by longtime SF fans is proportional to the urgency felt by feminists, racial minorities, gays, transgendered people, and supporters of all these groups to enter into negotiations about the future. Both emotions contribute to the level of social energy that fuels the work of James Morrow, Gwyneth Jones, Raphel Carter, Karen Fowler, Ursula K. Le Guin, Geoff Ryman, Nicola Griffith, Eleanor Arnason, and a host of fine writers whom I have not been able to work into any of the preceding chapters. Their work represents the leading edge of SF at the turn of the twenty-first century, not only because of inventiveness and stylistic excellence, but also because theirs is the stage on which our culture debates its nature and direction.

WORKS CITED

CHAPTER 1

Aldiss, Brian, with David Wingrove. *Trillion Year Spree: The History of Science Fiction.* New York: Avon, 1986.

Bornstein, Kate. *Gender Outlaw: On Men, Women, and the Rest of Us.* New York: Routledge, 1994.

Broderick, Damien. *Reading by Starlight: Postmodern Science Fiction.* Popular Fictions Series. London and New York: Routledge, 1995.

Cioffi, Frank. *Formula Fiction? An Anatomy of American Science Fiction, 1930–1940.* Contributions to the Study of Science Fiction and Fantasy, Number 3. Westport, CT: Greenwood, 1982.

Ellison, Harlan. *Dangerous Visions.* Garden City, NY: Doubleday, 1967.

Garber, Marjorie. *Vested Interests: Cross-Dressing and Cultural Anxiety.* New York: Routledge, 1992.

Haraway, Donna. *Simians, Cyborgs, and Women: The Reinvention of Nature.* New York: Routledge, 1991.

Laqueur, Thomas. *Making Sex: Body and Gender from the Greeks to Freud.* Cambridge: Harvard UP, 1990.

Russ, Joanna. "Images of Women in Science Fiction." *Images of Women in Fiction: Feminist Perspectives.* Ed. Susan Koppelman Cornillon. Bowling Green, OH: Bowling Green State UP, 1972. 79–94.

White, Hayden. *The Content of the Form: Narrative Discourse and Historical Representation.* Baltimore: Johns Hopkins UP, 1987.

Williams, Anne. *Art of Darkness: A Poetics of Gothic.* Chicago: U of Chicago P, 1995.

Wolfe, Gary K. *Critical Terms for Science Fiction and Fantasy: A Glossary and Guide to Scholarship.* New York and Westport, CT: Greenwood, 1986.

CHAPTER 2

Aldiss, Brian W., with David Wingrove. *Trillion Year Spree: The History of Science Fiction.* New York: Avon, 1986.

Alkon, Paul K. *Science Fiction before 1900: Imagination Discovers Technology.* Studies in Literary Themes and Genres No. 3. New York: Twayne, 1994.

Austen, Jane. *Northanger Abbey. The Novels of Jane Austen.* Edinburgh: Grant, 1911.

Fetterly, Judith. *The Resisting Reader: A Feminist Approach to American Fiction.* Bloomington and London: Indiana UP, 1978.

Franklin, H. Bruce. *Future Perfect: American Science Fiction of the Nineteenth Century.* Revised ed. New Brunswick, NJ: Rutgers UP, 1995.

Gunn, James, (ed.). *The Road to Science Fiction 1: From Gilgamesh to Wells.* New York: Mentor, 1977.

Hawthorne, Nathaniel. "The Artist of the Beautiful." *Future Perfect.* Edited by H. Bruce Franklin. 39–60.

———. "Rappaccini's Daughter." *Science Fiction: A Historical Anthology.* Ed. Eric S. Rabkin. Oxford and New York: Oxford UP, 1983. 161–192.

Hoffmann, E. T. A. "The Sand-Man." *Science Fiction: A Historical Anthology.* Ed. Eric S. Rabkin. 75–112.

Loudon, Jane Webb. *The Mummy! A Tale of the Twenty-Second Century.* Intro. and Abridgment by Alan Rauch. Ann Arbor: U of Michigan P, 1994.

Melville, Herman. "The Bell-Tower." *Future Perfect.* Edited by H. Bruce Franklin. 140–153.

Moers, Ellen. *Literary Women.* Garden City, NY: Doubleday, 1976.

O'Brien, Fitz James. "The Diamond Lens." *Future Perfect.* Edited by H. Bruce Franklin. 285–306.

Philmus, Robert M. *Into the Unknown: The Evolution of Science Fiction from Francis Godwin to H. G. Wells.* Berkeley and Los Angeles: U of California P, 1970.

Poe, Edgar Allan. "The Facts in the Case of M. Valdemar." *Future Perfect.* Edited by H. Bruce Franklin. 106–114.

———. "How to Write a Blackwood Article. A Predicament." *Great Short Works of Edgar Allan Poe.* Ed. G. R. Thompson. New York: Harper, 1970. 193–215.

———. "Mesmeric Revelation." *Collected Works of Edgar Allan Poe. Vol. 3: Tale and Sketches 1843–1849.* Ed. Thomas Ollive Mabbott. Cambridge, MS: Harvard UP, 1978. 1024–1042.

Shelley, Mary. *Frankenstein; or, The Modern Prometheus.* Third ed., revised. London: Colburn, 1831.

Stowe, Harriet Beecher. *Uncle Tom's Cabin; or, Life Among the Lowly.* Edited by Elizabeth Ammons. New York: Norton, 1994.

Suvin, Darko. *Metamorphoses of Science Fiction: On the Poetics and History of a Literary Genre.* New York: Yale UP, 1979.

Williams, Anne. *Art of Darkness: A Poetics of Gothic.* Chicago and London: U of Chicago P, 1995.

CHAPTER 3

Arnason, Eleanor. Letter. *New York Review of Science Fiction* 81 (May 1995): 21–22.

Barnes, Arthur K. "Green Hell." *Thrilling Wonder Stories* June 1937: 91–100.

Beynon, John [John Beynon Harris]. "The Perfect Creature." *Tales of Wonder* 1 [undated— June 1937]: 116–27.

Binder, Eando [Otto Binder and Earl Binder]. "The Chemical Murder." *Amazing Stories* April 1937: 91–114.

———. "Strange Vision." *Astounding Stories* May 1937: 46–56.

Cramer, Kathryn. "On Science and Science Fiction." *The Ascent of Wonder: The Evolution of Hard Science Fiction.* Edited by David G. Hartwell and Kathryn Cramer. New York: Tor, 1994. 23–28.

del Rey, Lester. "Introduction: The Three Careers of John W. Campbell." *The Best of John W. Campbell.* Edited by Lester del Rey. Garden City, NY: Doubleday, 1976. 1–6.

Edwards, John. "The Planet of Perpetual Night." *Amazing Stories* February 1937: 15–57.

Farley, Ralph Milne [Roger Sherman Hoar]. "A Month a Minute." *Thrilling Wonder Stories* December 1937: 14–26.

Fearn, John Russell. "Menace from the Microcosm." *Thrilling Wonder Stories* June 1937: 14–30.

———. "Metamorphosis." *Astounding Stories* January 1937: 90–114.

———. "Seeds from Space." *Tales of Wonder* 1 [June 1937]: 17–39.

Godwin, Tom. "The Cold Equations." *Astounding Science Fiction* 1954. Reprinted in *The Science Fiction Hall of Fame, Volume I.* Edited Robert Silverberg. New York: Avon, 1970. 543–69.

Hamilton, Edmond. "A Million Years Ahead." *Thrilling Wonder Stories* April 1937: 92–97.

Hawthorne, Nathaniel. "The Birth-Mark." *Mosses from an Old Manse.* Vol. 10 of *The Centenary Edition of the Works of Nathaniel Hawthorne.* Edited by William Charvat et al. Columbus: Ohio State UP, 1962–1988. 36–56. 22 vols.

———. "The Man of Adamant." *The Snow Image and Uncollected Tales.* Vol. 11 of *The Centenary Edition.* 161–169.

Keller, Evelyn Fox. *Reflections on Gender and Science.* New Haven and London: Yale UP, 1985.

Kuttner, Henry. "When the Earth Lived." *Thrilling Wonder Stories* October 1937: 90–100.

Larbalestier, Justine. "The Battle of the Sexes in Science Fiction: From the Pulps to the James Tiptree, Jr. Memorial Award." Diss. University of Sydney, 1996.

Lemkin, William. "Cupid of the Laboratory." *Amazing Stories* August 1937: 79–112.

Long, A. R. [Amelia Reynolds]. "The Mind Master." *Astounding Stories* December 1937: 41–45.

Macfadyen, A., Jr. "The Endless Chain." *Astounding Stories* April 1937: 56–72.

Mulvey, Laura. "Visual Pleasure and Narrative Cinema." *Screen* Autumn 1975; Reprinted in *Literary Theory: An Anthology.* Edited by Julie Rivkin and Michael Ryan. Malden, MS: Blackwell, 1998. 585–95.

Poe, Edgar Allan. "The Colloquy of Monos and Una." *Tales Volume III.* Vol. 4 in *The Complete Works of Edgar Allan Poe.* Edited by James A. Harrison. New York: AMS, 1965. 200–212. 17 vols.

———. "The Conversation of Eiros and Charmion." *Tales Volume III.* Vol. 4 in *The Complete Works.* 1–8.

———. *Eureka. Marginalia–Eureka.* Vol. 16 in *The Complete Works.* 179–354.

———. *The Narrative of Arthur Gordon Pym. Tales Volume II.* Vol. 3 in *The Complete Works.* 5–245.

———. "Some Words with a Mummy." *Tales Volume V.* Vol. 6 in *The Complete Works.* 116–38.

Pragnell, Festus. "Man of the Future." *Tales of Wonder* 1 [June 1937]: 57–65.

Raymond, K. [Kaye]. "The Comet." *Astounding Stories* February 1937: 98–105.

Rose, Walter. "By Jove." *Amazing Stories* February 1937: 75–106.

Schachner, Nat. "City of the Rocket Horde." *Astounding Stories* December 1937: 112–35.

Scheer, George H. "The Crystalline Salvation." *Amazing Stories* June 1937: 92–119.

———. "The Last Ice." *Amazing Stories* October 1937: 71–96.

Skidmore, Joseph Wm. "Murder by Atom." *Amazing Stories* June 1937: 13–15.

Smith, E. E. "Doc." *First Lensman.* 1950; Reprint, New York: Pyramid, 1964.

———. *Galactic Patrol. Astounding Stories,* 1937–38. Revised 1950 and reprinted, New York: Pyramid, 1964.

Stableford, Brian. "The Last Chocolate Bar and the Majesty of Truth: Reflections on the Concept of 'Hardness' in Science Fiction (Part I)". *The New York Review of Science Fiction.* 71 (July 1994): 1, 8–12.

Stone, Leslie F. "The Great Ones." *Astounding Stories* July 1937: 52–71.

Stuart, Don A. [John W. Campbell, Jr.]. "Forgetfulness." *Astounding Stories* June 1937: 52–71.

Williamson, Jack. "Released Entropy." *Astounding Stories* August 1937: 8–30.

Willey, Robert [Willey Ley]. "At the Perihelion." *Astounding Stories* February 1937: 41–76.

Winterbotham, R. R. "Specialization." *Astounding Stories* August 1937: 31–36.

CHAPTER 4

Andrae, Thomas. "From Menace to Messiah: The Prehistory of the Superman in Science Fiction Literature." *Discourse: Journal for Theoretical Studies in Media and Culture* 2 (summer 1980): 84–111.

Atheling, William, Jr. [James Blish]. *More Issues at Hand.* Ed. James Blish. Chicago: Advent, 1970.

Berger, Albert I. *The Magic That Works: John W. Campbell and the American Response to Technology.* San Bernardino, CA: Borgo, 1993.

Bleier, Ruth. *Science and Gender: A Critique of Biology and Its Theories on Women.* New York: Pergamon, 1984.

Blish, James. *Jack of Eagles.* 1952: reprinted. New York: Avon, 1958.

Card, Orson Scott. *Wyrms.* New York: Tor, 1987.

The John W. Campbell Letters. Chapdelaine, Perry A., Sr., Tony Chapdelaine, and George Hay, editors. Vol. I. Franklin, TN: A.C. Projects, 1985.

Carter, Paul A. *The Creation of Tomorrow: Fifty Years of Magazine Science Fiction.* New York: Columbia UP, 1977.

Darwin, Charles. *The Descent of Man: And Selection in Relation to Sex.* 2nd ed. Akron, OH: Werner, 1874.

Dick, Philip K. "The Golden Man." 1954; reprinted in *Second Variety: The Collected Stories of Philip K. Dick, Volume 3.* New York: Carol Publishing Group, 1987.

Frisby, Elisabeth Stein. "Nietzsche's Influence on the Superman in Science Fiction Literature." Ph.D. Diss. Florida State University, 1979.

Hamilton, Edmond. "The Man Who Evolved." 1931; reprinted in *Before the Golden Age.* Edited by Isaac Asimov. Garden City, NY: Doubleday, 1974. 23–39.

Haraway, Donna. *Primate Visions: Race and Nature in the World of Modern Science.* New York: Routledge, 1989.

Heinlein, Robert A. "Gulf." 1949; reprinted in *Assignment in Eternity.* New York: Signet, 1953. 7–67.

James, Edward. *Science Fiction in the 20th Century.* New York: Oxford UP, 1994.

Kuttner, Henry. "The Piper's Son." 1945; reprinted in *The Best of Kuttner I.* London: Mayflower, 1965. 179–201.

Letson, Russell. "Locus Looks at Books: Reviews by Russell Letson." *Locus* 37 (November 1996): 61.

Moskowitz, Sam. *Seekers of Tomorrow: Masters of Modern Science Fiction.* Cleveland and New York: World, 1966.

Newman, Louise Michele. "The Problem of Biological Determinism (1870–1890)." *Men's Ideas/Women's Realities: Popular Science, 1870–1915.* Ed. Louise Michele Newman. Athene Series. New York: Pergamon, 1985. 1–16.

Page, Norvell W. "But without Horns." 1940; reprinted in *Five Science Fiction Novels.* Edited by Martin Greenberg. New York: Gnome, 1952. 13–109.

Robinson, Frank M. *The Power.* Philadelphia: Lippincott, 1956.

Spencer, Herbert. "Psychology of the Sexes." *Men's Ideas/Women's Realities: Popular Science, 1870–1915.* Edited by Louise Michele Newman. New York: Pergamon, 1985. 17–24.

Tymn, Marshall B., and Mike Ashley, editors. *Science Fiction, Fantasy, and Weird Fiction Magazines.* Westport, CT: Greenwood, 1985.

Van Vogt, A. E. *The Silkie.* New York: Ace, 1969.

———. *Slan.* 1940; reprinted, New York: Berkley, 1968.

Weinbaum, Stanley G. *The New Adam.* 1939; reprinted, New York: Avon, 1969.

Williamson, Jack. *Wonder's Child: My Life in Science Fiction.* New York: Bluejay, 1984.

CHAPTER 5

Beauvoir, Simone de. *The Second Sex.* Trans. and edited by H. M. Parshley. London: Cape, 1953.

Bunn, Geoffrey C. "The Lie Detector, *Wonder Woman* and Liberty: The Life and Work of William Moulton Marston." *History of the Human Sciences* 10 (1997): 91–119.

Butler, Octavia E. *Xenogenesis.* Book Club edition, consisting of *Dawn, Adulthood Rites,* and *Imago.* New York: GuildAmerica, n.d. Original publication, New York: Warner, 1987, 1988, 1989.

———. *Mind of My Mind.* Garden City, NY: Doubleday, 1977.

———. *Patternmaster.* New York: Avon, 1976.

———. *Wild Seed.* Garden City, NY: Doubleday, 1980.

Cixous, Hélène. "The Laugh of the Medusa." Trans. Keith Cohen and Paula Cohen. *New French Feminisms: An Anthology.* Ed. Elaine Marks and Isabelle de Courtivron. Amherst: U of Massachusetts P, 1980. 245–64.

Clifton, Mark. "Star, Bright." 1952; reprinted in *The Mathematical Magpie.* Revised edition edited by Clifton Fadiman. New York: Simon, 1981. 70–96.

Donawerth, Jane. *Frankenstein's Daughters: Women Writing Science Fiction.* Syracuse, NY: Syracuse UP, 1997.

Gotlieb, Phyllis. *Sunburst.* New York: Fawcett, 1964.

Haraway, Donna J. "A Manifesto for Cyborgs." *Simians, Cyborgs, and Women: The Reinvention of Nature.* New York: Routledge, 1991. 19–81.

Henderson, Zenna. "Gilead." *The Magazine of Fantasy and Science Fiction,* 1954; reprinted in *Ingathering: The Complete People Stories.* Edited by Mark and Priscilla Olson. Framingham, MA: The NESFA P, 1995. 39–63.

———. "Interlude: Lea 1." *Ingathering.* 1–12.

Irigaray, Luce. "The Power of Discourse and the Subordination of the Feminine." In *This Sex Which Is Not One.* Trans. Catherine Porter, with Carolyn Burke. Ithaca, NY: 1985. 68–85.

———. "This Sex Which Is Not One." Trans. Claudia Reeder. *New French Feminisms.* 99–106.

Kress, Nancy. *Beggars and Choosers.* New York: Tor, 1994.

———. *Beggars in Spain.* New York: Avon, 1993.

———. *Beggar's Ride.* New York: Tor, 1996.

Kuttner, Henry, and C. L. Moore (as Lawrence O'Donnell). "The Children's Hour." *Astounding Science Fiction* 1944; reprinted in *A Treasury of Great Science Fiction* Vol. 1. Edited by Anthony Boucher. Garden City, NY: Doubleday, 1959. 255–87.

Marston, William Moulton (as Charles Moulton). *Sensation Comics* No. 2 (February 1942); reprinted in *Wonder Woman Archives Volume 1.* New York: D.C. Comics, 1998. 31–44.

———. "Why 100,000,000 Americans Read Comics." *The American Scholar* 13:1 (winter 1943–44): 35–44.

Merril, Judith. "That Only a Mother." *Astounding Science Fiction,* 1948; reprinted in *Children of Wonder.* Ed. William Tenn (Philip Klass). New York: Simon, 1953. 207–16.

Moore, C. L. "No Woman Born." *Astounding Science Fiction* 1944; reprinted in *The Best of C. L. Moore.* Edited by Lester Del Rey. Garden City, NY: Doubleday, 1975. Citations in text are from Ballantine Edition, New York, 1976. 236–88.

———. "Shambleau." *Weird Tales,* 1933; reprinted in *The Best of C. L. Moore.* 1–32.

———. "Tryst in Time." *Astounding Stories,* 1936; reprinted in *The Best of C. L. Moore.* 131–58.

Reynolds, Richard. *Super Heroes: A Modern Mythology.* Jackson: University Press of Mississippi, 1992.

Riviere, Joan. "Womanliness as a Masquerade." *The International Journal of Psychoanalysis* 10 (1929); reprinted in *Formations of Fantasy.* Edited by Victor Burgin, James Donald, and Cora Kaplan. London and New York: Methuen, 1986. 35–44.

Robinson, Lillian S. "Looking for Wonder Woman." *ArtForum International* Summer, 1989: 100–103.

Sargent, Pamela, (ed.). *More Women of Wonder: Science Fiction Novellas by Woman about Women.* New York: Vintage, 1976.

———. (ed.). *The New Women of Wonder: Recent Science Fiction Stories by Women about Women.* New York: Vintage, 1978.

———. (ed.). *Women of Wonder: Science Fiction Stories by Women about Women.* New York: Vintage, 1975.

Shiras, Wilmar. *Children of the Atom.* New York: Grove, 1953.

Tuck, Donald. *The Encyclopedia of Science Fiction and Fantasy Through 1968.* 3 vols. Chicago: Advent, 1974, 1978, 1982.

Weinbaum, Stanley G. "The Adaptive Ultimate." *Astounding Stories* 1935; reprinted in *A Martian Odyssey.* Selected by Sam Moskowitz. New York: Lancer, 1966. 42–70.

CHAPTER 6

Arnason, Eleanor. *Hearth World.* Unpublished manuscript.

———. "The Lovers." *Isaac Asimov's Science Fiction Magazine* July 1994; reprinted in *Flying Cups & Saucers: Gender Explorations in Science Fiction & Fantasy.* Edited by Debbie Notkin & The Secret Feminist Cabal. Cambridge, MA: Edgewood, 1998. 16–42.

———. *Ring of Swords.* New York: Tor, 1993.

Bradley, Marion Zimmer. *The Shattered Chain: A Darkover Novel.* New York: Daw, 1976.

Bradley, Marion Zimmer, and John Jay Wells (Juanita Coulson). "Another Rib." *The Magazine of Fantasy and Science Fiction* June 1963: 112–27.

Bryant, Dorothy. *The Kin of Ata Are Waiting for You.* 1971 as *The Comfortor;* reprint, San Francisco: Moon, n.d.

Bujold, Lois McMaster. *Ethan of Athos.* Riverdale, NY: Baen, 1986.

Burdekin, Katharine. *Swastika Night.* 1937; reprint, Old Westbury, NY: The Feminist P, 1985.

Burwell, Jennifer. *Notes on Nowhere: Feminism, Utopian Logic, and Social Transformation.* American Culture, Vol. 13. Minneapolis: U of Minnesota P, 1997.

Chandler, A. Bertram. *Spartan Planet.* Also titled *False Fatherland.* New York: Dell, 1969.

Charnas, Suzy McKee. *Motherlines.* New York: Berkley-Putnam, 1978; reprint, New York: Berkley, 1979.

————. *Walk to the End of the World*. New York: Ballantine, 1974; reprint, New York: Berkley, 1978.

Cooper, Edmund. *Gender Genocide*. Also titled *Who Needs Men*. New York: Avon, 1972.

Delany, Samuel R. *Stars in My Pocket Like Grains of Sand*. New York: Bantam, 1984.

Evans, Arthur B. "The Vehicular Utopias of Jules Verne." *Transformations of Utopia: Changing Views of the Perfect Society*. Edited by George Slusser et al. AMS studies in cultural history; no. 5. New York: AMS, 1999. 99–108.

Fowler, Karen Joy. "Game Night at the Fox and Goose." *Black Glass: Short Fictions*. New York: Holt, 1998. 228–42.

Friend, Beverly. "Virgin Territory: Woman and Sex in Science Fiction." *Extrapolation* 14 (1972): 49–58. Revised as "Virgin Territory: The Bonds and Boundaries of Women in Science Fiction." *Many Futures, Many Worlds: Theme and Form in Science Fiction*. Edited by Thomas D. Clareson. Kent, OH: The Kent State UP, 1977. 140–63.

Gearhart, Sally Miller. *The Wanderground: Stories of the Hill Women*. 1979; reprint, London: The Women's P, 1985.

Gilman, Charlotte Perkins. *Herland*. 1915; reprint, New York: Pantheon, 1979.

Griffith, Nicola. *Ammonite*. New York: Ballantine, 1992.

Heinlein, Robert A. *Space Cadet*. New York: Scribner's, 1948; reprint, New York: Ballantine, 1978.

Hollinger, Veronica. "(Re)reading Queerly: Science Fiction, Feminism, and the Defamiliarization of Gender." *Science-Fiction Studies* 77 (March 1999). Special Issue on Science Fiction and Queer Theory.

Jones, Gwyneth. Review of *Flying Cups and Saucers (Gender Explorations in Science Fiction and Fantasy)*. *The New York Review of Science Fiction* 127 (March 1999): 12–14.

Ketterer, David. "Utopian Fantasy as Millennial Motive and Science-Fictional Motif." *Studies in the Literary Imagination*. Special Issue on "Aspects of Utopian Fiction." Vol. 6, No. 2 (Fall 1973): 79–103.

Lane, Mary Bradley. *Mizora: A Prophecy*. 1890; reprint, Boston: Gregg, 1975.

Le Guin, Ursula K. *Always Coming Home*. New York: Harper, 1985.

————. *The Left Hand of Darkness*. New York: Walker, 1969.

————. "The Matter of Seggri." *Crank! Science Fiction and Fantasy* 3 (spring 1994): 3–36.

Mitchison, Naomi. *Solution Three*. London: Dobson, 1975.

Moskowitz, Sam, ed. *When Women Rule*. New York: Walker, 1972.

Moylan, Tom. *Demand the Impossible: Science Fiction and the Utopian Imagination*. New York: Methuen, 1986.

Pearson, Carol. "Women's Fantasies and Feminist Utopias." *Frontiers: A Journal of Women's Studies*. Vol. 2, no. 3 (fall 1977): 50–61. Revised as "Coming Home: Four Feminist Utopias and Patriarchal Experience." *Future Females: A Critical Anthology*. Edited by Marlene S. Barr. Bowling Green, OH: Bowling Green State U Popular P, 1981. 63–85.

Pearson, Wendy. "Alien Cryptographies: The View from Queer." *Science-Fiction Studies* 77 (March 1999). Special Issue on Science Fiction and Queer Theory.

————. "Identifying the Alien: Science Fiction Meets Its Other." *Science-Fiction Studies* 77 (March 1999). Special Issue on Science Fiction and Queer Theory.

Piercy, Marge. *Woman on the Edge of Time*. New York: Knopf, 1976.

Roberts, Robin. *A New Species: Gender and Science in Science Fiction*. Urbana, IL and Chicago: U of Illinois P, 1993.

Russ, Joanna. "*Amor Vincit Foeminam*: The Battle of the Sexes in Science Fiction." *To Write Like a Woman: Essays in Feminism and Science Fiction*. Bloomington: Indiana UP, 1995. 41–59.

————. *And Chaos Died*. New York: Ace, 1970.

————. *The Female Man*. New York: Bantam, 1975.

————. "The Image of Women in Science Fiction." *Images of Women in Fiction Feminist Perspectives*. Edited by Susan Koppelman Cornillon. Revised ed. Bowling Green, OH: Bowling Green U Popular P, 1973. 79–94.

————. "Recent Feminist Utopias." *Future Females*. 71–85.

————. *To Write Like a Woman: Essays in Feminism and Science Fiction*. Bloomington: Indiana UP, 1995.

————. "What Can a Heroine Do? Or Why Women Can't Write." *Images of Women in Fiction Feminist Perspectives*. Edited by Susan Koppelman Cornillon. Revised edition, Bowling Green, OH: Bowling Green U Popular P, 1973. 3–20.

————. "When It Changed." *Again, Dangerous Visions*. Vol 1. Garden City, NY: Doubleday, 1972. Reprint, New York: Signet, 1972. 266–81.

Russell, Frances Theresa. *Touring Utopia: The Realms of Constructive Humanism*. New York: Dial, 1932.

Ryman, Geoff. *The Child Garden, or A Low Comedy*. New York: Tor, 1989.

————. "O Happy Day!" 1985; reprinted in *Unconquered Countries: Four Novellas*. New York: St. Martin's, 1994. 153–90.

Sargent, Lyman Tower. "An Ambiguous Legacy: The Role and Position of Women in the English Eutopia." *Future Females*. Edited by Marleen Barr. 88–99.

Sargent, Pamela. *Women of Wonder: Science Fiction Stories by Women about Women*. New York: Vintage, 1975.

Sheldon, Raccoona [Alice]. "Your Faces, O My Sisters! Your Faces Filled of Light!" *Aurora: Beyond Equality*. Edited by Vonda McIntyre and Susan Anderson. New York: Fawcett, 1976. Reprinted in *Out of the Everywhere: And Other Extraordinary Visions*. James Tiptree, Jr. New York: Ballantine, 1981. 34–52.

Tiptree, James Jr. [Alice Sheldon]. "Houston, Houston, Do You Read?" *Aurora: Beyond Equality*. Reprinted in *Worlds Apart: An Anthology of Lesbian and Gay Science Fiction and Fantasy*. Edited by Camilla Decarnin, Eric Garber, and Lyn Paleo. Boston: Alyson, 1986. 40–104.

Sussex, Lucy. "My Lady Tongue." *The Women Who Walk Through Fire: Women's Fantasy & Science Fiction Vol. 2*. Edited by Susanna J. Sturgis. Freedom, CA: Crossing, 1990. 208–55.

Tepper, Sheri S. *The Gate to Women's Country*. Garden City, NY: Doubleday, 1988; reprint, New York: Bantam, 1989.

Varley, John. *Steel Beach*. New York: Putnam's, 1992.

Weinstone, Ann. "Science Fiction as a Young Person's First Queer Theory (review–essay)." *Science-Fiction Studies* 77 (March 1999). Special Issue on Science Fiction and Queer Theory.

West, Wallace G. "The Last Man." *Amazing Stories,* February 1929: 1030–1040.

Williams, Lynn F. " 'Great Country for Men and Dogs, but Tough on Women and Mules': Sex and Status in Recent Science Fiction Utopias." *Women Worldwalkers: New Dimensions of Science Fiction and Fantasy*. Edited by Jane B. Weedman. Lubbock, TX: Texas Tech P, 1985. 223–35.

————. "Separatist Fantasies, 1690–1997: An Annotated Bibliography." *Femspec* 1:2 (2000): 30–42.

Wittig, Monique. *Les Guérillères*. Trans. David Le Vay. New York: Viking, 1971.

Wylie, Philip. *The Disappearance*. New York: Holt, 1951; reprint, New York: Pocket, 1952.

CHAPTER 7

Barr, Marleen S. "Revamping the Rut Regarding Reading and Writing about Feminist Science Fiction: Or, I Want to Engage in 'Procrustean Bedmaking.' " *Extrapolation* 41:1 (spring 2000): 43–50.

Barrow, Craig, and Diana Barrow. "*The Left Hand of Darkness:* Feminism for Men." *Mosaic* 20:1 (winter 1987): 83–96.

Bradley, Marion Zimmer. *Darkover Landfall.* New York: Ace, 1972.

———. *The World Wreckers.* New York: Ace, 1971.

Brennert, Alan. "The Third Sex." *Pulphouse 3,* 1989; reprinted in *The Year's Best Science Fiction: Seventh Annual Collection.* Edited by Gardner Dozois. New York: St. Martin's, 1990. 385–401.

Butler, Judith. *Gender Trouble: Feminism and the Subversion of Identity.* London and New York: Routledge, 1990.

Butler, Octavia. *Xenogenesis,* Book Club edition, consisting of *Dawn, Adulthood Rites* and *Imago.* New York: GuildAmerica. n. d. Original publication, New York: Warner, 1987, 1988, 1989.

Carter, Raphael. "The Angel's Dictionary." Home page. March 1998 <http://www.chaparraltree.com/raq/angels.shtml>. 28 May, 2000.

———. "Congenital Agenesis of Gender Ideation, by K. N. Sirsi and Sandra Botkin." *Starlight 2.* Edited by Patrick Nielsen Hayden. New York: Tor, 1998. 91–106.

———. "M. Manners' Guide to Excruciatingly Correct Behavior toward (and by) Androgynes, or, Brothersister Raphael Explains it All to You)." Home page. March 1998 <http://www.chaparraltree.com/raq/manners.shtml>. 28 May, 2000.

Delany, Samuel R. "Aye, and Gomorrah . . ." in *Dangerous Visions,* edited by Harlan Ellison. Garden City, NY: Doubleday, 1967; reprinted in *The Road to Science Fiction #3: From Heinlein to Here.* Edited by James Gunn. New York: Mentor, 1979. 449–59.

Elshtain, Jean Bethke. "Against Androgyny." *Feminism and Equality.* Edited by Anne Phillips. Oxford: Blackwell, 1987. 139–59.

Eskridge, Kelley. "And Salome Danced." in *Little Deaths.* Edited by Ellen Datlow. London: Orion, 1994; reprinted in *Women of Other Worlds: Excursions through Science Fiction and Feminism,* edited by Helen Merrick and Tess Williams. Nedlands, WA: U of Western Australia P, 1999. 148–61.

———. "Identity and Desire." *Women of Other Worlds: Excursions through Science Fiction and Feminism.* Edited by Helen Merrick and Tess Williams. Nedlands, WA: U of Western Australia P, 1999. 176–82.

Gelpi, Barbara Charlesworth. "The Politics of Androgyny." *Women's Studies* 2:2 (1974): 151–60.

Harris, Daniel A. "Androgyny: The Sexist Myth in Disguise." *Women's Studies* 2:2 (1974): 171–84.

Heilbrun, Carolyn. *Toward a Recognition of Androgyny.* New York: Knopf, 1973.

Jones, Gwyneth. "Balinese Dancer." *Asimov's Science Fiction* Sept. 1997; reprinted in *The Year's Best Science Fiction: Fifteenth Annual Collection.* Ed. Gardner Dozois. New York: St. Martin's, 1998. 288–305.

Lamb, Patricia Frazer, and Diana L. Veith. "Again, *The Left Hand of Darkness:* Androgyny or Homophobia?" *Erotic Universe: Sexuality and Fantastic Literature.* Edited by Donald Palumbo. Contributions to the Study of Science Fiction and Fantasy, Number 18. New York: Greenwood, 1986. 221–31.

Le Guin, Ursula K. "Coming of Age in Karhide." reprinted in *The Year's Best Science Fiction: Thirteenth Annual Collection.* Edited by Gardner Dozois. New York: St. Martin's, 1996. 70–86.

———. "Is Gender Necessary? Redux." *Dancing at the Edge of the World: Thoughts on Words, Women, Places.* New York: Grove, 1989.

———. *The Left Hand of Darkness.* New York: Harper, 1969, 1976.

———. "Winter's King." *The Wind's Twelve Quarters.* New York: Harper, 1975. 93–117.

Pateau, Francette. "The Impossible Referent: Representations of the Androgyne." *Formations of Fantasy.* Edited by Victor Burgin, James Donald, and Cora Kaplan. London and New York: Methuen, 1986. 62–84.

Rhodes, Jewell Parker. "Ursula Le Guin's *The Left Hand of Darkness:* Androgyny and the Feminist Utopia." *Women and Utopia: Critical Interpretations.* Edited by Marleen Barr and Nicholas D. Smith. New York: University Press of America, 1983. 108–20.

Secor, Cynthia. "Androgyny: An Early Reappraisal." *Women's Studies* 2, No. 2 (1974): 161–69.

Sturgeon, Theodore. *Venus Plus X.* New York: Pyramid, 1960.

Sturgis, Susanna. "Notes of a Border Crosser." *Women of Other Worlds: Excursions through Science Fiction and Feminism.* Edited by Helen Merrick and Tess Williams. Nedlands, WA: U of Western Australia P, 1999. 103–14.

Varley, John. "Options." *Blue Champagne.* New York: Berkley, 1986.154–82.

———. *Steel Beach.* New York: Ace, 1992.

Weil, Kari. *Androgyny and the Denial of Difference.* Charlottesville: UP of Virginia, 1992.

Woolf, Virginia. *A Room of One's Own.* New York: Harcourt, 1929.

———. *Orlando.* New York: Harcourt, 1928.

CHAPTER 8

Baudrillard, Jean. *Simulations.* Trans. Paul Foss, Paul Patton, and Philip Beitchman. Foreign Agent Series. New York: Semiotext(e), 1983.

———. "Two Essays." Trans. Arthur B. Evans. Special Issue "Science Fiction and Postmodernism." *Science-Fiction Studies* 18 (1991): 309–20.

Cox, F. Brett. "The Brute Facticity of the Corpse: James Morrow, Science Fiction Writer." Special Issue: "The Divinely Human Comedy of James Morrow." *Paradoxa* 5 (1999): 16–24.

Delany, Samuel R. "*Paradoxa* Interview with James Morrow: Blinded by the Enlightenment." Special Issue: "The Divinely Human Comedy of James Morrow." *Paradoxa* 5 (1999): 132–49.

Haraway, Donna. *Simians, Cyborgs, and Women.* New York: Routledge, 1989.

Hayles, N. Katherine. *Chaos Bound: Orderly Disorder in Contemporary Literature and Science.* Ithaca: Cornell UP, 1990.

Jameson, Fredric. *Postmodernism, or, The Cultural Logic of Late Capitalism.* Durham, NC: Duke UP, 1991.

Johnson, Mark. *The Body in the Mind: The Bodily Basis of Meaning, Imagination, and Reason.* Chicago: U of Chicago P, 1987.

Jones, Gwyneth. *Deconstructing the Starships: Science, Fiction and Reality.* Liverpool Science Fiction Texts and Studies 16. Liverpool: Liverpool UP, 1999.

———. *North Wind.* London: Gollancz, 1994.

———. *Phoenix Cafe.* London: Gollancz, 1997.

———. *White Queen.* 1991; Orb Edition, New York: Tor, 1994.

Lakoff, George, and Mark Johnson. *Philosophy in the Flesh: The Embodied Mind and Its Challenge to Western Thought.* New York: Basic, 1999.

Lakoff, George, and Mark Turner. *More Than Cool Reason: A Field Guide to Poetic Metaphor.* Chicago: U of Chicago P, 1989.

McHale, Brian. *Postmodernist Fiction.* New York: Methuen, 1987.

Morrow, James. *Blameless in Abaddon.* New York: Harcourt, 1996.

———. *The Eternal Footman.* New York: Harcourt, 1999.

———. *Towing Jehovah.* New York: Harcourt, 1994.

Science Fiction Studies. Special Issue on "Science Fiction and Postmodernism." 55 (November 1991).

Wertheim, Margaret. *Pythagoras' Trousers: God, Physics, and the Gender Wars.* New York: New York Times Books, 1995.

CHAPTER 9

Bacon-Smith, Camille. *Enterprising Women: Television Fandom and the Creation of Popular Myth.* Philadelphia: U of Pennsylvania P, 1992.

———. *Science Fiction Culture.* Philadelphia: U of Pennsylvania P, 2000.

Bainbridge, William Sims. *Dimensions of Science Fiction.* Cambridge: Harvard UP, 1986.

Bradley, Marion Zimmer. "Responsibilities and Temptations of Women Science Fiction Writers." *Women Worldwalkers: New Dimensions of Science Fiction and Fantasy.* Edited by Jane B. Weedman. Lubbock: Texas Tech P, 1985. 25–41.

Broderick, Damien. *Reading by Starlight: Postmodern Science Fiction.* Popular Fictions Series. London and New York: Routledge, 1995.

Brooke-Rose, Christine. A *Rhetoric of the Unreal: Studies in Narrative Structure, Especially of the Fantastic.* Cambridge: Cambridge UP, 1981.

Cadigan, Pat. *Synners.* New York: Bantam, 1991.

Clute, John. "The Norton Book of Science Fiction." *TLS.* 11 March 1994. 24.

Dery, Mark. "Slashing the Borg: Resistance Is Fertile." 1996. Home page. 7 June 2000. <http://ww. dds.nl/~n5m/texts/markdery.htm>.

Dozois, Gardner, (ed.). *Modern Classics of Science Fiction.* New York: St. Martin's, 1991.

Duncan, Andy. "Think Like a Humanist: James Patrick Kelly's 'Think Like a Dinosaur' as a Satiric Rebuttal to Tom Godwin's 'The Cold Equations.'" *The New York Review of Science Fiction* 94 (June 1996): 1, 8–11.

Godwin, Tom. "The Cold Equations." *Astounding Science Fiction* 1954. Reprinted in *The Science Fiction Hall of Fame, Volume I.* Robert Silverberg, editor. New York: Avon, 1970. 543–69.

Greenblatt, Stephen. *Shakespearean Negotiations: The Circulation of Social Energy in Renaissance England.* The New Historicism: Studies in Cultural Poetics, no. 4. Berkeley and Los Angeles: U of California P, 1988.

Gunn, James, (ed.). *The Road to Science Fiction.* Volumes 1–4. New York: NAL, 1977–1982. Rpt. Clarkston, CA: White Wolf, n.d.

Gustavsson, Dan. "Why We Need a New *Star Trek* Series." 1997. Home page. 7 June 2000. <http://home1.swipnet.se/~w-15935/why/htm>.

Hamon, Philippe. "Un discours constraínt," *Poétique* 16 (1973) 411–45.

"I Love LeGuin, But. . . ." 21 Feb. 2000. Amazon.com: Customer Reviews: The Norton Book of Science Fiction: North American Science Fiction 1960–1990. 29 March, 2000. <http://www.amazon. com/exec/obidos/ts/boo...id=1-72/104-0278027-0418834>.

Hartwell, David G., and Kathryn Cramer, (eds.). *The Ascent of Wonder: The Evolution of Hard Science Fiction.* New York: Tor, 1994.

Hartwell, David G., and Milton T. Wolf, (eds.). *Visions of Wonder.* New York: Tor, 1996.

Huntington, John. *Rationalizing Genius: Ideological Strategies in the Classic American Science Fiction Short Story.* New Brunswick, NJ: Rutgers UP, 1989.

Jenkins, Henry, III. "Star Trek Rerun, Reread, Rewritten: Fan Writing as Textual Poaching." Close Encounters: Film, Feminism, and Science Fiction. Edited by Constance Penley, et al. Minneapolis: U of Minnesota P, 1991. 171–202.

Jones, Diana Wynne. *Archer's Goon.* New York: Greenwillow, 1984.

Le Guin, Ursula K., and Brian Attebery, (eds.). Karen Joy Fowler, consultant. *The Norton Book of Science Fiction: North American Science Fiction, 1960–1990.* New York: Norton, 1993.

Nixon, Nicola. "Cyberpunk: Preparing the Ground for Revolution or Keeping the Boys Satisfied?" *Science-Fiction Studies* 57 (July 1992): 219–35.

"The Norton Book of PC Science Fiction." Nov 18, 1998. Amazon.com: Customer Reviews: The Norton Book of Science Fiction: North American Science Fiction 1960–1990. 29 March, 2000. <http://www.amazon.com/exec/obidos/ts/boo...id=95451172/sr=1-72/104-0278027-0418834>.

Penley, Constance. "Brownian Motion: Women, Tactics, and Technology." In *Technoculture.* Edited by Constance Penley and Andrew Ross. Cultural Politics, Vol. 3. Minneapolis: U of Minnesota P, 1991. 135–61.

Perkins, Timothy D. "An Open Letter to the Producers of Voyager." 15 May, 1995. Home page. 2 June 1997. <http://www.ccnet.com/gaytrek/openletter.html>.

Russ, Joanna. *How to Suppress Women's Writing.* Austin: U of Texas P, 1983.

Schweitzer, Darrell. Letter to the Editor. *The New York Review of Science Fiction* 99 (Nov 1996): 23.

Shippey, Tom, (ed.). *The Oxford Book of Science Fiction Stories.* New York and Oxford: Oxford UP, 1992.

Silverberg, Robert, (ed.). *The Science Fiction Hall of Fame Volume I.* New York: Avon, 1970.

Stableford, Brian. "A Review of *The Norton Book of Science Fiction: North American Science Fiction, 1960–1990* edited by Ursula K. Le Guin and Brian Attebery." *The New York Review of Science Fiction* 62 (Oct 1993): 1, 3–7.

Tulloch, John, and Henry Jenkins. *Science Fiction Audiences: Watching* Doctor Who *and* Star Trek. Popular Fiction Series. London and New York: Routledge, 1995.

Willis, Connie. "Schwarzschild Radius." 1987; reprinted in *The Norton Book of Science Fiction.* Ed. Ursula K. Le Guin and Brian Attebery. New York: Norton, 1993. 689–704.

Wolfe, Gary K. *Critical Terms for Science Fiction and Fantasy: A Glossary and Guide to Scholarship.* Westport, CT: Greenwood, 1986.

INDEX